The Battle of Actium
31 BC

The Battle of Actium 31 BC

War for the World

Lee Fratantuono

Pen & Sword
MILITARY

First published in Great Britain in 2016 by
Pen & Sword Military
An imprint of
Pen & Sword Books Ltd
47 Church Street
Barnsley
South Yorkshire
S70 2AS

Copyright © Lee Fratantuono, 2016

ISBN 978 1 47384 714 9

A CIP catalogue record for this book is available from the British Library.

Typeset in Ehrhardt by
Replika Press Pvt Ltd, India
Printed and bound in England
by CPI Group (UK) Ltd, Croydon, CR0 4YY

Pen & Sword Books Ltd incorporates the Imprints of Pen & Sword Aviation, Pen & Sword Family History, Pen & Sword Maritime, Pen & Sword Military, Pen & Sword Discovery, Pen & Sword Politics, Pen & Sword Atlas, Pen & Sword Archaeology, Wharncliffe Local History, Wharncliffe True Crime, Wharncliffe Transport, Pen & Sword Select, Pen & Sword Military Classics, Leo Cooper, The Praetorian Press, Claymore Press, Remember When, Seaforth Publishing and Frontline Publishing.

For a complete list of Pen & Sword titles please contact
PEN & SWORD BOOKS LIMITED
47 Church Street, Barnsley, South Yorkshire, S70 2AS, England
E-mail: enquiries@pen-and-sword.co.uk
Website: www.pen-and-sword.co.uk

For KMG

många tankar men så få ord

Contents

Preface and Acknowledgments

The present volume is a study of one of the most famous battles in history; the naval engagement of Antony, Cleopatra, and Octavian at Actium. Its aim is to explicate what might well have happened in the waters off northwestern Greece, where the future course of the Roman Republic was charted, and where the lives of three of the most celebrated figures of ancient history converged in one fateful struggle for dominance over the waters of the Mediterranean.

John M. Carter's 1970 monograph, *The Battle of Actium* has a somewhat misleading title, despite its cover illustration of a warship; the subtitle, *The Rise and Triumph of Augustus Caesar* gives away the book's omnibus concern with the entirety of the struggle by which the man history knows best as 'Augustus' came to power in Rome (or restored the Republic, or served as its first citizen, or conquered disorder, etc., etc.). Carter's book is a wonderful introduction to a difficult period in Roman history, and the product of careful investigation of the surviving primary historical sources on Actium – in particular the full-scale accounts in Plutarch's *Life of Antony* and Dio Cassius' *Roman History*. As a general primer on a subject of vast and enduring interest, Carter's book has worn its years well, and it remains an important guide to the events of the transition from Roman Republic to Empire.[1]

My interest in Actium has romance as its genesis: the twin lures of poetry and cinema, of the poets of Augustan Rome and the cinematic depiction of the battle in Mankiewicz's 1963 *Cleopatra*, a film that despite its numerous problems of both film quality and historical accuracy, was a contributing factor to my early interest in antiquity. Before long, I was reading numerous studies of Actium out of sheer interest in knowing as much as possible about what happened at the battle, and learning that frustration was a common experience for those who would study the events of 2 September, 31 B.C.E. It seemed unbelievable that so major an event in military history should be so poorly understood, and that so many questions should linger about the events of that September day. Questions such as whether or not Antony and/ or Cleopatra always planned an attempt at escape from entrapment, and just how great a role in the battle was played by Egypt's most famous queen seemed surprisingly vexed, especially given the ever expanding bibliography, much of which was derivative of a few of the seminal debates from the early to mid-twentieth century, especially those of Kromayer and Tarn, the main scholarly opponents of the twentieth century on the problem of what happened at the battle.

My study of Actium took a new turn quite unexpectedly, when I commenced a dissertation on Virgil's *Aeneid*. My topic was Book 11, one of the more understudied and unappreciated sections of the epic. In the process of explicating the mysteries of the cavalry battle that is extensively narrated in that book of epic verse, I realized that were significant parallels between Virgil's poetic exercise in the description of an equestrian engagement and our surviving evidence for what happened at Actium. More generally, I realized that a close study of the allusions and references to Actium in the poets, Virgil and Horace in particular, were a potential source for serious inquiry into the military situation at Actium. It seemed that the poets of Augustan Rome, notoriously condemned by some as mere propagandists of the victorious regime, deserved to be taken seriously as witnesses and sources of evidence alongside the 'traditional' accounts preserved in the ancient historians. Further investigation into the appearance of Actium in these contemporary works, the earliest literary references to the battle that we possess, seemed to justify the investment of interest and attention. In short, I did not initially approach Virgil with an expectation to find much about Actium other than the celebrated appearance of the battle on Aeneas' shield, and the mention of the site of the battle in the course of Aeneas' wanderings westward from Troy to Italy. What I discovered about the Virgilian treatment of Actium lore was thus both surprising and unsurprising; Actium emerged as a key event in the unfolding of the depiction of the Virgilian vision of the nature of Augustan Rome.

It is a pleasure then, to turn to Actium as a subject of separate study and investigative research. It is my hope that this book will be of interest to a wide range of possible readers, including both those primarily interested in Roman military and naval history, and those with a particular love for Virgil and his contemporary poets of Augustan Rome. The notes try to blend elements of respect for diverse audiences; those with both more and less knowledge of Roman history, and Latin language and literature, are begged for the indulgence that a book of intentionally diverse aims may require. For ultimately, the desired audience of this work is anyone with a love for the wonder of the study of ancient military history, a field of justly popular interest and enduring appeal. Devotees of Cleopatra may be pleased to find a reading of Egypt's queen that concludes that for all her many faults, her military performance at Actium may have been impressive; certainly the Augustan poets were capable of respectful admiration, even as they were willing to criticize the behaviour of both queen and lover.

The plan of the book is to provide commentary and analysis on surviving records and references to the war in ancient literary and historical sources; first the Greek and then the Latin. In the latter case, prose evidence is followed by poetic. Consideration of the evidence is followed by a reconstruction of the battle and some treatment of the question of how certain possible myths and fantasies may have developed in the aftermath of the engagement. A brief afterword considers certain aspects of Roman naval technology and practice, with particular attention to the innovations in strategy and hardware that were implemented by Marcus Vipsanius Agrippa.

Simply put, in terms of the scholarly debate on Actium, this book offers a close analysis of hitherto unconsidered evidence in support of the general argument that Actium was a difficult battle in which both sides fought ably and well, and enjoyed a chance at decisive victory. Conclusions derived from the 'evidence' of Virgil's eleventh *Aeneid* must of course be considered speculative given the nature of the narrative of that book. But what emerges from attention to what may seem an unlikely source is a reinforcement of the views of those scholars who have taken Actium seriously as a battle between forces that may well have possessed reasonable chance of success; those historians who believe that the battle that irrevocably changed the Roman world was no mere escape attempt by Antony and Cleopatra from desperate circumstances of blockade and privation.

Readers will not find herein a comprehensive account of the aftermath of Actium, let alone of the story of Antony and Cleopatra more broadly conceived (and in the other temporal direction, there is no detailed account of what brought Antony and Octavian to blows in the first place). The worlds of literature, the arts, music, television and film have all responded to the mystique and appeal of various aspects of the story. There are selective references here and there to material culture, but the bulk of the attention is on the ancient literary and historical evidence for Actium. In this regard too, it bears noting that there is no systematic consideration of archaeological or art historical evidence (though here too, some is mentioned in passing). This book's *raison d'être* is to be found in the new analysis it offers based on a study of the allegorical aspects of Virgil's *Aeneid* 11, and the single volume treatment of Actium it offers almost half a century after Carter, years in which good work has been done on various aspects of Actium. Much of this work has been on the importance of Actium in Augustan ideology, together with related work on the significance of the god Apollo, the patron deity of Actium, in the development of the Augustan mythology. Those topics are not the particular consideration of this volume, though as with other aspects of the story, they will merit attention here and there as we proceed through a study of the battle.

Scholarly references have been made to a variety of bibliographical items on both Actium and its sources; these notes cannot aspire to comprehensiveness, but they do try to provide an introduction and guide to the major resources for further study. Again, some of the silence is to avoid excess length that would only retell stories and episodes that have already been well treated in the scholarly tradition.

This book would not have been possible without the assistance and support of numerous individuals. Philip Sidnell was a wonderfully supportive editorial presence through the acquisition and composition process. My former classics students Cynthia Susalla, Marissa Popeck and Michael McOsker were an invaluable help, and I can only hope that I have satisfied the first in my treatment of Marcus Antonius. Lisa Mignone is both Roman historian and friend, and her comments and criticisms are always welcome. Discussions with Daniel Picasso about Roman and military history never fail to inspire new ideas and novel ways of looking at old problems, while Blaise Nagy has shared his wisdom with me on matters historical for almost a quarter century. The late Karl Maurer of the University of Dallas, scholar of Thucydides and Propertius, is a deeply missed academic conscience; so also my first teacher of Roman history, Gerard Lavery of The College of the Holy Cross. The work of Professor Carsten Lange of Aalborg University in Denmark never fails to impress, and to him I owe the example of his own studies of Actium. The same is true of Adrian Goldsworthy, especially in his work on late republican and early principate biography, a trio of volumes that repay repeated examination.

Lastly, this book owes much to a dear friend whose help for many years now has made all the difference, and to her it is fittingly dedicated.

Lee Fratantuono
Delaware, Ohio, U.S.A.
6 June, 2015

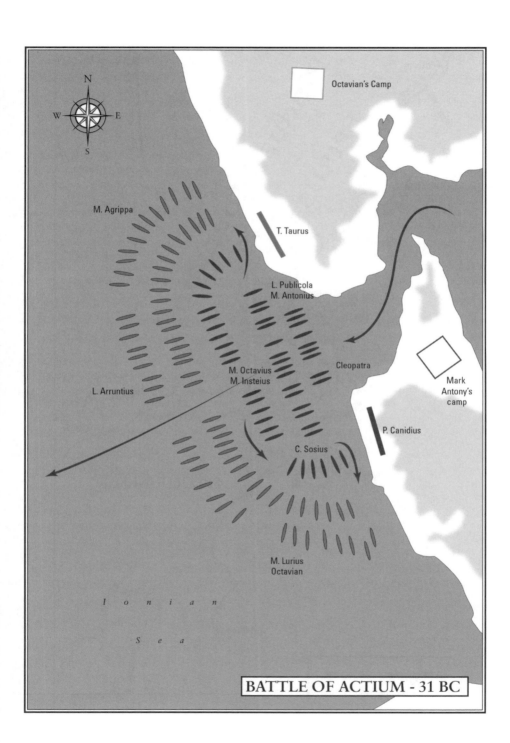

Octavian's Camp

M. Agrippa

T. Taurus

L. Publicola
M. Antonius

L. Arruntius

M. Octavius
M. Insteius

Cleopatra

Mark
Antony's
camp

P. Canidius

C. Sosius

M. Lurius
Octavian

I o n i a n

S e a

BATTLE OF ACTIUM - 31 BC

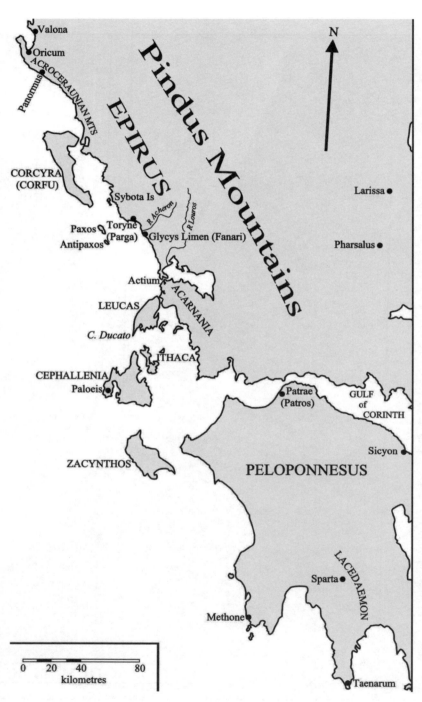

Greece West Coast.

Introduction: Octavian and the Winning of a World

A Most Crucial Engagement

On the second day of September, 31 B.C.E., two naval forces (or some might prefer to say three) faced each other for several hours of a tense morning and early afternoon off the coast of northwestern Greece. It may in fact have been well into the afternoon before much of anything happened; we cannot be certain if fighting continued into the night. But by dawn the next day, at the very latest, the fate of the known world had likely been decided. Neither Rome nor Egypt would ever be the same, and a case could be made that 2 September was the birthday of the Roman Empire. For good reason, the scholar Christopher Pelling opens the introduction to his edition of Plutarch's *Life of Mark Antony* with the observation that 'Actium was one of those battles that mattered.' It also remains one of the most shrouded in enigma, controversy and continued debate.

Or Not Much of a Battle?

Few today outside of the realm of ancient history and classics are aware of the significance of what took place on that late summer day in the waters off Actium. Even within the fields of ancient military history and Augustan studies, there is a general lack of familiarity with exactly what happened when those two or three fleets of warships met in battle; if indeed, some would say, it was even much of a battle. For there are scholars of Roman history who would argue that Actium was not, in the end, all that impressive a campaign or battle; that in fact Actium was hardly a battle at all, and that more accurately it could be called a desperate attempt at escape from an increasingly intolerable position.

For those who think that Antony and Cleopatra intended nothing much more than to escape to Egypt (with at best a vain hope for some success in whatever clashes accompanied the flight), Actium was a victory for the ultimate losers, since they did manage to extricate themselves from difficult circumstances with at least some of their fleet. Even those who would subscribe to this view, however, acknowledge that Actium was at the very least the beginning of the end for resistance to Octavian. For the end result of Actium is, as often in military history, what is best known: Octavian won, and Antony and Cleopatra lost, though in this case 'loss' on 2 September meant the beginning of a strange year of survival that would end only in a very different place indeed, in the tomblike palaces and monuments of Alexandria, in Egypt.

By the end of the summer of 30 B.C.E., the Roman Octavian, the future Augustus, had a mythology that would be the envy of any would-be master of the world. And within a relatively short period of time after that August, he had an impressive array of poetic tributes that to this day form an important surviving corpus of Latin literature. The future Augustus had survived some of the most challenging and difficult days in Roman history theretofore, and he was, in several important regards, the undisputed master of his world. He was not yet thirty-three years of age, and his lifelong friend and confidante Agrippa was not much older. If anyone were 'seasoned' by years in the waters off Actium, it was Antony; but long experience under Julius Caesar would not be enough to win the day or the war.[1]

Part of the 'problem' of Actium is the relative paucity of surviving sources, leaving aside for now the question of the *reliability* of said sources, and the fact that the very nature of the battle seems to work against an appreciation of why exactly Octavian won, not to mention how he managed to do so in the face of significant obstacles and threats to his forces. For Actium was no mere engagement in a longer civil war, no mere continuation of what had already been a century of internecine struggles between rival Roman generals and commanders. Actium was a mighty clash between the forces of Rome and the East, between Rome and Egypt; and Egypt, in these days, meant Cleopatra. Most of what has been written about Actium in both the scholarly and the popular literature has been presented as something of a footnote, albeit a long footnote, to the romantic entanglement between the Roman military and political hero Mark Antony and the self-styled daughter of Isis, the Ptolemaic Queen Cleopatra (or to be more precise, Cleopatra VII Philopator). Actium was a foreign war, perhaps more than it was a civil; Actium was the last great resistance of a Hellenistic monarchy to the Roman Republic. Those monarchies had taken shape in the years after the premature death of Alexander the Great in 323 B.C.E. and the resultant breakdown of his empire; indeed scholars refer to the period from the death of Alexander to the death of Cleopatra as the

'Hellenistic Age' – 323–30 B.C.E. After the death of Cleopatra, the history of Egypt becomes the history of a part of the *imperium Romanum*, a unique part, to be sure, but not an independent political or military entity.

New Twists on a Familiar Romance

The present study is not a rehash of the love affair of the Roman triumvir and his Egyptian queen, though aspects of the affair will of course be relevant to our story (indeed, a reasonable case could be made that the love affair precipitated the collapse of the position of both Antony and Cleopatra). Nor is the present study a survey of Roman history from the death of Julius Caesar to the rise to power of his adopted son and heir Octavian, though that complicated and fascinating lore will also be directly relevant to our tale. Still less is it a history of naval warfare in the late Republic and early Empire, though that too, will of course be of interest and concern.

Some of what we shall consider in these pages will be specimens of the propaganda of the nascent reign of the man we can rightly call Rome's first emperor; propaganda that we may conclude was effective precisely because it was rooted in essential truths. It has become fashionable in some circles to look askance at Octavian as a merciless, self-interested tyrant with little in the way of attractive qualities, and to engage in a healthy amount of revisionism with respect to certain aspects of the story of the last Roman civil war of the age before Christ, but herein we shall explore the thesis that Horace and Virgil were essentially correct in their characterization of events surrounding Actium, and that the Cleopatra who emerges from the pages of both poets was glorified in part for having done her part, after all, for securing the world for Octavian. We may find in the end that the wishes of Octavian and Cleopatra in the last days of the latter were not entirely disparate; both victor and vanquished had a vested interest in seeing the glorification of the defeated as a formidable adversary, as even the greatest foreign threat to Rome since Hannibal, a noble enemy who had to be defeated, to be sure, but who posed a significant enough peril for the future *princeps* of Rome that he could be justly praised for a tremendous accomplishment.

The book you hold will seek to explicate one of the most mysterious battles in history, arguably the most important battle in Roman history, and the one about which we would seem to know the least among the major engagements. Along the way there will be a fair amount of evaluation and analysis of popular, romantic images; most notably of Cleopatra fleeing the scene of battle, and of her lover Antony sacrificing his chance for victory by chasing after the object of his erotic desire. What remains after the investigation will be revealed to be no less thrilling and inspiring as any possibly romanticized fantasy of epic verse, especially when we investigate the reasons for why certain aspects of the story may well have been altered almost immediately in the aftermath of the battle. We shall see how key events from the Battle of Actium may well have inspired elements of the accounts of how the whole drama ended, with the suicide of Cleopatra in Alexandria less than a year after the naval engagement; perhaps the death that mattered the most in the drama, the end of the queen who may well have been the more important figure in the resistance to Octavian in its last months.[2]

One Latin Word

Throughout, we shall see how the best and most reliable accounts of what happened at Actium and Alexandria may well be preserved in the very poetry that the victor commissioned to celebrate his victory: historical verse that preserves tantalizing clues as to what took place in the waters made red with what some have considered not so much blood after all, but more than enough to ensure a new world order that would usher in the reign of the longest serving emperor in Roman history. Prominent among those verse memorials of the battle and its aftermath is the eighth book of Virgil's epic *Aeneid*, where the drama of Actium is central to the glorious decoration of the shield of the Trojan hero Aeneas; and also the eleventh book, where, as we shall see, the struggle in the waters off northwestern Greece may well be depicted in poetic allegory. Indeed, the earliest surviving literary evidence for the war comes in the pages of Augustan verse, and in the case of the earliest example of such poetry, we shall see how a single word in a poem influenced one of the major scholarly reconstructions of the battle.

Names Matter

Where and how should one begin such a story? One place might be Nola, Italy, in 63 B.C.E., where and when Octavian, the putative hero of our story, was born. Names matter. Throughout this book for the sake of convenience we shall refer to Octavian by a name we know he disliked, or at least eschewed. For 'Gaius Octavius Thurinus'[3] would become 'Gaius Julius Caesar' before he was twenty years of age, and on the day he would win his naval victory at

Actium, he would be known by exactly the same name as the more famous Julius Caesar who had been slain on the Ides of March in 44 B.C.E. No one could have predicted that he would live until August of 14 C.E.; after some forty-four years as the first man of the Roman state, the *princeps* who would no doubt have bristled at any suggestion that the Roman Republic was no more, that the Empire had taken its place.

'Thurinus' derives from 'Thurii' in Tarentum, in southern Italy; the story went that Octavian's father had helped to suppress a band of outlaws who were survivors from the infamous slave revolt of Spartacus, together with former partisans of the equally notorious Catiline.[4] The name *Thurinus* was thus something of an honorific, and not a particularly glorious one for the future sole master of the Roman world; indeed, as we shall see, Antony would taunt his young adversary with the rather undignified if not ignoble appellation. On the other hand, the name had undeniable charm as a tribute to the defence of Italy and the 'old days' of the Republic, and just as one Octavian had helped to defend Rome from a marauding rabble, so another would preserve the Republic from an even more ambitious would-be opponent.

The young Octavian was born into a Republic that had been at war with itself intermittently for several decades (and not without more than its share of foreign entanglements). The Republic itself was a little more than four hundred years old; before that, Rome had been one of several, if not many, Mediterranean kingdoms. We can be reasonably suspicious that the Romans of Octavian's day knew not so very much more than we do about those days of the monarchy, days shrouded in myth and legend more than scientific inquiry and history; days that today we know best through the surviving work of the Augustan historian Livy. The salient point was this: the Romans decided that kings were not for them. In 509 B.C.E., (the dates cannot be pressed too closely) the last of the kings was expelled, and the Republic was born with the rule of a pair of leaders, the so-called Roman consuls. And over the course of the next several centuries, a world was reborn and renewed, a world that was increasingly becoming Roman. Monarchy became an increasingly unthinkable proposition in the western reaches of the Mediterranean, while in the East, Alexander's bequest was the aforementioned patchwork of rival kingdoms of various size.

And the centuries rolled on, years and decades filled with such storied names as Pyrrhus, Hannibal, Mithridates, Spartacus, Marius and Sulla, Crassus and Pompey. They were years filled with struggles between patricians and plebeians at Rome, of conquests of Macedonians and Carthaginians, of Samnites and Numidians. The survival of the Republic, at least as an impressive Mediterranean power, would be threatened by various forces both internal and external. Some would call it miraculous that the Republic survived for well over four centuries, and that in fact it achieved far more than mere survival. For Rome achieved nothing less than the attainment of the pre-eminent position in the known world.

Gaius Julius Caesar may well be the figure most responsible for the eventual transition from a Republic to an Empire, though one cannot put a definitive date on when the one became the other, or even what exactly it was that defined Empire to the exclusion of Republic. In some ways the one never ended, while the other was merely an outgrowth of forces that had been at play for decades in different spheres of Roman life. But we can be suspicious, if not certain, that men like Caesar and Octavian/Augustus would not have entirely understood such a question as 'When did the Republic end?', or 'When did the Empire begin?' Actium is as reasonable an event as any of several others to choose as a convenient signpost on the timeline, so long as we qualify the date with numerous clarifications. And, too, there is the problem that the central figure in our story, the man who would be Augustus, nurtured the title *princeps* as his favourite appellation, the image of the future *pater patriae* or father of the fatherland as the first citizen. Thus we can fairly call the system that Augustus established the 'principate', the management of Rome by the *princeps* as first man of the Republic. It was the end of a long and variegated series of constitutional and legislative wrangling, and the constant threat of war, and throughout the story, we are reminded of how difficult it may have been in the years after the death of Caesar to predict what exactly would emerge from the maelstrom of historical controversies. One could hardly be faulted for thinking that the young Octavian might not survive some of the more challenging years in Roman history; certainly one could not be expected to think that he would be the father, in essence, of a new political system that would represent a transformation of the Republic into something markedly different from what had preceded it.

Octavian's adoptive father was assassinated on the Ides of March in 44 B.C.E. Julius Caesar was assassinated in large part because the senatorial aristocracy became convinced that he had aspirations to restore the monarchy. Indeed, less than a month before he was stabbed to death, it would seem that Caesar had turned down a calculated offer of a diadem, a royal crown, after testing a crowd to see the reaction to the idea of his being invested with the symbol of monarchical power. The man who had teasingly (?) offered Caesar the crown was none other than Mark Antony, his trusted friend and political ally. Caesar, for his part, was due to leave Rome to lead a mighty expedition against the Parthians a month later, and his enemies decided at last to act before he could leave (with Antony) on that military adventure in modern Syria, Iraq and Iran. There might well be the risk, after all, that the Parthians would see to Caesar's end just as they had eliminated his onetime partner in power Marcus Licinius Crassus. We cannot be sure exactly what Caesar's full intentions were for his Parthian expedition; perhaps he sought a complete conquest of their empire. Likelier might have been some sort of accommodation with them on terms that were eminently favourable to Rome.

Certainly Caesar's enemies were worried in the spring of 44 B.C.E. about political and domestic concerns, strains on the governmental system for which they blamed Caesar (and to some extent his lackey Antony). But the greater peril seemed to be that Caesar would triumph in the East, and that in consequence his supreme power in Rome would be unassailable, especially given his ambitious friend and ally in war, the popular Mark Antony. Caesar, after all, had won tremendous victories already in his career; he was supported by loyal soldiers, and a populace that seemed genuinely to appreciate his munificence and good nature; and he had an increasingly public relationship with a woman much his junior in years, though perhaps not in intellect and wit. This last detail of the final years of Caesar may have been a significant factor in his undoing. Caesar had won impressive victories in the West; he was known as a military hero in numerous Gallic campaigns, indeed for having fought in Britain (though his adventure there was not nearly as successful or noteworthy as in Gaul), and now he had the riches of the East either at his disposal or in line for the taking. He was also ageing, and possessed of an innate desire to rival the accomplishments of Alexander; the stuff of romance to be sure, but no less compelling and true for all the epic fantasy.

Caesar was suspected of monarchical ambitions for more reasons than a mere story about a crown (especially one that he had rejected after all, once the crowd started to protest). Caesar was well known for having engaged in a sexual affair with Cleopatra of Egypt, a royal woman more than thirty years younger. He had brought Cleopatra to Rome and lived with her more or less openly. He even had a son with her, a boy rather blandly named or at least nicknamed Caesarion, Greek for 'Little Caesar'; not a citizen of Rome, of course, but the son of the most powerful man in the Republic.[5] This was arguably the start of a new dynastic arrangement that was at least vaguely reminiscent of Alexander's affair with Roxane and the dream of a nuptial union of East and West. Whatever it was, it was most certainly not Roman in the traditional sense. The conspirators of the Ides and their supporters, the Brutuses and Cassiuses of both honour and infamy, had their own romantic dreams, visions of what they considered a restoration of the lost purity and splendour of the Republic of old. That Republic may have been well on its way to the grave even before Caesar came to power, but it exerted a powerful pull and hold on many a Roman politician. It is not for nothing that a later historian would meet his downfall for claiming that the ringleaders of the conspiracy to kill Caesar were the last of the Romans. Dante would place Brutus and Cassius together with Judas in the lowest circle of hell, doomed to be masticated for eternity in the mouth of Satan; the poet of the *Inferno* considered them the worst examples of traitors and of treacherous behaviour. Dante's view was by no means universally shared in the early years of what would become known as the Julio–Claudian dynasty. Caesar had been betrayed, for sure, and tales and rumours that Brutus was his biological son could only have increased the sense of violation and treachery. But Caesar had also managed to convince more than a few Romans that he posed a serious threat to the safety and security of the Republican system. We do well to remember that when Caesar defeated Pompey at Pharsalus, there were still more than a few Romans who were willing to fight and to die for what they saw as the salvation and redemption of the Republic. The contrast to the aftermath of the defeat of Antony and Cleopatra would be telling. It would be many years in fact, before the Pompeian resistance to Caesar's ghost would be entirely put down.

For reasons that cannot be definitively explicated (but that invite speculation and analysis of our evidence), on his death Caesar did not leave anything to Caesarion, or to Cleopatra, in his will.[6] Certainly, it would have been contrary to all Roman tradition and precedent, let alone of questionable legality. Nor did he bestow any bequests on Mark Antony, for reasons that will prove interesting too, on speculation. No, Caesar named Octavian as his heir, a fairly obscure son of a Roman senator, a fairly unknown quantity in Roman politics, a man whose only obvious claim to Caesarian favour was a somewhat tenuous family connection to Caesar, and the qualities that Caesar had perceived in the young man in the relatively limited interactions they had enjoyed. Romans had adopted other Romans with abandon for generations before Caesar; in the case of what happened in the months before the Ides of March, this much is certain: neither Caesar nor Antony expected the great Julius to die anytime soon, let alone in the Theatre of Pompey where Caesar was stabbed to death by his senatorial colleagues. Caesar had proven to be remarkably resilient since the days of pirate adventure and entanglement in the political drama of the civil war between Sulla and Marius, and luck had more than once sided with the hero of the Gallic campaigns. Octavian may well have been surprised by the news of the death, and certainly it plunged him into a both potentially rewarding and likely perilous situation; it was not without reason that his friend Agrippa was quite concerned about his friend's travel to Rome in the wake of the assassination.

Adolescence in the Crucible

Octavian was nineteen and had a new name. He did not however, have so very much of Caesar's money. This was in part because Antony did a fair amount of wheeling and dealing in the days immediately after Caesar's death to ensure that his own extensive debts would be paid (at least in part) by the generous sums of money in both the Roman treasury and Caesar's will. This outright theft was made possible in part because Antony was actually in Rome on the day of Caesar's assassination, as was Cleopatra, while Octavian was in the East, studying in Greece, and following the more or less normal career of a Roman nobleman in educational training and preparation for a career in politics and the law courts. In an interesting coincidence, the beginning of the accomplishment of Octavian's destiny would come while he was alone in Greece, with his two great enemies alone in Italy; a reverse of what would be the case a mere baker's dozen years later, when Antony, Octavian, and Cleopatra would all meet at Actium. The name of Caesar was a questionable advantage for Octavian, but it was also a name that seemingly might just as easily lead to his untimely death.

What happened to this trinity of historical worthies between 44 and 31 B.C.E.? In simple terms, they would emerge as fierce enemies. Antony and Cleopatra would commence their own love affair, and at least two children would be born from their union; Alexander the Sun and Cleopatra the Moon (Alexander Helios and Cleopatra Selene), names that evoke in part the Roman military hero's fantasies of becoming the new Alexander. Antony would seek to do what Caesar had failed to accomplish; subdue Parthia and extend Roman rule over the East. In this military endeavour, he would fail miserably, and Cleopatra would be part of the disaster. Antony would sign a solemn pact with Octavian to rule the Roman Republic in what some would call contrived emergency circumstances, as part a committee of three, a triumvirate, though it would soon become clear that only two of the three men really mattered. It was an age of dramatic historical change, and also of the rise of intensely talented artists in prose and poetry, men who would become key figures in what has often been called the Golden Age of Latin literature. It was a season of giants, both in the realms of the political and military, and the arts and culture. It was a world that would leave a lasting impact on all that came after it. To name but one inheritance, the very months of July and August that we use are due to the legacy of Julius and Augustus.

Some men would have time for the arts and the composition of verse in several genres, and others would be preoccupied with affairs of state. Almost from the beginning, Antony and Octavian would clash, though their clashes would be mitigated by the fact that they had conveniently agreed more or less to split the world between them, with Octavian in Rome and Antony in the East, where Caesar's protégé had both a natural recruiting ground for his Parthian expedition, and the no doubt welcome presence of his new lover, Cleopatra. Further, Antony agreed to one of the typical marriages of political alliance with Octavian's sister Octavia (the Romans were never creative about women's names), a marriage that seemed to portend peace between rival Romans, but which spelled only disaster for the understandably jealous Cleopatra. Antony would divorce Octavia; he would move to recognize the dynastic rights of the son of Cleopatra and Caesar over eastern territories that Cleopatra and he coveted, and in short, he would commence a dangerous game of chess with Octavian.

The strategy of Antony at least would seem to have been to capitalize on weariness and war fatigue. Would Octavian really move to subject the Roman world to another round of civil wars? For in the dozen or so years since Caesar died, Rome was consumed with enough civil and foreign strife as it was: 1) the conspirators who had killed Caesar now faced Caesar's heir, Octavian, and his erstwhile ally Antony; 2) the sons of the late Pompey the Great, greatest foe of the now equally late Caesar, were carrying on their own wars against the Republic they saw as now dangerously close to being a reborn monarchy; 3) various small kingdoms in the Roman East, not to mention North African realms, were taking advantage of the Roman civil strife to free themselves from financial and political arrangements with Rome that seemed increasingly disadvantageous to them; 4) Octavian himself had made enemies in Rome, on the one hand with those who resented the tremendous power of a teenager who had been left in daily charge of the problems of administering Rome, and on the other hand with those veterans who (not unreasonably) expected to be paid with coin and land for their long and arduous service.

In short, it is a miracle that Octavian survived the period from 44 to 31 B.C.E. Antony's strategy of hoping that Octavian would not want to add yet another war to the already long catalogue of wars and military struggles was tied to confidence in the belief that if he *did* try to do anything other than sit back and let his ostensible rival and his mistress take the Roman East, there would be plenty of opportunities for someone to do to the adopted son what had been done to the father. For one thing seemed certain to Antony: Octavian was no Caesar. It may not have occurred to Antony that he was no Caesar either, at least not in matters military.

And looming over it all was the enigma of Cleopatra, the lover first of Caesar and then of Antony; the woman who may in the end have been the greatest help of all to Octavian. Cleopatra would provide an outstanding means to secure what no other major Roman Republican civil combatant had accomplished; the redefinition of civil conflict as nothing less than a great clash between East and West, a foreign conflict *non pareil*. Actium and Alexandria would close the Mediterranean basin off as a Roman lake, as a truly labelled *mare nostrum*. Actium and Alexandria would be the final, definitive clash between Rome and what remained of the dream of Alexander. During the years just before this engagement of East and West in the strife of arms, a complicated political and propaganda war would be fought between Antony and Octavian, a war in which the latter would come out the better.

By the summer of 31 B.C.E., tensions had never been higher. The conspirators who had killed Caesar were more or less all dead or exiled; the marriage alliance that had helped to preserve some measure of peace between Antony and Octavian was no more. The expedition in Parthia had been a dismal failure, which meant that for Antony, cash reserves came only from Cleopatra and the riches of the realms she held as sovereign.[7] Octavian meanwhile, had a gift whose value could not be underestimated: Antony was living openly in Alexandria, in Egypt, with a foreign queen. Caesar, it is true, had brought her and her son to Rome, but Caesar had never drawn up a will that bequeathed anything to what the Roman aristocracy considered his mistress and bastard. Antony was not so wise, it might well seem, either in *les affaires politiques* or *les affaires d'amour*.

What historians call the 'Donations of Alexandria' may have been the last straw for Octavian and his friends in Rome.[8] Antony had been foolish enough, it would seem, to try to legitimize his relationship with Cleopatra and the rights of Caesar's son by her, and by extension, the rights of his own children with Egypt's queen. From a military point of view, Antony had also done something that was eerily reminiscent of what had happened when Caesar and Pompey had clashed; he began to move troops in quantity to Greece. Warships, many of them Egyptian, left Alexandria and other eastern ports and began to converge on Greece, specifically the northwest and the coast of what today extends past the Greek frontier to Albania.[9] The message was clear enough: the fleet and the ground forces were poised either to defend Greece from invasion, or to invade Italy and threaten the security of Rome herself. Of course the problem would be to hold Greece, if defensive action was the chosen strategy, and an invasion of Italy would have posed difficulties of its own. Antonian naval bases were established in a cordon around Greece; the triumvirs had agreed that Antony was the master of the Roman East, and the one responsible for negotiating anything that needed to be negotiated with Cleopatra of Egypt, but soon enough, Antony's forces could be depicted in Octavian's propaganda as a knife poised against Italy, a knife wielded by Egypt's queen. It did not matter whether or not the queen ever intended an Italian invasion and rule in Rome; what mattered was that her armed forces were manoeuvering dangerously close to the Italian coast, and that she was moving military units through the Roman East without the approval of the Roman Senate; the client queen of Rome was an all too easy target for the label of potential foreign invader.

Octavian and Antony had divided the world, to be sure, but the clear understanding had been that there was still one Republic. Increasingly, it became easier for Octavian to present the actions of Antony as the manoeuvres of one who was smitten with a sworn enemy of Rome, an Egyptian queen who was rumoured to have said that one day she would pass laws on the Capitoline Hill in Rome; a story that may have been invented by Octavian's active and well-rehearsed propaganda machine, but a report that was credible in part because of the massive military presence that Antony built up with his lover in Greece. And Antony had permitted Octavian to be in charge in Rome, a strategy designed in part, no doubt, to capitalize on the young man's relative inexperience and the hazards of domestic politics and the needs of angry veterans. The Octavian of the first Virgilian eclogue may be a god to one of the pastoral interlocutors, but Virgil's poem, with its backdrop of the land confiscations and other measures taken to satisfy the anger and resentment of military veterans in Italy, belies a quite perilous situation for the future *princeps* and first emperor of Rome. Still, if there were what some would call a 'home field' advantage, it was Octavian's; Antony handed that to him, aided mostly by his affair in Egypt.

Antony vs. Octavian

Some notes here may be useful. In the summer of 31 B.C.E., Antony on paper was conceivably stronger than Octavian. He was arguably the more popular of the two men with the Roman military rank and file, and the East was financially better off; indeed, significantly better off than Octavian's Italy, Spain, and Gaul. In terms of manpower, Antony had tremendously better reserves of recruits from which to augment his forces, and the capacity to pay them (though the question of just how good the recruits were in comparison to Octavian's reserves is a significant one). While there were Roman senators with Antony and other trappings of the Roman Republic, it was also clear that in the East, the word of Antony and Cleopatra was law, while in Rome, Octavian had to dance around the Senate and the apparatus of the Republic in a delicate political ballet in which more than a few players wanted to see the Republic restored for good and all. It could reasonably be argued that Antony, like Caesar before him, was less willing than Octavian to play within the republican system. Octavian was willing to endure long senate debates and hearings; he was at home in Italy more than anywhere else in the Roman world. For Antony, in many respects Athens was a more welcome home than Rome; Alexandria was more appealing than Capua or Antium, Brundisium or Misenum, and increasingly, the Roman world was aware of his philhellenic preferences.

But there was an undeniable romance to all this, a quality of the theatrical and the heroically appealing. Put another way, it seemed that Caesar's friend and military ally Antony, was poised to become the new Caesar (if not the new Alexander); he had even taken the mistress of his late master, while Octavian was a poor imitation indeed of Pompey, an adolescent who had barely any military experience at all in comparison to his rival, Antony. Indeed, at one battle during the campaign against Caesar's assassins, he had been driven from his command tent and forced to hide in a marsh until Antony could save him. Inexperienced and young, Octavian was also rumoured to be sickly; throughout his life, he would be plagued by real or psychosomatic bouts of ill health that would cause significant constitutional crises in Rome, and the birth of what would become *the* perennial problem of early Roman imperial history: what would happen if the soon to be great Augustus would die?[10] The problem of the Augustan succession is a recurring, key concern of the Augustan poets,

Virgil and Horace; it would remain a matter of contention and crisis for much of Augustus' life as *princeps*. Some would say that Octavian's system was inherently unstable in that it made no provision for the orderly transfer of power from one generation to another; perhaps the principal cause for this seeming lack of foresight was the desire to maintain what some would identify as the pretence of republican government.

Notwithstanding all that, Antony had perhaps equally glaring faults and liabilities, not least his losses in Parthia, the seemingly eternal enemy of Rome where the would-be Caesar had not enjoyed anything close to the successes of his mentor. And there was Cleopatra, no friend she to more than a few of Antony's supporters from Rome. Antony was ageing too, and he had far less on his *curriculum vitae* than Caesar had had. There was also the problem of his drinking, an alcoholism that even prompted him to write a short work *De Sua Ebrietate*, 'Concerning His Intoxication.'[11] Alexander had suffered from alcohol related problems, too; excess in wine and carousing cannot have helped Antony in the difficult military and political circumstances of 32–30 B.C.E.

By the summer of 31 B.C.E., Antony and Cleopatra had significant military forces throughout the East, with particular concentrations of naval and ground forces in western Greece. Some wags might well have noted that while Antony was clearly in the running to become the next Caesar, he was also in Greece and not in Italy; in other words, he was where Pompey had waited for Caesar. The crucial difference was that Pompey had fled Italy under duress; Antony had travelled to the East of his own free will (or at least his own free will as manipulated by Cleopatra). As we have seen, by this point in his life at least, he was far more at home in Athens than in Rome; Greece was for him a dream of a place in comparison to his native Italy.

Antony had a sizable force that seemed to taunt the *de facto* Western Roman Empire with an invitation to attack and be destroyed. The choices Octavian faced seemed all bad: 1) invade and risk significant destruction and quite possibly an overall loss; 2) defend Italy from the threat of invasion at significant financial and manpower costs that would likely spell economic collapse and military revolt; 3) come to some arrangement with Antony and Cleopatra that would give them complete control over the eastern third of the Roman Empire, with likely the same economic consequences to follow as with the second option. In other words, die and/or pay now or later.

Octavian and his childhood best friend Marcus Vipsanius Agrippa chose the first option, and the gamble would prove more than justified. They also decided that they would pursue a course of action that had been more or less off the Roman military table of 'safer' and 'more reliable' options for decades: naval warfare. Rome had tremendous experience in the construction and use of warships, but there had been no truly great naval wars for some time. The reasons for this were several and specific. First, ancient navigation was tremendously dependent on the luck and fortune of a given ship or fleet in dealing with weather in an age where meteorological predictions were crude and elementary at best. Octavian himself had lost not one, but two entire fleets off Sicily while he was engaged in the thankless task of finishing off Pompey's rebel son and his pirate flotilla. During the great conflict between Rome and Carthage too, entire fleets had been lost due to storm and tempest. Especially in time of financial exigency and monetary constraint, naval warfare might well have seemed a reckless and imprudent course of action. Octavian had had impressive successes at sea, but he had also suffered significant disasters, and Antony and Cleopatra posed a far more serious challenge to his ingenuity and stamina than Sextus Pompey. Arguably though, Octavian had the best advantage of all; he did not have Cleopatra on his side as a liability. The sources present a picture of Antony's Roman officers practically begging for him to send the queen away, and their position was more than justified, financial backing from Alexandria notwithstanding.

War on the Water

Octavian and Agrippa seem to have been fascinated by naval conflict, a fascination that likely came about after the forced engagements with Sextus Pompey. Some of this fascination may have been born from the experience of the loss of those fleets off Sicily. But whatever the genesis of the interest, the schoolboy fast friends started playing with boats (both real and toy) on bodies of water (both real and artificial). For many of those crucial thirteen years between the Ides and Actium, Octavian and Agrippa were practising for naval war. The immediate reason was the conflict with Sextus Pompey. The more important one would soon become the battle with Antony and Cleopatra. In short, there would be sound military reasons for a naval engagement (or even several), but the element of romantic adventure as West clashed with East would have been a prominent consideration on the minds of many. Rome had been founded (at least in one sense) after the naval voyage of Trojan exiles from the ruined city of Priam to Hesperia, the almost magical dream of a western land and a new home. Now, a voyage would take place in the opposite direction, as Rome faced the hazards of the East in dramatic marine combat.

By the summer of 31 B.C., Octavian and Agrippa were arguably far more competent at naval warfare than their Eastern foes; they had the aforementioned extensive experience in conflict with the marine forces of Sextus Pompey. Still, they lacked the financial reserves of their opponents, and there was still the tremendous risk that fleets could be lost despite the best of admirals and helmsmen. After all, from October to May it was only the bravest or most foolhardy of Roman ships that did much more than skirt the coasts of the Mediterranean; the hazards and risks were simply too high and not nearly cost effective enough to justify travel. According to lore, Caesar had surprised Pompey (and his own officers) by commandeering a boat to take him from Italy to Greece at the height of a storm (a tale dramatically related by the Roman poet, Lucan); he had more or less allowed propaganda to celebrate how the goddess Venus had protected her descendant Caesar. Venus, after all, was a goddess of islands and had, according to the ancient tales of mythology, floated on a conch shell to Cyprus, which became sacred to her in consequence. Caesar was descended from Iulus or Julus, the grandson of Venus, and so arguably his adopted son Octavian was under the protection of the goddess. But Octavian was sensitive to another god, another deity who conveniently had a temple in the vicinity of where Antony and Cleopatra were massing their fleets: the Apollo of Actium and Leucas. The god Apollo would become the key figure in the Augustan mythology that would be born in the waters of Actium.[12]

Leucas is an impressive place. White marble cliffs mark the heights where a temple of Apollo gazes over the harbour and shores of Actium. The island protects the natural port and safe anchorage for ships. Apollo was not particularly associated with mariners or navigation; his temple on the island long predated the time when the area was used as a staging ground for landing and transporting troops. But no doubt Octavian remembered that in the very first book of Homer's *Iliad*, it was the god Apollo who launched deadly arrows that brought plague to the Greeks after they had dishonoured a priest of the god. Apollo presided, as it were, over the action of the great Homeric epic; he was a war god who had to be appeased by victorious military forces.

Antony and Cleopatra had chosen the best place to anchor their vessels and house their troops either for defensive or offensive operations; they may too have appreciated the patronage of the site and the temple of Apollo that gleamed in the morning son: the white cliffs reflected the sun's light, and Apollo after all, was a god of the sun. And if Rome were born from the destruction of Troy, then who better to defend Rome than the god who had been responsible for the defence of the Trojans at the very start of the greatest of ancient epic poems?

East vs. West

Troy; East and West; Homer and epic: these images no doubt occurred to Octavian and Agrippa on long nights of anxiety after the training of troops and appeasement of the rancorous Senate, and veterans in Rome. Greece had done battle with Troy just as the Greeks of a later age did battle with the Persians; there was a profound awareness that Europe and Asia were separate, and clashed at rather regular intervals in human history, including the great, quasi-mythical struggle that had spelled destruction and ruin for Troy. This is the stuff of romance, but it is also rooted in history (even if for the Greeks and Romans, 'history' might well be more accurately labelled 'mytho-history' for the seminal events in the settlement of the Mediterranean. Certainly the victors contribute the prevailing mythology, and there are no epics that celebrate the descent of Antony from Anton and Hercules, though in Virgil's epic *Aeneid*, Hercules would play a key role as part of the crafting of the image of the conquest of chaos and disorder, and the establishment of peace and even serenity.

From the ruins of Troy came the exile band that had traveled to Italy and intermarried with the native Italians; from their union came the long line of kings and rulers that would culminate in the founding of Rome by Romulus. One of the key details in that process of the birth of Rome from the ruins of Troy, was the idea that Troy was truly dead and that Trojan customs and habits were suppressed in favour of native Italian language and lore. In other words, the Rome that emerged was not a new Troy in the strict sense. In the last book of Virgil's *Aeneid*, this would be exactly the point that would be settled in the final discussion of Jupiter and Juno at the climax of the unfolding of the divine machinery of the epic.

There is evidence that Julius Caesar took his Trojan lineage seriously. It was a mark of Roman blue bloods to trace one's family back to the mythical ancestors from Troy and Asia Minor; Caesar was apparently particularly proud of how he was descended from not just any Trojan, but from *the* Trojan: Aeneas' own son, Iulus (hence Iulius or Julius). The specific evidence of Caesar's pride in his Trojan lineage was the fact that he was accused of entertaining the idea of transferring the capital of Rome from Rome to Troy. By Caesar's day, Troy was a mere tourist site, and not a very impressive one at that; the poet Lucan has an account in his ninth book, of Caesar visiting Troy and seeing overgrown ruins, and barely a village on the site of the once great city and glory of the East. It seems that Caesar raised the idea of this shift of symbolic capital and rebuilding of the long dead city in February of 44 B.C.E. as part of his preparation for the campaign in Parthia: in other words, Caesar would conquer the East that had once been under the sway of Troy, and he would restore the glory of the ancient Troy that had distantly been responsible for the eventual birth of Rome. He, the descendant of the son of Aeneas and grandson of Venus, would take his place as the restorer of the glories of his ancient and storied lineage.

Some scholars have scoffed at the idea that Caesar actually ever raised or seriously considered this move from Rome to Troy (or for that matter, to Alexandria), or that anyone would have cared enough about the idea to add it to the list of reasons to kill the dictator. I think that the idea was very real and all too concerning for the Roman senatorial aristocracy, and I think that Octavian was acutely aware of the reality that in Roman historical and mythological lore, Troy was truly and forever dead. Troy, after all, was associated with the fanatical worship of the Great Mother Goddess Cybele, whose devotees and priests would castrate themselves in frenzied liturgical rites. In other words, Troy was all too closely associated with a simple and powerful paradigm: the bizarre religious rites of the East *vs.* the sober traditions of Rome and Italy. Cleopatra was uncomfortably close to the image of the dead Troy, of the strange liturgical traditions and practices of a world that was far removed from the Italy of the poet Virgil's *Georgics*.

The idea seems to have occurred to Octavian and Agrippa, then, that what was shaping up to be another civil war in Rome was actually a foreign war that fit quite neatly into the paradigm set at Troy in the distant mythological past, the same struggle that the Greek historian Herodotus celebrated in his history of the war between the Greeks and the Persians. West and East were clashing in mighty array; the real battle here was not between two Romans, but between Rome and the East. This would be another Trojan War as it were, or more precisely, another Greek naval victory over the Persians, another Salamis. This great naval victory would spell the defeat of the resurgent East, and confirm, or rather seal, Roman rule over the eastern Mediterranean. Rome after all, was not merely geographically located in the middle of the Mediterranean, at the very meeting point of West and East, Rome was the child of the union of Troy and Italy, and too, in an important sense, the offspring of the celebrated mythological affair between Venus and Mars. We shall see that in no small part, the Battle of Actium and its subsequent celebration and related propaganda was an attempt by the victors to come to terms with the diverse origins of the Roman people and state; an attempt not so much to rewrite history, as to offer a commentary both on what took place and why. Actium would become the centrepiece in nothing less than a commentary on the history of Rome, of how the Roman state had come to the point in its destiny where Octavian was the man of the hour, the man needed by his Roman brethren to save them from disasters both foreign and domestic.

Legend says that before the Battle of Zama, Hannibal and Scipio met for some time in private discussion. There is no such record of any communications between Antony and Octavian on the day of Actium. There is no evidence of what might have constituted the last communication between the two men whose alliance had always been political and expedient rather than heartfelt and rooted in friendship, beyond some reports of challenges and offers of single combat. Nor was there any evidence of what it was in the thoughts and minds of either man before the day they finally clashed, on 2 September in 31 B.C.E. It is likely, though, that in Octavian's mind was something of the larger issues of ethnicity, of Roman *versus* Trojan, of West *versus* East. This would have been all the more apparent given the nature of the fleet that Octavian found when he set up the first attempts of a blockade of the harbour at Actium: the ships Antony and Cleopatra manned included huge vessels that far exceeded the size of anything in the Roman fleet, ships that were identified by the terrifying images of the great anthropomorphic gods of ancient Egypt: the jackal-headed Anubis prominent among them, ready to send Roman sailors to the underworld in the waters off northwest Greece. If Antony had a vision of how he could be a new Alexander and unite the East and West in one great world empire, Octavian was dreaming of the preeminence of Italy.

What it was that happened on 2 September, 31 B.C.E. has been shrouded in mystery and romantic drama for more than two thousand years. We shall now begin to examine the extant evidence, and to seek to determine exactly how it was that by the end of that late summer day, a thirty-two year old with a perhaps more than unlikely background was the more or less undisputed master of the Roman world.[13]

Part One

Greek Historical Sources

Chapter 1

The Evidence of Plutarch

O ur methodology will be to examine closely the surviving literary attestations of the naval conflict at Actium, with a view to reconstruction and analysis of what might have happened.[1] We shall begin with sources written in Greek, before moving to those in Latin. The reason for this is because the surviving Greek sources offer the two longest and most connected narratives of the battle; those of Plutarch and Dio Cassius. Most study of Actium has centred on the evidence of these two accounts, which in large part agree with each other, though they admit to significant difficulties of interpretation. Some shreds of information and reference to Actium can be gleaned too from other sources, but our main concern, other than the narratives in Plutarch and Dio, will be to examine the earliest body of evidence concerning Actium; the references to the battle in the poets of Augustan Rome, Horace, Virgil, and Propertius.[2]

A Narrative from the Life of Antony

Much of what we know about the conflict between Octavian, Antony and Cleopatra is due to the magnificent achievement that is Plutarch's *Life of Antony*.[3] *The Life* was almost certainly composed sometime early in the second century C.E., when Plutarch was in his 50s or 60s, well over a century after the engagement at Actium. It relies on sources that are now lost or at best fragmentary, and it presents a host of difficulties for reconstructing what exactly took place at the battle. But it provides a convenient starting point for inquiry, not least because it is unquestionably the single most influential source for contemporary impressions and understanding of Actium.[4] We should remember that we are reading biography and not history of course, and that Plutarch is interested in what we might call the moral dimensions of his story of the rise and fall of Antony, a story in which Cleopatra will play a fatal role.

Actium is a battle where the outcome is not in dispute, but the rationale for the conflict, and the intentions of at least Antony and Cleopatra, are very much matters of controversy and doubt. Plutarch offers an abundance of detail, including passages that have been discussed and studied by numerous scholars of ancient history and classics. We shall move through both Plutarch and our other sources now, with annotated consideration of their accounts of the battle.

Plutarch's Actium narrative begins in paragraph 60 of *The Life*. Octavian made his preparations (Plutarch does not detail them; a significant omission for us), and a vote was taken to make war on Cleopatra, and to remove Antony from the command that he had given over to a woman. Octavian claimed that Antony had been drugged, and that the war was actually against the eunuch Mardion, Pothinus, Iras the hairdresser of Cleopatra, and Charmion, figures not mentioned anywhere else in the evidence, though three of the four would have a persistent afterlife in the long and colourful reception of the lore of the queen and her doomed lover.

Omens

Portents preceded the battle, as typically in Roman historical narratives; significantly, the last of the omens recorded by Plutarch concerns Cleopatra's flagship, the *Antonius*. Here swallows were said to have made a nest under its stern; the birds were attacked by other swallows, and the nestlings were destroyed. The image may well have been inspired by a simile of the poet Virgil at *Aeneid* 12.473-480, where the hero, Turnus is assisted by his divine sister Juturna in battle against Aeneas. Juturna takes the place of her brother's charioteer Metiscus, and proceeds to drive Turnus around the battlefield, essentially keeping him out of the line of fire and the perils of war (she rightly fears for his life). Virgil compares her to a black swallow that flies through the massive halls of a rich lord, seeking food for her hungry nestlings. The goddess is determined to protect her brother, but in fact the image of the swallow in the wealthy dwelling evokes the idea of Juturna seeking out (safe) targets on the battlefield for her brother.

Earthquake portents and the sweating of statues are not uncommon in Roman historiography; bird battles are more difficult to parallel. The only other source that mentions the swallow omen is the second-third century C.E. Roman historian, Dio Cassius (whom we shall consider in detail below), and he notes only the nesting of the birds on the ship, not the seemingly internecine avian war.[5] Whether or not the bird was especially associated with the goddess Isis, the omen seemed to be a dark and ominous indicator of imminent disaster.

Forces Arrayed for War

Plutarch proceeds to the marshalling of forces: Antony had no fewer than 500 vessels. The exact specifications of the ships is not noted, except that many were 'eights' and 'tens,' presumably with reference to the number of men on the oars, but in fact we cannot give definitive explanation of the exact disposition of the sailors on the individual ship types, or the exact way in which the banks of oars were arranged. Antony had 100,000 infantry and 12,000 cavalry; he also had a number of foreign kings in his service: Bocchus of Libya, Tarcondimotus of Upper Cilicia, Archelaus of Cappadocia, Deiotarus Philadelphus of Paphlagonia, Mithridates of Commagene, Sadalas of Thrace, and Amyntas of Lycaonia and Galatia.[6] The potentates Polemon of Pontus, Malchus of Arabia, Herod the Great, and Artavasdes of the Medes all sent aid. Antony had the firm support of the great (and lesser) monarchs of the East, at least on paper and in theory.

The principal problem in Plutarch's rendition of Antony's forces is that no clear distinction is made in the narrative as to the number of men and horse; we have no idea if the figures given include the foreign contingents. What is clear is that Antony outnumbered Octavian; the latter is credited with having 250 ships (half the force of Antony), 80,000 infantry, and an equal number of cavalry.

Plutarch is our source for the explanation that it was decided to fight on water and not land so as to please Cleopatra.[7] In Plutarch's view it is a proof of Antony's slavery to Cleopatra that he decided to do this, even when he was both far superior to Octavian on land, *and* in dire need of men to staff his ships.[8] It would seem that Antony was stronger (relative to his foe) on sea than land, given his possession of twice as many ships as Octavian; on land, if Plutarch can be trusted, the two men were equal in cavalry, and Antony had an extra 20,000 men. The question may indeed rest on just how well manned and staffed those many ships were, and also if the allied and subject kings contributed ground forces that are not included in Plutarch's numbers.[9] For the question of relative strength at sea hinged on the ability of the naval commander to man his vessels, the ability to have enough men ready to serve not only as rowers, but also as 'marines' for the inevitability raiding of enemy ships. All the ships in the world would be meaningless to Antony and his lover if they had no crews to fill them.

All that said, control of the sea was no mere romantic or adventurous gamble; there was good long-term strategic reason to assert naval supremacy.

In Plutarch, Octavian sends an invitation to Antony to come and enjoy an unopposed landing; he promises to withdraw a distance of one day's cavalry journey to permit Antony both a safe passage and time to set up a camp to prepare for a battle in southern Italy. Antony counteroffers with a demand for single combat, a heroic gesture of Homeric and Virgilian proportions, or at least that the battle be fought at Pharsalus in Greece, the site of the celebrated battle between Caesar and Pompey in August of 48 B.C. It is likely that some of the point of the offer of single combat was an attempt by the older, more experienced Antony to poke fun at his younger, sickly adversary. The desire to settle everything by single combat had been proposed in the *Iliad* in the case of Menelaus and Paris, and in Virgil's *Aeneid* it constitutes the climactic scene of the poem, as the Trojan Aeneas confronts the Rutulian Turnus, but there would be no such drama at either Actium or Alexandria. An offer of single combat was not to be taken seriously, except when it was.

If we can trust the historicity of the offers, it would seem that on the surface, Octavian wanted to fight in Italy, and Antony in Greece; indeed, at the very place where Caesar had defeated Pompey.[10] Plutarch locates Antony's force at Actium, near the so-called City of Victory (Nicopolis) that would be founded by the victor after the campaign. Actium was the promontory that guarded the *Ambracius Sinus* or 'Ambracian Gulf'; it was a natural enough locale in western Greece for a naval base, with an entrance that does not even measure a half-a-mile in length (and was thus easy to defend ably with towers and other fatal threats to those who would try to launch a frontal assault).[11] There was a celebrated temple of Apollo at Actium, a feature of the locale that is noted by Thucydides in his great history of the Peloponnesian War.[12]

Octavian meanwhile, is credited with making the crossing of the Ionian Sea ahead of Antony (if the latter actually intended one at this point), and landing at Torune in Epirus.[13] The exact location of Torune is disputed; Plutarch records that Cleopatra made an obscene joke about how it was of no concern that Octavian was now sitting on a ladle.[14]

The identification of Torune was likely complicated by the presence of Torone to the north (a location likely too far north to be the landing and settlement place of Octavian's force). Cleopatra's jests aside, Antony and his officers were disturbed by the news; certainly they had lost the strategic initiative and were now (at least for the moment) on the defensive. In Plutarch's version, Octavian essentially answers Antony's challenge for settling matters in Greece; he preemptively crosses the Ionian Sea. Antony was clearly surprised by the speed of the naval operation and amphibious landing; soon enough he manages something of a 'show piece' display of naval strength to conceal his serious deficiencies in crews, a ruse that succeeds in forcing Octavian to withdraw his naval force after its first sortie.[15]

Defections ...

At this point in his narrative, Plutarch notes the defections of Gnaeus Domitius Ahenobarbus and of kings Amyntas and Deiotarus Philadelphus, certainly signs of increasing worry and displeasure with the course of affairs.[16] Perhaps curiously, Plutarch observes that Antony's navy was always unlucky, and indeed perpetually late in rendering aid.[17] As we shall see soon enough, this may well constitute a reference to other episodes in the larger Actian campaign. There may be an allusion too, to the hope for additional allied support. Plutarch relates that Antony was compelled to pay attention to his land army in the face of naval disappointments; the point in context would seem to be that failure to achieve a quick victory at sea forced a revision of strategy and the prospect of a more or less protracted land campaign. Publius Canidius Crassus, Antony's commander for land forces, urged that Cleopatra be sent away, and that the army depart for Macedonia and Thrace. This recommendation is presented as a change of mind on Canidius' part; certainly it reflects growing irritation in Antony's ranks with the Egyptian queen.[18] Specifically, Plutarch cites Canidius' advice that Antony withdraw to await help from Dicomes of the Getes, Thracian tribesman from what is today part of Bulgaria and Romania. The mention of the Getes may reflect any aforementioned disappointment in the matter of naval reinforcement, and it comes with Canidius' explicit admonition to abandon the sea and prepare for a stand on land.[19] Plutarch's narrative is replete with evidence for the disagreement and disputes in Antony's camp, news of which would have been a significant part of the reports of the defectors to Octavian. The provenance of the intelligence however, is no good reason to doubt its truth; if anything, a telling detail in the preliminaries to Actium is the evidence we have that Octavian and Agrippa may have originally disagreed on the battle strategy. Agrippa won, or more pointedly, it seems that Octavian was willing to yield to Agrippa, whereas it is not entirely clear that Antony was always (or even often) able to do the same with respect to his lover. The history of the victors would of course admit of no serious dissension in Octavian's camp, but the evidence does provide good reason to believe that one side enjoyed far more cooperation and collegial planning sessions than the other.

In Antony's camp, Cleopatra won the day to be sure, and the decision was taken to fight at sea; for Plutarch, the queen was already planning an escape.[20] The key detail here may be that Cleopatra disposed of her forces where they would most easily be able to flee; perhaps if she had departed in accord with Canidius' recommendation, her force would have been expected to stay behind to aid Antony (especially in time of deficiencies in manning ships).[21] Certainly it is plausible that the same queen who wanted a fight on the water would also want a ready escape plan in the face of disaster. Those who condemn her for fleeing should be reminded that she could not very well return to the Ambracian Gulf; her situation there would arguably have been even more hazardous than Antony's.

... and Ambush.

Plutarch also records a story that Antony was nearly ambushed and captured alive by Octavian's forces during a private walk he took between walls extending from his naval base to his camp; a slave apparently advised Octavian that such an ambush would be possible. In the end, the ambush failed and Antony was successful in making his escape. The story is somewhat odd and not otherwise attested; certainly it speaks to the pervasive atmosphere of treachery and deceit in the camp.[22] We have no record of attempts on the queen's life; one suspects that her assassination was at least contemplated by some in Antony's command, but the truth is that we know surprisingly little about the life of the queen while she was with Antony on his expeditions.

At this point, Antony burns many of his vessels, but sixty of his Egyptian ships are certainly saved.[23] The best and largest ships of the fleet were outfitted with 20,000 infantry and 2,000 archers. The burning of the vessels can be explained as a costly measure in the face of a serious shortage in manpower; some would prefer to imagine that there was fear of desertion. Certainly there would be a reasonable fear of losing the unmanned vessels to Octavian, but the squandering of resources must have weighed heavily on some. In the immediate aftermath of this incendiary culling, a centurion questions Antony's decision to fight at sea; the commander makes no reply, but he does order that sails be taken on board the vessels, allegedly to allow for a quick pursuit of the (faster) ships of Octavian in the event of victory.[24]

Fleet Opposed Action.

The date was 29 August, 31 B.C.E. Plutarch notes that on that day, and for the triduum thereafter, the sea was tempestuous and windy. On the fifth day, 2 September, B.C.E., the weather was at last calm, and the battle was waged now that naval manoeuvres were possible. As we shall see, the calm weather of the morning would not last through the day. Weather determined the day of battle; any of the days from 29 August to 1 September could have been the date for the engagement.

Antony commanded the right wing of his fleet; Lucius Gellius Publicola was with him. 'Coelius' was on the left; this appears to be a mistake.[25] Marcus Octavius and Marcus Insteius were in the centre. On the other side, Marcus Vipsanius Agrippa was on the left, Caesar on the right. *with no mention of the centre command.*[26] Canidius commanded Antony's land force; Titus Statilius Taurus, Octavian's. As it happened, the land armies would have very little to do but watch and wait for news of what happened on the water.

Antony visits his ships in a small vessel; he urges them to rely on their bulk by not moving and by retaining their position as if it were a land battle. If attacked, the ships were to hold position at the narrow mouth of the gulf; none of this of course, is compatible with the idea of a breakout, at least not for the main body of Antony's force. The mouth of the *sinus* was eminently easy to defend, which of course meant that it was also all too easy to blockade.

Octavian is said to have left his tent to visit his ships, and to have met a man driving an ass, who when asked for his identity said that he was Good Fortune, and his beast of burden was Victory.[27] He was soon brought to his right wing in a small vessel, and was surprised to see Antony's fleet as if at anchor; the implication being that either he expected a breakout or an active engagement. Agrippa was prepared for either eventuality, and he had an array of strategies ready for battle.

Octavian kept his own fleet eight stades from the enemy; he was unsure, after all, as to Antony's exact strategy.[28] It was now the 'sixth hour', that is, about high noon. The wind rose from the sea, and Plutarch would have us believe that Antony's men were impatient, and they set the left wing in motion (Sosius' command). The manoeuvre apparently pleased Octavian, who ordered his right wing to back up so as to draw in the Antonian ships, hoping for a chance to encircle them.

Inevitably, the navies drew closer together, but Plutarch emphasizes that there was no ramming or crashing of vessels. He blames this first on the unwieldy nature of Antony's ships, and second on the related point that Octavian's were so much more maneuverable, and so for Plutarch, the battle really was like a land battle, or the siege of a walled town.[29] One would also not want to commit oneself too quickly to a particular strategy before the enemy had had a chance to show his hand. Antony's larger ships we should remember, would have posed a formidable threat to Octavian at close quarters, for all their vulnerability.

Plutarch gives a brief description of the actual manner of fighting. He states that three or four of Antony's ships were engaged with one of Octavian's, and that the men were fighting with wicker shields and spears, with poles and firebrands; Antony's forces are said to have fired catapults from wooden towers.[30] It may seem odd that so many of Antony's ships were after but one of Octavian's; perhaps it was felt necessary to block in and check the progress of the smaller, swifter vessels; their great advantage in speed and manoeuvrability needed to be neutralized.

Meanwhile, Agrippa is said to have drawn out his left wing; the encirclement strategy was well underway. Publicola advanced, and was thus cut off from the centre as Agrippa withdrew ever more to the left. The centre fell into confusion – the details are not specified – and engaged with Arruntius. Plutarch finally names the commander of Octavian's centre, a name the commentators note should have been provided earlier. As we shall explore soon enough, Plutarch may well have imitated the narrative of Virgil's allegoricized Actium, where his Arruns appears seemingly out of nowhere in pursuit of the heroine Camilla. As we shall see, Arruntius may have been a commander who more than earned his salary at Actium.

The Departure of Cleopatra.

Plutarch makes clear that at this point in the battle, the outcome was far from certain, indeed with an equal balance of fortune. But suddenly the sixty ships of Cleopatra hoisted sail for an escape through the midst of the battle.[31] Plutarch says that Cleopatra's ships were stationed behind Antony's larger vessels, and that they caused great confusion to their own forces as they suddenly pushed through, and Octavian's forces were said to be amazed as they saw Cleopatra's ships take advantage of a favourable wind to make for the Peloponnesus. Readers hoping for details to explain exactly how Cleopatra managed to make her escape will be disappointed; Plutarch offers no clear indications.

There is the detail or clue that Cleopatra took advantage of the wind. The wind was certainly reasonably predictable, but it could not be counted upon to allow for flight. The narrative is reasonably clear, then: the battle was evenly matched, and the queen made her escape as the wind allowed. It is easy to see how the scholarly community has come to what we might call a majority view that the plan from the start had been flight.

Infamously, Antony's reaction to the flight of his lover was to commandeer a five-oared galley in the company of Alexias the Syrian and Scellius, and to pursue Cleopatra.[32] Cleopatra takes note of the pursuit, and raises a signal; Antony approached and was taken on board her flagship.[33] We should note that Plutarch wastes no opportunity to make a moral judgment on Antony; his decision is entirely ascribed to the action of a lover who was considered his woman to be a part of him, or perhaps better, himself a part of her. One could argue that it is a relatively easy step to move from Plutarch's scene of Antony's evident surprise to Dio's account where the whole matter had been decided in advance by the two lovers. By the end of the day, the two leaders were safely away from the Ambracian Gulf, and the stuff of legends had transpired in the windy waters off Actium and Leucas.

We should also observe that Plutarch states clearly enough that the centre was in confusion as a result of action on Antony's right; Arruntius was engaged with the middle of the Antonian fleet. But the biographer also notes that Cleopatra's action of plunging through the middle *also* caused confusion. Certainly it is possible that there could have been what we might term a 'double confusion' in the mess of war, but as we shall see, it may well be that Cleopatra's forces responded to a crisis in the centre caused by the shift of resources and attention to the right wing.

Octavian's swift Liburnian ships pursue Cleopatra (the winds were no doubt working in the queen's favour); Antony takes over naval tactical operations and orders the flagship to face Octavian's vessels. All were held off except for that of Eurycles the Laconian, who was the most active of Antony's opponents, indeed who stood on deck with a spear as if to strike down the Roman. The scene in Plutarch is dramatic; Antony asks who it is who is so zealous to kill him, and he is told that it is none other than the son of Lachares, who can now avenge the death of his father.[34] Eurycles, in any event, did not ram Antony's ship, but that of Cleopatra's 'other' naval commander, and that vessel, and another besides, were captured together with significant treasures.

At the Entrance to the Underworld.

Antony meanwhile made his escape, only to spend three days alone on the prow, either in anger or shame in the face of Cleopatra. They landed at Taenarum, the modern Cape Matapan in the southern Peloponnesus, a legendary entrance to the underworld.[35] The couple are soon eating and sleeping together again, when word arrives that some transports have arrived from the battle, with word that the fleet was destroyed, the land army still intact. The detail about their reunion has a bit of a quality of the pathetic about it; this is the beginning of the long and languid months of waiting and what some would call pointless preparation. Certainly Octavian and Agrippa had more intelligence in the aftermath of the battle about what was happening, with everyone except perhaps, Antony and Cleopatra themselves; one imagines the lovers were largely in the dark for some time about most everything.

After some additional details about Antony's affairs (in particular, the order given to the land forces to withdraw via Macedonia into Asia), Plutarch provides some valuable further details about the engagement at Actium. The Antonian fleet is said to have held out for some time against Octavian after the departure of the two leaders; the seas appear to have become stormier, and the struggle was over at around four in the afternoon.[36] There were 5,000 dead, and 300 ships were captured; Plutarch cites Octavian himself for this detail.[37] If Antony had started with close to 500 ships and had suffered the capture of 300, then some 200 either escaped or were among those burned before the battle. Sixty Egyptian ones were certainly not subject to pre-battle pyromania, and may well have escaped; Eurycles captured two of these (and more may have been lost in the escape manoeuvres). The main problem is not so much how large Antony's original fleet was, but exactly which ships were burned (if indeed the story is reliable).

The detail about the high seas/stormy conditions is interesting. Was the wind that aided Cleopatra's flight especially strong? Were conditions exactly favourable for an escape in the general direction of Alexandria, and far more challenging for a battle on the Antonian right wing, or indeed in the centre? What sort of discomfiture was caused by the high seas to Octavian and Agrippa? Was the end of the battle hurried along by the weather? What was the exact disposition of Octavian's fleet on the night of the battle/the morning after?

The Aftermath.

In any case, the news of Antony's flight was apparently a shock to his men, especially when they considered that he still had 19 legions and 12,000 cavalry.[38] The latter number is of course the same as that given at the start of the battle; either Plutarch was careless in his recollection, or the horsemen were not part of the manning of the vessels.[39] Another interesting detail is that only a few of Antony's men were aware of his flight. This is certainly a reminder that in ancient battles, the availability of reliable information and intelligence was at a premium. It may be indicative of a sense of shock that anyone would have simply left the scene so abruptly, especially in pursuit of Cleopatra. Sober consideration might have reached the conclusion that Antony would be in potentially grave and imminent danger if he had retreated back to the Ambracian Gulf, and that flight to Egypt might well seem preferable (again, these decisions would have been fairly quickly settled, and in difficult circumstances). Scholars of course can debate endlessly the question of what would have happened if Antony had chosen to follow in Caesar's footsteps and fight on land, rather than to pursue his engagement of what to many has seemed a hopeless battle and most fortunate, and indeed skilled extrication operation. In contrast to the war between Caesar and Pompey, this conflict of a Caesar would not in the end, see any great land battle in Greece.

But Plutarch certainly paints a picture of a battle that Antony could have won, and Cleopatra with him, had only queen and lover not ran. This is in fact the summation that the biographer makes in his comparison of Antony and Demetrius Poliorcetes, where he observes that Demetrius was forsaken by others, while Antony did the forsaking of his friends and supporters.[40] The final word of Plutarch on Antony could perhaps not be more damning; Antony is to be considered more noble than Demetrius because at least he died before Octavian could capture him, though his death was still the death of a coward.[41] We may contrast these sentiments with the description of Cleopatra's death and its effect on Octavian, scenes that we will consider later as part of our study of the immediate aftermath of Actium.[42]

Chapter 2

The Lost Appian

A Tantalizing Loss.

Appian of Alexandria was born near the end of the first century C.E. He was a friend of Marcus Cornelius Fronto and a reasonably successful minor official under Antoninus Pius. He is known today principally for his work on Roman history, a twenty-four book work that devoted Books 13-17 to a narrative of the Roman civil wars; Books 18-21 concerned Roman wars in Egypt.[1] Of this original work, all of the Egypt books are lost; the five books on the civil wars survive. While there is valuable information on the conflict between Antony and Octavian, we have nothing of the historian's account of the actual campaigns.

A few references to Actium occur in the extant portions of Appian. At 13.5-6, the historian notes that it was after Actium that Octavian took control from Antony of all the provinces from Syria to the mouth of the Adriatic, and that Actium was both the climax of the civil wars and the commencement of his Egyptian history.

At 16.38, Appian gives a brief vignette of Marcus Valerius Messalla Corvinus in the context of the proscriptions of the second triumvirate. Messalla refused to accept command of the remnant forces of Brutus and Cassius, but sided with Antony; he remained with Antony until the dominance of Cleopatra. He then defected to Octavian and was suffect consul after Antony was deposed from power; at Actium he held a naval command against his former friend.

At 16.42, Appian describes how Metellus was a commander at Actium under Antony; he was taken prisoner and was not recognized. His son, also named Metellus, was in Octavian's service, and held his own command at the battle. After the son realized that his father was a prisoner in Octavian's camp, he urged his master either to spare his father or to kill the son as a proxy sacrifice; Octavian spared them both, though Metellus *pater* had been highly critical of Octavian, and had refused all requests to defect from Antony.

At 16.49, Marcus Lollius is noted as having served as an officer under Octavian at Actium; his story is not unlike Metellus'. He had served under

Brutus and been proscribed; he was saved when he pretended to be a slave and was purchased by one Barbula. Barbula eventually learned of the ruse and was able to intercede with Agrippa to obtain pardon for Lollius from Octavian. Later, Barbula fought for Antony at Actium and pretended to be a slave when captured. He was saved in turn by the intercession of Lollius.

The son of Lepidus was sent to Octavian on a charge of treason while the latter was at Actium (16.50); the son of Cicero was the one who announced the victory at Actium from the same rostra where his father's head had once been displayed during the proscriptions (16.51).

These are the only references to Actium in Appian, and they yield but little information that adds to our picture of the battle; we would give much to have access to the complete account of the engagement from the lost Book 18, a narrative that no doubt was of significant value to our next source, Dio Cassius, the author of the second of our two surviving detailed records of the battle.

Chapter 3

The Evidence of Dio Cassius

Another Narrative of Battle.

Dio Cassius Cocceianus was born in Bithynia in Asia Minor around the year 150 C.E., or some three decades after the death of Plutarch; he died in 235.[1] The son of the Roman governor of Cilicia, Dio had a storied career under several emperors in turbulent times. Today, he is best remembered for what remains of his eighty-book history of Rome.[2] Fortunately for the student of Actium, we possess Book 50 of the history, which contains another extended account of the battle, this one composed in the decades after Plutarch's *Life of Antony*, and so plausibly dependent at least in part on that lengthy version. Dio in fact offers what is the second of our two longer extant narratives of the battle; comparison is both frustrating and enlightening. Much of what we can hope to think we know about Actium is owed to Plutarch and Dio; the accounts have more in common than not, but the differences are quite significant. For various reasons Dio is not as widely known as Plutarch, but our knowledge of Actium (already plagued by a paucity of sources) would be far poorer, absent the survival of his account.

Book 50 of Dio opens with a summary of the reasons for the conflict between Antony and Octavian; it does not take the historian long to note the problem of Cleopatra, indeed specifically with the question of the children from her whom Antony had acknowledged as his own, and the reference to Cleopatra's son by Caesar as 'Caesarion' or 'Little Caesar'. Letters and harangues followed back and forth across the Mediterranean, together with envoys, a source, Dio notes, of ready access to information about the respective plans of the rival Romans. Open conflict came in 32 B.C.E., the year of the consuls Domitius and Sosius; the latter praised Antony on the first of the year, and spoke ill of Octavian. Octavian is said to have stayed away from Rome at first (a wise and prudent course of action); when he finally came to the capital, he was calm and condemnatory of Sosius and Antony. Soon enough Sosius and Domitius were off to Antony together with other senators; the perhaps inevitable conflict was drawing inexorably closer.

Others travelled in the opposite direction and made their way to Octavian; again, Dio takes care to note that among these were men who knew more than a little about Antony's plans.[3] Prominent among these refugees from Alexandria were Marcus Titius and Lucius Munatius Plancus; Dio notes that they may have been in conflict with Cleopatra.[4] This is all in Plutarch (60.2-3), especially the famous story of the deposition of Antony's will and the revelation that he wanted to be buried in Alexandria, the crowning argument of Octavian's propaganda against his onetime partner in power.

When war was finally declared against Cleopatra, Dio is careful to note that Antony had superior forces.[5] Active bribery is cited as a way to weaken the already inferior forces of Octavian; Octavian was thus compelled to pay his own men more to retain their loyalty. The inevitable portents are noted; in Dio, there is a dramatic detail that a monkey entered the temple of Ceres.[6] There was an eruption of Etna, and a massive (85 Greek feet) serpent in Etruria was killed by lightning after it had done much damage in the north of Italy. Little children fought the forthcoming battle in Rome for two days; the Antonians were defeated.[7]

The year 32 B.C.E. in Dio was an eventful one then, not least in terms of portentous events; on the military front, Antony is said to have intended to come to Italy in force, only to fall into trouble at Corcyra.[8] Dio notes that Antony found that Octavian had already arrived, and that he suspected that this was the main body of his rival's force and not some mere advance guard on reconnaissance, and so he withdrew to the Peloponnesus, spending the winter at Patrae. Caesar sent a letter to Antony offering the terms of withdrawal, a day's journey on horseback either in Greece or in Italy. Dio makes clear that the offer was not meant to be taken seriously, and that even Antony laughed at the proposal and noted that it was virtually unenforceable. It is difficult to know what to make of these stories of agreed upon landing spots and withdrawal to permit both armies to assemble; it would have been difficult if not impossible for Antony to utterly prevent Octavian's landing in Greece (easier to block access to Italy); certainly for the sake of morale on both sides there was a desire to appear to be eager to settle the whole matter as quickly as possible, to appear free from fear of a clash.

The consuls for 31 B.C.E. were Octavian and Marcus Valerius Messalla Corvinus; Antony by now had of course been deposed. Dio notes that it was near the start of the year when a fanatic rushed into the theatre and seized the crown of the dead Julius Caesar; he was at once torn to pieces by a mob.[9] A wolf was killed in the Temple of Fortune.[10] A dog killed and consumed another dog at a horse race; numerous fires broke out that may have been deliberate acts of arson. Omens are born of the fundamental human problem of lack of knowledge of the future; ominous events are all too easy to discern both forwards and back in time. The Romans may well have been among the more superstitious of peoples; in the case of Actium, propaganda and Cleopatra aside, there would be deaths and suffering for Romans on both sides of the battle.

Dio offers more details of the events of the winter of 31 B.C.E. Octavian left from Brundisium and advanced to Corcyra; he is said to have planned to have surprised Antony at Actium.[11] It is possible that the northern strategy was in part a response to the idea that Antony would have expected a stronger showing in the south first, a force that would have wreaked havoc with the routes from Egypt to Greece.

In any case, a storm compelled Octavian to withdraw. With the coming of spring, Antony made no moves; Dio notes that he had suffered deaths from disease and desertions, and that his fleet was polyglot and difficult to manage. Certainly this must have been true, at least in part; Antony would have had an enormous difficulty in managing an army such as he had in Greece to face a rather monolithic opponent (even if Octavian had auxiliaries and other forces that would have been recruited from outside Italy).[12]

A Crucial Engagement.

Agrippa now managed to seize Methone in the Pelopponesus, where he killed the client king Bogud; from this vantage point he was able to watch for commercial arrivals in Greece, and even to launch raids here and there on Greek soil; the south was now in Octavian's sights as much as the north. Octavian took great encouragement from these successes, and assembled a main force at Brundisium that soon enough crossed the Ionian Sea, not in the direction of Agrippa's force at Methone and the Pelopponesus, but again for Actium, where Dio notes that the majority of Antony's fleet was at anchor. Corcyra was now taken without resistance, and Octavian had another base, and a formidable one.[13] Antony had done the correct thing and established a cordon of bases to guard the East from any naval attacks from Italy; now one by one his possessions were taken away in what appears to have been a lightning series of raids. The desertion of Corcyra is easily criticized today, though resistance there may well have been futile at this point. If there were questions of strategy to debate, it might be the matter of whether or not Antony should have invested in more defence of bases that could then be seriously contested, or if he should have been considering his own invasion, of Italy. Some of the problem may have been manpower; it is conceivable that Antony simply did not have the forces to defend everything he needed to cover, and that Octavian thus had an easier time taking the initiative. Dio reports that Octavian made daily excursions to Actium, though no enemy ships appeared to challenge him. We should remember that in an age without satellites and radar, with intelligence coming mostly from actual eyewitness contact and desertions, Antony's forces would have very little sense of what Octavian and Agrippa were planning in any given strike or voyage. Still, the scene is clearly enough set: initiative was slipping away step by step from one side, as the other has an increasingly free hand in travel and expedition. The seas were being ceded, one station at a time.

Dio's Octavian made a demand now either for surrender or for battle; his Antony refused the former out of confidence in his abilities, but the latter out of fear; certainly Octavian seems to have seized the initiative. Antony proceeded to fortify Actium and to establish his main naval base there; Dio notes a story that he cannot verify that ships were ever conveyed over land into the inner harbour (the Ambracian Gulf). Dio describes both the geography of the place and its sacredness to Apollo; the stage was being set for the climactic clash.

Antony does not engage the enemy at once; Dio makes clear that Octavian was eager for a quick engagement either on land or at sea, all in the hope of winning a victory before Antony's forces could be massed at Actium (both men after all, had manpower problems, and Octavian's men were always in need of pay and other concessions to keep them happily in his employ and service). Interestingly, Dio relates that once Antony's cavalry had arrived and had more or less pinned down the enemy, Octavian launched a diversionary raid in the direction of Macedonia, a raid that allowed Agrippa the opportunity to move more or less unopposed to seize Leucas and the Antonian ships there. The Patrae Islands were also taken by Agrippa, in an engagement against Quintus Nasidius that is cited without detail.[14] Again, the loss of additional naval bases would have constituted a potentially grave peril to Antony. One gathers from the surviving evidence that one side had a very detailed plan, and the other a less than certain grasp of the ideal strategy to pursue. Agrippa displayed a far better sense of the rationale of naval manoeuvres, of the need to take bases and either to hold them or to deprive the enemy of their use.

Marcus Titius and Statilius Taurus launched a charge against Antony's cavalry and won a land victory to match Agrippa's naval conquests; soon enough, both Deiotarus and Domitius defected.[15] Dio's Antony grows more and more suspicious of treachery; he orders the death of the Arabian king, Iamblichus, and hands over Quintus Postumius to be ripped to pieces.[16] Antony himself sets out in pursuit of King Amyntas and Quintus Dellius (who had been sent to Macedonia and Thrace to find recruits); the implication is that he no longer trusted them, and perhaps that he was fearful of the consequences if they defected. (The poet Horace, as we shall see, would make much of the loss of the Galatian cavalry of Amyntas.) The picture is one of the collapse of the land situation side by side with the naval; there is no indication that Antony had any effective initiative to take, merely that he was responding to the increasingly dire situation set into motion by his enemies. More and more of his men and allies were looking for exit strategies as the noose was tightened.

At last, there was a glimmer of hope and chance for success. Lucius Tarius Rufus, one of Octavian's naval commanders, was attacked by Sosius.[17] Sosius appears to have had the right strategy in mind; Agrippa had been allowed to seize islands with relatively little resistance, and he was quickly achieving strategic dominance, and the far more formidable position. Sosius displays impressive tactical skills as well; he is said to have waited for a thick mist to conceal his numbers, and to have sailed just before dawn against the enemy. Sosius won the engagement and was in pursuit of his quarry when he encountered Agrippa, who saved Octavian's forces. King Tarcondimotus died in this battle, and, Dio would seem to have us think, Sosius as well.[18] Some scholars think that this action of the campaign was the source for the reference in Horace's ninth epode (which we shall discuss below in detail) for the apparent defections/retreats of Antonian forces before Octavian.[19] This encounter may well have been the most serious threat that Antony posed to Octavian in the skirmishes and engagements before Actium; it was exactly the sort of aggressive response that Antony needed to have exercised once he realized Agrippa's offensive strategy.

But Antony returns to his camp, and he is defeated soon enough by Octavian's advance cavalry; both on land and sea the situation is decidedly bleak for his forces. Soon enough Antony holds a council of war, and Cleopatra is said to have urged that the best positions should be fortified, while Antony and she should flee to Egypt. Here the omen of the swallows is cited; the birds had made their nest on her flagship as well as around her tent; milk and blood had also been observed to flow from beeswax. Dio's Cleopatra was nervous and frightened by the portents; the decision was taken to flee in such a way that was neither entirely secretive nor openly anxious.[20] The picture is one of near total desperation and exhaustion; there is no readily apparent way to win the day, and no effective response to the vice in which Octavian's forces seemed to hold Antony on land and sea. Battle would need to be offered, either on land or at sea; if you decide between the two, then the fate of your ships hangs in the balance either way; boats are not easily transported, disassembled, or otherwise disposed, unless you are willing to abandon or destroy them.

Thus the ruse of the naval battle seems to have been invented; a naval engagement would allow for the chance to flee without seeming to flee. If there were resistance, they would need a strong naval force to secure the breakout; only the best of the ships would do, and so the rest were burned.[21] Valuables were boarded on the vessels destined for flight and escape (not to mention sails); Antony at last addressed his men. Before offering any comment on Antony's speech, we should underscore that Dio's account of the preliminaries to the battle is the only extant source that offers an account of some pre-engagement strategy planning for what some might think a 'fake' encounter; only in Dio do we find war council strategizing that involves an active intention to use a battle as mere 'cover' to escape the scene.[22] We have no idea what source Dio had for the narrative here, if indeed he did not invent some of it to explain later events; the council of war and the subsequent speeches to the army are part of the tradition of classical (especially Greek) historiography; certainly there were such meetings and speeches, though the content can only have been reported to the victors by either defectors or survivors.

Dio's account of Antony's speech is long and largely devoid of any clues regarding the progress of the battle; Antony notes *inter alia* that his forces are significantly larger than Octavian's, and that he himself is a far superior commander.[23] Antony particularly notes how his naval forces are far superior to Octavian's, while Octavian has the better position on land; for this reason, he has decided to challenge his enemy on the water, and not with infantry and cavalry in a land engagement. Antony notes that victory at sea would ensure victory on land.

One might question the Antonian argument that Octavian was superior on land, but the basic outline of the supremacy of naval combat in the present circumstances may well be the correct argument (again, the Cleopatran argument was arguably the sound one). There is more to the picture, to be sure, especially the relationship of the naval struggle to that on land, but a case can be made for the position that Antony and Cleopatra needed a naval victory to secure any lasting chance of Octavian's ultimate defeat. The fate of the ships must have been among the most pressing concerns for Antony and the queen; it was unthinkable that Octavian should gain control of a large portion of the

Antonian fleet without a fight. And while we do not have evidence to reach a definitive conclusion, we can be reasonably certain that neither queen nor disgraced triumvir had much in the way of additional ship strength readily available in the eastern Mediterranean; again, this was not the age of standing navies (though Agrippa was changing that). Among the naval lessons that may be learned from Actium is this; if you bring your fleet to a particular point on the map, you must be prepared either to defend the position or to withdraw. But in the case of ancient navies, defensive naval action was always fraught with difficulties; the victory usually went to the one with the initiative though, as the Romans had illustrated so well in the First Punic War; dogged determination could also win the day. In the present circumstances, there would be no such determination after 2 September.

Dio notes that Antony had all of his most powerful allies and friends placed on the boats, so as to avoid any possibility of rebellion against his command on land.[24] Archers, slingers, and heavily-armed foot soldiers also embarked on the ships. Dio's Antony learned from the knowledge of how Octavian had defeated Sextus Pompey in Sicily; he purposely built his ships to be higher than Octavian's, with towers that could be manned for marine siege warfare. Octavian's intelligence learned much of this of course, and Dio relates his alleged speech to his own men. Much of the speech is concerned, not surprisingly, with the question of Antony's enslavement to Cleopatra; much of it is a paean to the glory of the old Roman spirit. Octavian notes that Antony has taller ships, and that in consequence they are less manoeuverable.[25] This is one of the oddest details in the overall picture we have of the battle; surely Antony and his captains would have realized that Octavian and Agrippa were prepared for a conflict against larger ships, and that they had a strategy for responding to such a threat; if we can believe our sources, Antony's naval battle plan was weakest precisely in the matter of having highly manoeuvrable, small crafts like the Liburnian galleys that would receive so much credit for Octavian's victory. Then again, Antony had hardly any experience in water fights compared to his rivals.

Octavian correctly notes that if Antony plans simply to sit in place in his ship-borne wooden towers, then soon enough his vessels will be assaulted by Octavian's siege works; defensive warfare will not suffice. He observes that Antony's ships are both too large to flee away successfully, and too bulky to chase down the enemy's vessels. After observing that Antony's ships have already been tested and found wanting in the waters off Leucas, he notes that Antony and Cleopatra are not really trying to fight a decisive engagement, but merely to break out and escape Octavian's blockade; the battle is thus as good as finished. So much for Plutarch's detail that Octavian's forces were astounded by anything they saw on the day of battle.

A Curious Strategy.

At paragraph 31 of his account, Dio begins to narrate the actual strategy that Octavian employed. He intended to let the enemy escape, with the plan to fall upon their rear as they took flight; he aimed to capture Antony and Cleopatra and thus dissuade the rest of the naval force from fighting.[26] Agrippa, however, was worried that they would not be fast enough to catch them, given that the enemy would be using sails, an interesting detail in light of the recurring emphasis on the relative sizes and manoeuvrability of the forces. Agrippa was certain he could win a victory though, in particular because a storm had struck Antony's fleet and not his own (one wonders if anyone considered that detail to be portentous).

Octavian listened to Agrippa (a recurring theme in the literary evidence), and had his own infantry board the ships; his friends were placed in swift boats that could move about quickly and spread news among the fleet.[27] We shall see later that the poet Horace may well have been in one of those small vessels. Soon the battle proper commences; Antony's forces move outside of the strait just a little, and make no further move. Octavian advanced, but Antony's fleet neither engaged him nor retreated. Dio notes that Antony made his battle line especially dense by close formation; Octavian was in doubt as to what to do (did he expect an attempt at flight?). Certainly he did not wish to fall into an Antonian trap by advancing too close to the large ships, with the attendant hazards from their elevated siege engines. The Antonian ships were a particular threat at close quarters, and Agrippa had seen what tall and threatening vessels could do in his campaigns against Sextus Pompey.

And so rather than risk an engagement, Agrippa ordered a pause, and his men waited; at some point then, he gave a sudden command to advance to his wings, and they moved forward in a crescent formation.[28] Dio states that the goal was either encirclement or disruption of Antony's battle line. Antony was worried about being outflanked, and so unwillingly he moved to engage Octavian; again, he had lost the initiative. We should remember that any crescent formation might recall nothing less than the bow of Apollo, the metaphorical weapon that would be launched against both Antony and Cleopatra. Octavian had speed and maneuverability on his side, and he could realistically hope to seek to outflank the enemy fleet, especially on the wing where Agrippa was in command. In naval combat you do not usually want to allow the opposing fleet to fight another day, if destruction is both safe and feasible; the goal, *ceteris paribus*, is the utter destruction of your foe.

Hit and Run Strikes.

Dio notes that in the ensuing conflict Octavian's ships were faster and thus capable of veritable hit and run strikes; they would ram ships and hope to sink them, but if they failed, they would simply move on to attack another and another in rapid, unrelenting succession. One side resembled cavalry (that is, Octavian's) and the other infantry (a telling description).[29] There was equal destruction and successful good fortune on either side; the battle seems for a while to have been more or less equally matched, given that Antony's men were able to launch attacks with archers and siege works on approaching ships. One strategy was to attempt to destroy an enemy bank of oars; there was always the risk of being sunk by stone and missile from the defending vessel. Ships that failed to ram and actually sink an opponent found themselves cut off and surrounded by enemy units. All of this is preface to Dio's clear indication that the battle was anyone's game for some time. We might observe that Dio's description of the difference in the tactics of the two forces (as occasioned by the differences in ship size) would perhaps mean that Octavian's navy needed to have an especially disciplined plan of both attack and retreat; throughout, one may recall that Agrippa, if anyone, was the likely naval genius on the water that day. Practiced manoeuvres and carefully launched attacks were the order of the day, at least to start; luring ships away from their battle position to seek to encircle them and (ultimately) to get to the rear was the plan of the day. There must have been a gingerly quality to the early manoeuvres, as Agrippa tested the Antonian fleet to see what, if anything, was their battle plan. Would there be some drive to the centre in the hopes of shattering Agrippa's battle line and allowing for some sort of attempt at encircling him? Would such an attempt simply result in Agrippa being able to wheel around and envelop the enveloper?

Dio notes that Cleopatra was at anchor in the rear, and that eventually she lost her nerve in the face of the ongoing hours of uncertainty (the anchors would have reflected the difficulty of sitting still, as it were, given the conditions and threat of wind and sea). For Dio, her decision to raise the signal to her Egyptians to flee was typical both for her gender and her race; the historian makes clear that until she fled, the battle was anyone's game. A favouring wind had arisen, and Cleopatra's forces raised sail and took to flight (Dio makes clear that the wind had arisen by chance; again, it would have been fairly predictable for location and season, but it could in no way be counted on as a certainty.)[30] Antony saw all this, and assumed not that Cleopatra had ordered the escape, but that they felt that they were being defeated, and so he pursued them. When others saw this reaction from their commander, they were confused, and soon enough they were in flight too, some of them even throwing down their siege towers into the water in the hope of making a swifter escape, unencumbered by the large machinery that had been intended for ship-to-ship combat. Every siege machine overboard was one less threat to Agrippa's ships. Once the Antonian vessels were clearly seeking a safe path out of the struggle, they could be considered targets of opportunity, though here too, there would have been significant danger for the pursuing ship that strayed within range of enemy fire.

Octavian's forces were not under sail, and so they could not pursue the Egyptians (Agrippa's worry was well founded), but they began to attack the Antonian ships that *were* at hand (presumably with greater vehemence than heretofore, and the renewed morale that came from the sight of the flight). At this point, Octavian orders fire to be employed against the enemy ships; Dio notes that until now, Octavian had wanted to try to seize Antony's vessels intact for the sake of treasure and loot.[31] This is the moment in Dio's narrative where the conflict takes on an especially violent nature, though the historian had noted that things had been fairly indecisive for a while before the queen's flight. Was the use of fire the decisive factor in deciding the battle? Had Agrippa learned how to employ pyrotechnics effectively in naval warfare, thus reducing the risk to his own ships? Fire would certainly have been an option in terms of seeking to slow down the enemy, especially an enemy under sail.

The Horrors of War.

A dramatic scene unfolds; fiery horror and incendiary hell awaits the combatants as the war reaches a feverish, blazing conclusion of destruction and death. The very ships become funeral pyres.[32] The details are quite specific here; men tried to use potable water to extinguish the fires from missiles and assault, but when the supply of drinking water was exhausted, they turned to the use of seawater, which created an even worse problem in many cases, especially since they did not have a sufficient supply of buckets and firefighting equipment on board ship. Bodies are used to extinguish the flames – and the whole situation becomes worse when the wind proves to be fierce and strong, a detail that accords with Plutarch's account of the high seas that eventually intervened to bring an end to the fight.[33] Again, the wind that aided Cleopatra's escape appears to have continued to increase in strength and force. If the wind helped in any planned escape, it also helped in making fire a most effective and risky weapon of potentially mass destruction.

Smoke inhalation kills perhaps the more fortunate of the victims of the fires; others are burned alive in their very armour. Some were drowned when they jumped into the water; others were killed by sea monsters (we do well to note that scenes of death and destruction at sea can certainly attract the interest and attention of sharks). Suicides ensue, and mutual pacts thereof. Only Dio among our surviving sources gives any real indication of the tremendous struggle and plight of the men who fought and died at Actium; only Dio provides any real rendition of the enormous suffering of the casualties of the engagement.[34] This is rhetoric and drama to be sure, but it is also a compelling enough description of the hell that an ancient naval battle might easily have been. For the 'personal' story of the Battle of Actium we must turn to Dio; we have no idea what the eyewitness accounts of the participants may have reported about what they saw and experienced on that day. Were the quinquennial celebrations of Actium attended by veterans who could report what they saw, however reliable the memories, from that late summer day?

The book ends with the observation that Octavian's men stayed as far away from the ruined Antonian ships as they could, until finally the desire for greed outweighed any considerations for safety, and many a man perished because of lust for wealth, a moralizing conclusion to the fiery narrative (in Dio, all men are equally susceptible to the dangers of greed and perilous lust for rapine). There is no narrative of successful pursuit of Antony and Cleopatra; in Book 51, Dio notes that ships were sent to apprehend the couple, but that they were not able to capture them. But Dio does take special care to observe the date, 2 September, 31 B.C.E., noting that he usually does not make particular mention of such calendar concerns. Dio understood the significance of what happened off the waters of northwestern Greece, even if his narrative might seem just as mystifying as that of his predecessor Plutarch.

We are left with more questions than answers, even if the two Greek writers have presented a more or less coherent account of the battle. We shall now turn to less often consulted sources of evidence, other voices that contribute to our knowledge of how exactly Octavian won his victory.

Chapter Four

Strabo's *Geography*

The Patron God Apollo.

W e can next consider the relatively few mentions of Actium in two additional Greek authors, Strabo and Josephus, neither of whom ever provided battle narratives (lost or otherwise) of which we are aware. But given the paucity of surviving sources of the battle, we do well to scrutinize every scrap of testimony.

Strabo is another voice of evidence in the reconstruction of the puzzle of Actium, and an early one. He was born in 64-63 B.C.E. and died c. 25 C.E. His historical works have not survived, and we have no idea if Actium was mentioned therein, at least in passing, but his immensely valuable *Geographica* is extant.[1] It is one of two great classical geographies that survive; the other is the Latin work of Pomponius Mela (first half of the first century C.E.); Pliny the Elder's *Natural History* also devotes considerable space to the subject. Strabo's *Geography* is an invaluable treasure trove of information about the world as seen through the eyes of a highly educated Greek of the imperial period.

Strabo mentions the death of Bogud at Methone, after Agrippa captured the place in the early stages of the Actian campaign; again, one of the more important episodes of the overall campaign in terms of its strategic significance.[2] And at 10.2.7-9, we find a description of the locale around Actium. The temple of Apollo is noted, as well as Leucas and the temple of Apollo Leucatas, where the strange rites of Leucadian sacrifice were said to be conducted in honour of the god, complete with hurling sacrificial victims off the promontory, with wings and birds attached to the unfortunate soul in the hope of lightening the flight, and more happily perhaps, with men in boats waiting to save the cast off. For Strabo, even writing in the wake of Actium, indeed far closer in time than Plutarch, it is the Apollonian connection of Actium that is most prominent, far more than any mention of the war.

At 17.1.11 we find a succinct and telling survey of Egyptian history; Antony entered Asia after Philippi and honoured Cleopatra even as a wife and with children; he undertook Actium with her and fled with her, and as for the aftermath, at 17.1.9–10, Strabo mentions Antony's time at Alexandria in the wake of his defeat.[3] Tantalizing details indeed, even in the absence of a continuous account.

Further, the settlement at Nicopolis is mentioned at 7.7.6 as a place where all the survivors of the many years of war between Rome and Macedon were finally settled; Strabo notes the battle of Actium in passing here with a detail that Cleopatra was present for it. The quinquennial games that were established in honour of Octavian's victory are also noted; the games that are celebrated in honour of Actian Apollo.

Strabo, like Josephus, had no obvious reason to dwell on battle narratives or strategy and tactics.[4] But he is a voice from relatively soon after the war, and for him the salient points worthy of mention are the importance of the patron god to the site of the battle, and the flight from conflict of both Antony and Cleopatra.[5] Apollo was an indelible part of the mythology that developed around the battle; Octavian had merely to note whose temple it was that loomed large over the victory. Venus may have been the patroness of the Julian *gens* or Roman clan, and indeed her role in the Actian victory was an acknowledged part of the propaganda in honour of the Augustan achievement, but it would be Apollo who would prove to be the most enduring figure in the pantheon of Roman patron gods of the naval clash at Actium.

Chapter 5

The Evidence of Josephus

The Flight from Actium and the Advice to Kill the Queen.

Titus Flavius Josephus was born Joseph ben Matthias in Jerusalem around 37 C.E.; he died c. 100, roughly contemporary with Plutarch. Josephus' principal works were a history of the Jewish wars in seven books, and the great *Jewish Antiquities* in twenty volumes.[1] Josephus is an invaluable source of information on a wide range of topics from classical antiquity; it is a tremendous boon that so much of his work survives.

Unlike Appian (let alone Plutarch or Dio), Josephus did not compose a detailed narrative of Actium. But more scattered references to the battle survive in his work than in what remains of Appian's history, and one detail at least is of significantly greater interest. In the *Contra Apionem*, a late work of the author that may date to early in the second century C.E., there is one important allusion to Actium.[2] Josephus notes that Apion criticized the Jews of Alexandria for their treatment of Cleopatra, when in fact he should have exercised his venom on Cleopatra herself. Regrettably the passage is marred by the lacuna common to all manuscripts of the work; we have a Latin translation of the sixth century C.E., which in places seems to have misunderstood the original Greek text. This translation notes that Cleopatra abandoned Antony at Actium, and that by her exercise of sexual passion and corruption she drove Antony to abandon his power and to follow after her to destruction. The problems in the transmission of the text of Josephus here make it difficult to assess his evidence critically; it is possible that Josephus constitutes the earliest attestation for the view that Cleopatra somehow was treacherous to Antony's cause by seeking the safety of escape.

There are brief mentions of Herod in the context of Actium in the *Jewish Wars*; first that the king was prepared to join forces with Antony at the start of the campaign, and second that Palestine suffered an earthquake in the spring of 31 B.C.E. that is said to have killed 30,000 and to have inspired an Arab invasion.[3] Note is also made of how after the battle and defeat of Antony, Herod told Octavian that he was staunch and steadfast in his loyalty to Antony, even to the point of promising him defensive aid after his defeat, but that he had advised his friend to kill Cleopatra.[4] Some of these details are also found in the *Jewish Antiquities*, where Josephus makes clear that Actium was a campaign for supremacy over the world;[5] Josephus notes that Cleopatra wanted Herod to fight the Arabs in the expectation that one or the other would be defeated, and that she could more easily absorb the territory of the victorious survivor.[6] In any case, the friendship between Octavian and Herod was soon enough secure; Herod is credited with the finance of many of the public buildings at the City of Victory, Nicopolis.[7]

The several Josephan references to Herod the Great are to be expected in works that focus on Jewish history and not on the civil war between Octavian and Antony *per se*, but the evidence of Cleopatra's flight (however problematic) is of particular note. The date of the *Contra Apionem* cannot be given with any certainty; it is difficult, too, to comment on the relative chronology of the work and Plutarch's life of Antony. But what emerges consistently from Josephus' pen is a dislike of Cleopatra and a condemnation of Egypt's queen; for the great Jewish scholar and Roman pensioner, Cleopatra's flight was the cause of Antony's defeat at Actium, and consequently of his loss in the struggle for the world; the shrewd and prudent Herod, for his part, likely would have shared Josephus' appraisal of Antony's lover; he alone is attested in surviving sources for having urged Antony simply to kill his Egyptian girlfriend. The narrative offers something of the reverse of the better-attested story that Octavian urged Cleopatra to see to the death of Antony during the Antonian campaign; here Herod is reported to have given advice that must have seemed wise in the final analysis.

Josephus' interest in Herod the Great is understandable enough, and the king clearly played an important role in the events surrounding the ultimate victory of Octavian in the East. Herod himself was friends with Nicolaus of Damascus, a Greek historian who was apparently a teacher of the children of Antony and Cleopatra. Nicolaus composed a universal history in 144 books, a work that was a significant source for Josephus in his own compositions. Nicolaus was prodigious, and he also authored a life of Augustus, some portions of which survive.[8] It seems likely that Nicolaus' universal history was challenged only by Livy in sheer size and volume; it is another of those many works we should very much like to have intact.

Nicolaus was a devoted friend to Herod; apparently a significant portion of his work was given over to a detailed (and likely encomiastic) consideration of the king's reign. While Nicolaus' surviving work does not offer any help in explicating what happened at Actium, at the very least it does afford a good reminder of how much we have lost of contemporary and 'recent' historical work from the Age of Actium, and of the friendly relationship that developed between the tutor of the children of the notorious couple and the victorious *princeps* Octavian, a man who would come to name a particularly fine date after the friend of Herod and author of what was likely the first biography of Augustus.[9]

Part Two

Roman Historical Sources

Chapter 6

Velleius Paterculus

A Neglected Voice.

Marcus or Gaius Velleius Paterculus had the good or bad fortune of living through some of the most interesting dates in Roman history; for the sake of convenience, if not absolute precision, we can assign his years to 20 or 19 B.C.E. – 31 C.E.[1] His *Historiae Romanae* in two books was ostensibly meant to celebrate the rise of his friend Marcus Vinicius to the consulship.[2] The first book suffers from the loss of a considerable lacuna; the second book offers an important surviving account of the affairs of Julius Caesar, Augustus, and Tiberius.[3]

Velleius was a military man, and had a career in the army before entering political life; his work seems to have been relatively little known, but for the student of Actium it offers an insight, however brief and of questionable sophistication, into the thoughts of a Roman author writing some sixty years after the battle. It provides in fact, the first extant historical narrative of the engagement in Roman history. We have no way of knowing for certain whether it was a source for Plutarch and Dio; in general Velleius seems to have been little read in antiquity. No one would call Velleius a 'great' historian; he cannot stand any comparison to such Latin rivals as Livy and Tacitus. Still, for Actium we must be content to scrutinize the relatively few sources we have.

For Velleius, Antony's decision to bring war to his *patria* or fatherland was a byproduct of his passion for Cleopatra.[4] Even in a work as brief as Velleius', there is room for mention of Antony in his guise as Father Liber or Bacchus, the wine god, and of processions in Alexandria where Antony was dressed in saffron and ivy, with the wand and wreath of the god.[5] Plancus defects to Caesar, but for Velleius, the defection is of one who was more or less in love with the idea of betraying his hosts and friends. Velleius' Plancus was a flatterer of the queen, and even played the part of Glaucus the mythological sea creature, complete with blue paint on his body and a fish's tail for a costume. Of all our Actian accounts, this is the most memorable in terms of the degradation of Romans at the court of the queen.

Actium for Velleius was the culmination of a victory that was long before decided.[6] Octavian's men are depicted as eager and ready; Antony's as depressed and weary. Octavian's men have provisions and supplies; Antony's are hungry and in want. Octavian has vessels that can actually be manoeuvred; Antony's look impressive, but in practice are a liability. Octavian welcomes defectors nearly daily; no one goes over to Antony's side.[7] The final victory is a foregone conclusion; the picture of Plancus in his Glaucus costume and blue paint is nothing less than a perverse omen of the future engagement and the defeat of Antony and his Egyptian whore. Certainly Velleius can be accused (all too easily in fact) of being a sycophant to the Tiberian regime, and thus to being prone to glorifying whatever served to bring the Augustan one to power, but that does not mean that he is incapable of telling us what actually happened.

Velleius records that Agrippa took Leucas, Patrae, and Corinth, twice with defeat of Antonian forces, and indeed that all of the victories occurred before the eyes of the Antonian navy (it is not entirely clear how much of the set of victories was due to naval combat and how much to defection). On the actual day of Actium, Octavian fights for the *salus* or salvation of the world, Antony for its *ruina* or destruction. Octavian's right wing was under the command of Marcus Lurius, with Arruntius at the left, an apparent discrepancy from Plutarch; Agrippa is said to have had the *omne arbitrium* or entire judgment/command of the fleet. We might recall here that in Plutarch, it was Agrippa on the left, Octavian on the right, and Arruntius in the centre.[8] One wonders if the apparent inconsistency is the result of Arruntius' having originally been on the left, only to respond to troubles in the centre and there to achieve his most noteworthy accomplishments, against Cleopatra.[9] Velleius is earlier than Plutarch, and it is possible that he records the correct disposition of forces; he assigns no specific commander to the centre, perhaps a reflection of the desire of the Octavians to focus on encirclement. Agrippa and Octavian are essentially given flying commands over the entire fleet, which may reflect a flattering desire to credit them with whatever successes were achieved anywhere in the battle.

Publicola and Sosius commanded Antony's fleet; Plutarch actually reverses the Velleian decision of breezily mentioning Antony's commanders. For we receive no indication in Velleius of where exactly Publicola and Sosius were stationed, let alone Antony. Meanwhile, Octavian's land forces were commanded by Taurus, and Antony's by Canidius, but once the battle starts, Velleius notes that only one side actually had such a thing as a leader; Antony's side had only soldiers. In succinct narrative, Velleius notes that Antony chose to follow the fleeing queen rather than the fighting soldier.[10] Antony's men fight valiantly even after the departure; Octavian is depicted as shouting at them from his ship essentially that it was pointless for them to continue the struggle. At last surrender came, but only after Octavian voluntarily promised them their lives and a pardon. Antony is nothing more than a *desertor*, a deserter from his own force; not without reason does the Mankiewciz *Cleopatra* have Richard Burton comment before his attempt at suicide that this is the 'final desertion'; the image was deeply ingrained in the tradition.

Velleius is frustratingly brief in his compendium, but he does make clear that Antony acted according to Cleopatra's wishes in the matter of the flight.[11] The land army was said to have surrendered too, once Canidius fled after Antony (he likely had no real hope of being pardoned or spared by Octavian, and escape may well have been in his immediate best interest). Absolutely no sense is given of how the battle commenced or progressed; all that matters is the flight of first the queen, and then her virtual slave. For Velleius, Canidius is essentially of a piece with his master; he runs too, in an exercise of what had become the hallmark of the cause. Canidius is something of an enigma in the historical record; he was loyal enough to remain with Antony in the period before Actium, despite his evident serious misgivings with all that was happening. In the end he may have made the fatal mistake of delay.

Velleius makes clear that the victory of Octavian was a victory for Rome and the world, and he makes the interesting observation that had he been able to do so, Octavian would have made exceedingly good use of victory either at the start of the triumvirate, or at the time of Philippi after the defeat of Brutus and Cassius; in other words (we may infer), had Antony not been a serious inconvenience.[12]

Velleius does address the question of Sosius, and with reference to Lucius Arruntius. The historian recalls that Arruntius' trusted pledge had once saved Sosius (i.e., in the proscriptions), and Arruntius is praised for being a man of ancient severity and old style dignity as one might say (*L. Arruntii prisca gravitate celeberrimi fides*), and that Octavian did spare Sosius after Actium, though only after struggling with his own inclination to clemency in the matter of someone who had already had one escape card, as it were. A final word is given to the case of Asinius Pollio, who is credited with having politely refused Octavian's invitation to go with him to Actium, noting that his past ties to Antony were too great (Roman *pietas*, we might say, at its finest), and that he would be the 'plunder of the victor,' the *praeda victoris*. In short, while we learn next to nothing about the course of the battle, we learn the essential actions of the queen and her lover, and even of their key ground commander – flight – and that the victor was exceedingly merciful, even when arguably, clemency was not required. Velleius takes care to note that Pollio had never even seen Cleopatra or assisted Antony's cause in any way after the settlement between the triumvirs at Brundisium, with the possible implication that he was eminently untainted by the worst excesses of the Antonian regime, and thus could aspire to win Octavian's respect for his loyal neutrality in the matter of his friend's war with the future *princeps*. The vignette is an interesting picture of a man whose own history of the civil wars, we should emphasize, would no doubt offer a fascinating insight into an age of shifting alliances and allegiances that were seemingly always in flux if not jeopardy.

Certainly in time for the sixtieth anniversary celebrations in honour of the victory then, the Velleian narrative was clearly set in what we might well call Augustan/Tiberian propaganda: Cleopatra had seduced and bewitched Antony, and Antony had willingly followed after the queen when she fled from battle in anxiety and fear for herself and her treasure. If anything seems to have been remembered about what actually happened on that early September afternoon, it is that Egypt's queen ran away.

Chapter 7

Lost Roman Sources

Fragmentary Historical Ghosts.

I f only we had Book 133 of Livy's *Ab Urbe Condita* or history of Rome from its foundation.[1] Livy does mention the closing of the doors of the temple of Janus in the wake of Actium;[2] otherwise the great Augustan historian is silent on the battle.[3] The closest we can come to Livy's version is the surviving record of those historians who seem to have borrowed heavily from his account, at least in its epitomized version.

The loss of Livy's account of the engagement is lamentable not only in light of the greatness of the historian, but also his proximity in time to the actual battle. Velleius Paterculus was born a decade after Actium; Livy lived through it. And what of Agrippa, Octavian's trusted admiral and friend? He is said to have composed an autobiography in at least two books, of which but the barest mention remains.[4] Presumably Actium featured prominently in the navy man's record of his life and achievements. As often, we have no idea when Agrippa's work was no longer available or at least being read; we have no clear sense of what influence his memoirs may have had on such men as Appian and Dio. Similarly we have no clear sense of when the 'complete Livy' was no longer available.[5]

Other fragmentary sources reveal nothing about Actium, but perhaps something of the character and personality of the players in the campaign and battle. Lucius Arruntius is cited as the author of a work on the Punic Wars in the style of Sallust. The evidence for this is from Seneca the Younger,[6] who notes that Arruntius was of a notable simplicity of life, *vir rarae frugalitatis*, a detail to which we shall return. The historian Arruntius may well be the same as the participant in the civil wars, or it may be his son, the man who is probably most famous because of Tacitus' remark at *Annales* 1.13.2 that he had both the ability and the will to assume command of the principate.

Quintus Dellius, the sometime friend of Antony, may have written a work on Antony's Parthian campaigns,[7] according to Seneca the Elder.[8] Dellius was the *desultorem bellorum*,[9] literally the performer who jumps from one horse to another in swift routine, and too, he was the author of lascivious letters to Cleopatra (and if Dio 49.39.2 can be believed, he had a sexual relationship with Antony as well). If the story of the Cleopatra epistles were true, any infatuation did not last long; Plutarch records that he fled from an alleged attack Cleopatra planned against him.[10]

Marcus Valerius Messalla Corvinus may have composed a work of history (in either Greek or Latin). He was certainly in charge of some units at Actium, as both Plutarch and Appian attest, but we have no way of knowing what, if anything, he wrote of his service.[11] Cornell's edition of the fragmentary historians gathers the surviving evidence for how Corvinus spoke against Anthony in a number of speeches, and how Antony's house on the Palatine was eventually given to Agrippa and him; Corvinus may have been responsible for dealing with Antony's renegade gladiators in Syria. When Augustus was named the *Pater Patriae* or 'Father of the Fatherland' in 2 B.C.E., it would be Corvinus who would propose the title. The *Panegyricus Messallae* (which may date to 31 B.C.E., the question is seriously disputed) is a testament to his success and fame; he had literary pretensions and a circle of writers about him that included Tibullus, but there is simply no way of knowing for sure what influence Corvinus had on the composition of Actium histories; one imagines that it would have been thought quite natural to consult with the great man on a battle in which he played a leading role, or for such a man to compose something on the struggle in which he had taken part.

Corvinus should also be noted for his comment to Octavian after Actium; when he was celebrated for having fought so bravely for Octavian, though a few years before he had fought equally well for Brutus at Philippi, he responded that he was always accustomed to serving the better cause. The comment speaks to the relative freedom of speech that was apparently able to be exercised in the Augustan principate, though the subject of the exact parameters and extent of such liberty remains a subject of controversy.

Precious little survives of the seventeen books of Gaius Asinius Pollio's account of the civil wars; he was an Antonian from an early stage of the quarrel with Octavian, and eventually joined the latter, though famously he refused the invitation to join Octavian at Actium.[12] Together with Livy, we would profit much from possession of Pollio's history. Pollio is perhaps most famous today from the first ode of Horace's second book, the theme of which is the composition of the historian's dangerous work on the civil wars, a celebrated ode that makes no reference to any of the engagements of civil strife in which Octavian was involved. We cannot be certain how far Pollio's work extended;

if it commenced in 42 B.C.E., small wonder that Horace commented on what a perilous enterprise it was to compose it.

It is quite unknown what, if anything, the ill-fated Titus Labienus Rabienus said about Actium. Aulus Cremutius Cordus almost certainly dealt with the battle in his own *Annales*, the notorious work in which he referred to Cassius as the last of the Romans.[13] Cordus is said to have commented on the fact that Messalla Corvinus had been allowed to make note of his own service under Cassius; unfortunately for Cordus, much had changed in the climate of Rome between the days of Augustus and those of Tiberius.

According to Suetonius,[14] Tiberius Claudius Nero Germanicus (better known simply as the Emperor Claudius) commenced a history in his early years with the encouragement of Livy. He started from the death of Julius Caesar, but then commenced again from the end of the civil wars (that is, from after Actium and the mopping up operations at Alexandria), since he felt certain familial constraints on his composition, not least his mother and grandmother. But he managed to produce two books of his first history, and forty-one of the second. The subjects of his Greek history are quite unknown.[15]

Aufidius Bassus composed a history that may have commenced with the civil wars or just after; it was continued by Pliny the Elder.[16] Bassus is cited by Seneca as a source for the tradition of Cicero's noble death in the face of Antony's proscriptive wrath.[17]

Chapter 8

Octavian Himself

Imperator Dixit.

According to Suetonius' life of Augustus, our hero Octavian wrote thirteen books of autobiography that took his life story down to the time of the Cantabrian War.[1] Plutarch mentions memoirs of Augustus in his comparison of Demosthenes and Cicero (3.1); they were said to have been dedicated to Agrippa and Maecenas, and are likely the thirteen books mentioned in Suetonius. The only fragments of the autobiography to survive that in any way concern Actium do not lend much to investigation of the battle. First there is the detail preserved by Servius in his commentary on Virgil's *Aeneid* 8.696, where Augustus is said to have written that Antony ordered his legions to keep watch over Cleopatra, and to obey her every nod and order. And then there is Plutarch's own statement that not more than 5,000 were killed and 300 ships captured, on the testimony of Augustus.[2] Certainly it is reasonable to expect that Augustus would have mentioned the Battle of Actium in some way in his remembrances; just how much and what he may have said is unknown.

We do possess the great *Res Gestae Divi Augusti* or 'Deeds/Achievements of the Divine Augustus,' a work known to us also as the *Monumentum Ancyranum* or 'Ankara Monument' from the inscription in Latin (and Greek translation) preserved in a temple there.[3] Here, early in the account of Augustus' accomplishments we find mention of the capture of 600 ships (larger than triremes);[4] it is just possible that the *naumachia* or mock naval battle of 2 B.C.E. that is referenced at 23, with thirty beaked triremes or biremes, other small vessels, and some 3,000 men in addition to rowers participated, was meant to be a celebratory reminder of Actium.

Augustus also notes that all of Italy swore an oath to him and asked for his leadership over the Actian campaign (25.2); laconically, he also observes that he added Egypt to the possession of the Roman people (27.1 *Aegyptum imperio populi Romani adieci*).

We do not possess Augustus' memoirs, and his own inscription is both instructive and devoid of much in the way of detail.[5] Suetonius' life of Augustus offers little more in the way of help. Suetonius was born around 69 or 70 C.E., and died sometime after 122; the *De Vita Caesarum* or lives of the Caesars, dates to near the end of the life of the famous secretary to the Emperor Hadrian.[6] His work is one of the most popular from classical antiquity; many of the images and scenes that he recreates from the lives of the Caesars have become part and parcel of the modern conception of who these men were, and why we should remember them.

Suetonius' *Augustus* claims that Antony was named a *hostis* or 'public enemy' before Actium;[7] David Wardle here notes that 'Suet. is wrong.' At some point before Actium one might think, Antony was perhaps given a more specific legal status; the surviving evidence does not allow anything beyond speculation and educated guesswork. Octavian won Actium, and without any details Suetonius thought worthy of preservation beyond the unique classical mention of the fact that the battle went on for so long that Octavian spent the night on board ship, a testimony either to a desire on the part of the author or his source(s) to praise Augustus, or to the fact that the battle was actually a much harder fought contest than one might be tempted to think; it was by no means typical for ancient navigators to spend the entire night on board ship.[8] One wonders if this was the story that prompted a comment in Horace about what seems to be seasickness and nausea.[9]

Chapter 9

Florus' and Eutropius' Detached Accounts

Livy's Stepchildren?

Florus is not on the lists of many readers of Roman history. We are not certain of his name, which may have been Lucius Annaeus Florus; his surviving historical work is a two-book epitome of Roman affairs, most especially her wars, from the time of Romulus until the closing of the temple of Janus by Augustus in 25 B.C.E.[1] The work is ostensibly an abridged version of Roman history; it is heavily indebted to Livy no doubt, but also to other sources.

Chapter 21 of Book 2 concerns Octavian's campaigns against Antony and Cleopatra. The brief survey opens in seemingly conventional enough fashion; the first word is *furor* or 'madness', the madness of Antony as he succumbed to his lust for Cleopatra. For Florus, Antony had actually come to hate war after his disastrous Parthian campaign; all he wanted was to relax in the presence of his royal lover.[2] But Cleopatra was not so detached from political and military concerns; Antony was drunk and his queen was contemplating the *imperium* or command of the Roman state. Antony soon becomes a *monstrum*, a portentous thing is not what we would call an actual monster; he dresses in gold and purple and puts aside his toga and other insignia of Roman identity.

The narrative of the battle campaign proper commences. Octavian crosses the sea from Brundisium, and quickly sets up his camp in Epirus and surrounds Actium, Leucas, Leucate, and the Ambracian Gulf. Florus records that Octavian had 400 ships, and his enemy less than 200, though larger in size. Antony's vessels are described as ranging from so-called sixes to nines,[3] with towers as if to mimic the outlay of cities and fortifications. Interestingly, Florus notes that the sea groaned and the winds laboured as the vessels advanced, a vivid description of the inherent difficulties for navigation that the lumbering hulks posed. The superbly impressive armaments of Antony's ships came at a price; there is something here of an almost pathetic response to the stories of Agrippa's great victories at Naulochus in the war against Sextus Pompey; overcompensation on a seriously debilitating scale.

Octavian's vessels were of twos to sixes in size, and thus more easily managed; Florus notes that they were thus able to do whatever was needed to disrupt Antony's ships and to respond to the changing vicissitudes of battle. Several of Octavian's ships would close on one of Antony's (this detail is attested elsewhere, and speaks to the cooperation and discipline displayed by Agrippa's crews); they would use both ramming power and fire to attack the enemy. The sea was soon strewn with the refuse and wreck of battle; purple and gold are everywhere in the water. Once again, there is an emphasis on fire as a decisive element in the victory; incendiaries may seem to be obvious enough offensive weapons in a naval battle, but the combination of wind and lack of skill with a less than well trained crew could easily make the weapon fatal both to attacker and attacked alike. *Prima dux fugae regina cum aurea puppe veloque purpureo in altum dedit.* The queen was the first leader of flight, with her golden vessel and purple sail.[4] In Joseph Mankiewicz's 1963 film *Cleopatra*, Canidius observes from land the flight of Cleopatra, and he notes to his companions that they 'saw the victor sail away on her golden barge'. The wealth of expedition was in the water, with the exception, it would seem, of Cleopatra's treasure on her flagship; the purple and gold of the queen flees away. Antony follows, and Octavian pursues them both, hot on their tracks.

What is interesting in Florus' epitome of the engagement is that despite the opening critical characterization of Antony and Cleopatra, there is no clear narrative of a flight that altered the course of battle or that came amid a hotly contested, evenly balanced struggle. One could read Florus and think that the war was simply a loss for Antony and his allies, despite their hard fighting, and that if any blame were to be assigned, it would be to the tactical decision to pit Antony's heavy ships against Octavian's lighter and more manoeuvrable ones. The lessons of Naulochus had been learned incorrectly by Antony and his captains; Agrippa was the master of naval innovation and adaptability.

Interestingly, Florus continues with the observation that neither the prepared flight of Antony and Cleopatra to the Ocean, nor the fortifications of Egypt, etc., were of profit to them: *itaque nec praeparata in Oceanum fuga*. The 'prepared flight' referenced here is almost certainly to the plan of Antony and Cleopatra to drag their ships across the Suez and into the Red Sea, so as to flee to Arabia or even India.[5] *Praeparata fuga*, however, may well remind some readers of the story of Cleopatra's (and Antony?) alleged plan to flee from Actium. Still, Florus' narrative, with its possible strong influence from Livy's lost history, points to a sober and rational account of a struggle that was perhaps never in real doubt given the differences in military hardware between the two sides, and a flight from the scene of battle that represented nothing more than a reaction to defeat. In the end, survival by no means guaranteed the chance to fight effectively another day.

Another Compendium.

And what of Eutropius? The name is unknown outside of specialty Roman and ancient history circles. He was the author of a fourth century abridgment or compendium of Roman history, the so-called *Breviarium*.[6] Eutropius set out to provide a complete version of Roman history from Romulus to his own day; he is arguably of greatest interest to scholars of the complicated history of the fourth century. The work is in ten books; Actium features in Book 7. It will not take long to work through the short account of the climactic battle.

7.1 of the history gives a brief and colourless, dry survey of how Antony fought the Persians and was defeated by the Parthians, in effect, when he withdrew because of pestilence and privations; he abandoned Octavian's sister and married Cleopatra. The Queen is blamed for the subsequent eruption of civil war, *cogente uxore Cleopatra*; Cleopatra his wife was the one compelling her husband by driving events, as it were. The Queen's goal was nothing less than ruling in the city; it was a woman's desire and greed for power and ambition that inspired her (*dum cupiditate muliebri optat etiam in Urbe regnare*). Antony was defeated by Augustus (the name is anachronistic) in a famous and celebrated naval battle (*navali pugna et inlustri*). Antony fled into Egypt and was in desperate circumstances, since everyone defected to Augustus. He soon killed himself, and Cleopatra procured an asp and ended her own life (in rather more dramatic fashion). Egypt was added to the *imperium Romanum*, and Cornelius Gallus was placed in charge as the first Roman judge (*iudicem*) over *Aegyptus*.[7]

Eutropius' account is uninspiring and unimaginative to be sure; the author's purpose was not to compose history on a grand scale. Still, we might note that there is no note whatsoever of Cleopatra's flight, shameful or otherwise, and no detail about anything other than a great naval campaign that ended in Antony's defeat. The queen is rather secondary to the former triumvir; the great tradition of her suicide is powerful enough to give her a noteworthy death scene however, even in the brief compass of the paragraph. Still, Cleopatra is painted in a decidedly negative light; she was the instigator of the war, and her motivations were allegedly all too characteristic of her gender. The Eutropian account is in the same tradition as Florus', and probably if not certainly inspired by the epitomized Livy.

Chapter 10

The Evidence of Orosius

The Gasps of Antiquity.

Paulus Orosius was a Spanish Christian priest and student of Augustine; he was born around 375 C.E. and died sometime after 418. He composed a great *Historiae Adversus Paganos*, a seven-book history of the world from its creation to the sack of Rome by Alaric in 410.[1] Orosius is hardly a household name even to scholars of ancient history; like most 'minor' figures, he has attracted some scholarly interest in recent years in work that attempts to take him seriously as a witness to history in a tumultuous age of upheaval and transition.[2] By one of the accidents of history, we are fortunate to have Orosius' work and its account of Actium, a version of the story that is usually considered alongside the narratives in Florus and Eutropius as examples of retellings of the Livian record (even if epitomized).

Orosius' Octavian crosses from Brundisium to Epirus with 230 beaked ships.[3] Agrippa was sent ahead to disrupt Antony's supply lines to Egypt; heavy merchant vessels from Syria and elsewhere in Asia and Egypt were captured. Methone is captured, despite a significant Antonian garrison. Corcyra was taken next; the Antonians who fled from that locale were chased down and defeated in a naval battle. Agrippa returned to Octavian, having accomplished many things, Orosius notes, in a most bloody fashion (*multisque rebus cruentissime gestis*).[4] The detail is interesting; it speaks of a certain savagery that is not noted in the other sources of Agrippa's preparatory campaigns (which we should note, are not well documented). There may be a hint of not so much hard fought campaigning, but the effective wiping out of Antonian resistance in the cordon of naval bases meant to defend his position.

Antony was demoralized by both desertions and famine, and thus decided to hasten the engagement; he attempts a land battle and suffers a defeat. On the third day after his repulsion, he moved his camp to Actium and decided on a naval battle – perhaps a reasonable enough change of mind after his recent loss. Two hundred and thirty beaked ships were on Octavian's side, Orosius again notes, and thirty more without *rostra*; there were also triremes equal in rapidity to Liburnian galleys, and eight legions to board the ships – as well as five praetorian cohorts. Antony, for his part, had 170 ships, with the recurring motif that what he lost in number he made up for in size. His ships posed a significant threat to an attacker, if the opponent were not prepared for dealing with large and formidable vessels.

Famosum et magnum hoc bellum apud Actium fuit: full of repute and great was that battle at Actium. For Orosius it started at the fifth hour, that is late morning, before noon, and it lasted until the seventh (perhaps around one in the afternoon) in a state of uncertainty. That two-hour period however, was filled with great slaughter; from the seventh hour on through the rest of the day and into the following night the struggle continued, and Octavian was increasingly in the ascendant as the conflict proceeded.

Prior regina Cleopatra cum LX velocissimis navibus fugit ... the return of the problem of the flight of Cleopatra and her sixty ships. She fled with her swiftest vessels, and Antony followed his wife (*uxorem*), with the praetorian insignia of his vessel having been removed. Only as dawn broke did Octavian definitely achieve his victory (*inluscente iam die victoriam Caesar consummavit*); 12,000 are said to have died, Orosius notes, from the losing side, with 6,000 wounded, of whom 1,000 would succumb to their injuries; an important reminder perhaps, of the limitations of ancient medicine and the treatment of the war wounded; there could have been no effective treatment of the seriously injured from the campaign.[5]

In general, one is struck at once by the affinity of Orosius' account with that of Florus. In both, the crucial detail about the flight of Cleopatra is rendered devoid of any overt critical judgment; in both accounts, the likely defeat of the Antonians is made clear before the Queen is said to have left.[6] Aside from the casualty figures (which stand out among the sources), the significant detail in the *Historiae* account is the extreme length of the prolonged battle, from late morning on the one day to dawn the next. Orosius alone of our surviving sources describes so lengthy an engagement; one is tempted to wonder whether or not the overnight struggle is more realistic than a relatively quick battle that was finished by about four in the afternoon. This was one of those battles that lasted a considerable time, and we have no record of how exactly Octavian's forces dealt with the problem of the fortified harbour of the Ambracian Gulf, of how the forces that may have retreated into the gulf would have surrendered.

Probably there was some involvement of land forces, and the voluntary destruction of the deadlier threats to enemy ships.

Orosius is in some ways the voice of a world that was both falling and fallen, a Rome that was simultaneously old and new, transformative and transformed. His account of Actium could easily have veered toward vivid contempt for Cleopatra, indeed for Antony as her paramour; instead we find a more sober than not account of a battle that remains more than a little mysterious as we arrive at the end of our examination of the 'historical' sources of the campaign. It is particularly interesting to consider Orosius side-by-side with Velleius as the first and last surviving Latin historical attestations of the battle.

Some details, to be sure, seem beyond question or doubt. Antony clearly had larger ships than Octavian; this would prove to a fatal error on his (and/or Cleopatra's) part, though his intentions may have been good.[7] One almost feels something of the era of the decline of the battleship in reading the insistent reports of how Octavian was able to defeat Antony because of his greater mobility and maneuverability;[8] it is as if large capital ships were virtually obsolete in the face of well trained, practised and polished swift marine bringers of death. Again, Antony was in some ways fighting Mylae and Naulochus; Agrippa and Octavian were demonstrating a new sort of naval warfare. It would be many a long year before there would be any need for marine fighting on this scale in the waters of the Mediterranean.

Octavian and Agrippa (perhaps we should say Agrippa alone) successfully encircled Antony's forces in a lightning campaign from Corcyra in the north to Methone in the south; one has the impression in reading some of the accounts that Octavian's side was better at reading a map. By the time the actual day of Actium arrived, it is reasonably certain that Octavian and Agrippa were in a far better strategic position than Antony, though victory was perhaps by no means assured. Still, by sheer length of the engagement, the Actium of Orosius is among the harder fought of the extant versions; there was resistance for some time after Antony and his queen departed, and by no means was the conflict an insignificant one.

But whatever exactly happened at the battle, Cleopatra and Antony certainly fled, and the queen first; the only question (though perhaps the major one) is whether or not she and/or he intended to flee from the start.

We shall turn now to the world of Latin poetry for further evidence at a reconstruction of just what took place on that fateful September day. First however, we may adduce one additional piece of our puzzle.

An Epilogue of Curious Evidence.

Here we shall note a strange reference in Pliny's *Natural History* (32.2-4), amid the author's ichthyological references on the world of fishes. Pliny opens his book with a study of the *echenais*, a very small fish (some six inches in length) that is said to have the power to withstand even the power of the wind and tempest, and to be able to check the course of vessels of war. Pliny notes that at Actium, this fish was said to have stopped the flagship of Antony, who was moving around in the process of exhorting his men and offering them encouragement, until he changed his ship for another one, and the fleet of Caesar made a more serious attack (*fertur Actiaco Marte tenuisse praetoriam navem Antoni properantis circumire et exhortari suos, donec transiret in aliam, ideoque Caesariana classis impetus maiore protinus venit*).

This fish is mentioned by Aristotle, as well in his history of animals (2.14), where the Loeb editor A.L. Peck comments, 'Probably a blenny or goby. Pliny also mentions the *echeneis* as frequenting rocks, its use as a love charm and to stop proceedings at law, and Aristotle's denial that it has feet; he confuses it, however, with the sucking fish, also called Echeneïs; it is, he says, believed to slow down ships by sticking to their hulls...cf. *N.H.* xxxiii.2, in which book he tells how Mark Antony's ship was held up by one at the battle of Actium, and Caligula's was similarly delayed on the way to Antium...' (with further extended notes). Aelian also mentions the fish in his treatise on animals (1.36 and 2.17).[9]

One wonders if the reference in Pliny is to some sort of grappling hook or other physical implement that was able to attack Antony's flagship (which would of course have been a key target in the battle); if Antony's ship was in some way disabled, whether by fish or manmade contraption, the story of the transfer of the flag, as it were, to a smaller vessel makes practical sense (as opposed to a mere jumping to a smaller and swifter boat in the effort to catch the fleeing Cleopatra). But it is difficult to see clearly and without possible objection how we move from fish to grapple. Does Pliny's evidence constitute one of the only specific details as to what exactly happened on the wing where he faced Agrippa? How exactly would Antony's crew and captains have been able to know that his flagship had been impeded from its progress by the echeneis (even several of them) at the very height of a raging battle? (Of course if the peril were known to experienced crews, this objection could be explained). Was the story in some way concocted or crafted as a means of explaining why Antony needed to transfer to another ship (in other words, to offer at least something of an explanation of Antony's actions in the face of serious criticism in the aftermath of the battle)? Perhaps all that is certain is that Pliny has preserved a detail about the actual situation on board Antony's flagship, a precious scrap of information about the circumstances in which the failed triumvir found himself.

Part Three

Actium in Verse

Chapter 11

The Shield of Aeneas

Bellona Raging.

If contemporary sources are to be valued, then certainly the surviving works of Augustan Latin poetry are to be treasured as evidence for the what and why of the events at Actium, even if looming over all is the problem of how one might do well to note that Octavian helped to finance the poetry by his patronage of the poets. As we have noted, they have the virtue of proximity in time to the events they narrate.

A word here though, is owed about poetry and propaganda. The argument has been made that the Latin poets, perhaps even the language itself, were irredeemably prejudiced against Cleopatra, and that certainly they could not be trusted for giving an account of what happened at Actium.[1] As we shall see herein, the evidence does not support this oft-repeated contention, at least in the matter of the depiction of Cleopatra. Of the three Augustan poets who concern themselves with Cleopatra – Horace, Virgil and Propertius – a certain nobility of the queen emerges in at least the first two. This nobility is all the more noteworthy given the patron who was financing the works of these poets, a patron who had every reason to want to craft a subtle portrait of a queen who was unquestionably worthy of condemnation, but also of a certain degree of respectful admiration that worked to the mutual advantage of victor and vanquished.

As for Virgil in particular, we might note that the twelfth century Byzantine scholar Tzetzes, names Virgil first among those who speak of Cleopatra, in an interesting list that refers to Virgil, Lucian, Galen, Plutarch, Diodorus, and George the Chronicler.[2]

Virgil's *Aeneid* is legitimately labelled an instant classic of world literature.[3] After the death of its author in September of 19 B.C.E., the work was more or less quickly prepared for posthumous publication, and its influence since then on literature and the arts is incalculable. In an important sense, the *Aeneid* is a paean to Roman history, a meditation on the glories and disasters of the Roman past; a poem that gazes optimistically to an Augustan future, even as it nervously looks back on the problems that have made Augustus something of a welcome relief to a nation increasingly weary of near constant civil and foreign strife. Ostensibly, it tells the story of how the Trojan exile Aeneas made his way to Italy and played a signal role in the foundation and development of the future Rome. As the verses of the epic proceed, it is easy to see how Augustus was imagined as a new Aeneas, a re-founder of Rome after decades spent in the shadow of the unspeakable horror of civil war. Aeneas fought against forces of disorder and chaos, and so did Augustus. Looming over all was the image of Jupiter as the bringer of the Olympian order that was established in contrast to the chaos of the rebellious Titans and Giants; Jupiter is the divine paradigm for the coming of peace and order.

For the student of Actium, the *Aeneid* offers a valuable description of the battle on the hero Aeneas' divinely forged shield, which is described in detail in Book 8 of the epic. The context is the manufacture of arms for Aeneas at the behest of his divine mother, Venus; the craftsman is none other than the master builder of the immortals, the god Vulcan.[4] The shield is a complicated work of art that displays many images from Roman history, Actium among them. There is an interesting backstory to the shield, in that it is forged by Vulcan at the behest of the wife who is notorious for her affair with the god Mars; the Romans are the children of the goddess of love, and her violent, martial paramour. And Vulcan will be sure to include his amatory rival in a prominent place on the shield that he forges for the son of yet another of his wife's lovers, Aeneas the son of Anchises.

The sea flows around the pictures on the shield; one might think of the ancient conception of the lands of the world surrounded by the River Ocean (8.671 ff.). The sea is splendidly depicted; it is gold and yet cerulean blue; white billows of the waves rise up as dolphins play. The scene could be eminently tranquil; there are no ships at first, but only the marine mammals, as they traverse the deep. We might even recall the verses in the opening book of the epic, where Neptune was said to have brought calm to the sea in the wake of the storm that Juno had instigated to harass Aeneas' Trojan fleet.[5] But then, 'in the middle' (8.675 *in medio*), fleets of bronze appear.[6] The contrast between the animals and the man-made works of war is striking; at once the reason for the warships is made clear; this is the scene of the *Actia bella*, the 'Actian wars.' The plural is both poetic and deliberate; the entire campaign is envisaged. Leucate is now ablaze with marshalled forces of war; the Latin *instructo Marte* (8.676) refers metonymically to Mars as the god of war; it is as if the very father of Romulus were present for this clash. There is more gold too, the waves gleam with gold, but the gold is the precious metal of ships and (conceivably) weapons.[7] The scene is splendid to the point of blinding; the intended effect serves in part to highlight the signal role of the god Apollo in the drama, the god of the sun, the patron of the white marble cliffs of Leucas that reflect the sun in radiant brilliance.

On one side is Augustus Caesar, and he is leading the *Italos*, the Italians. He has with him both father and people, *patribus populoque*, where the fathers are the senators of Rome (in clear evocation of the image of the Republic and the glories of the 'old' system that is to be rescued by Augustus' victory). He also has the Penates or 'household gods' of Roman religion, not to mention the divine favour of his father's star, and a portentous double flame on his head. The dramatic imagery refers to the signal signs of favour that were recorded and alleged in the wake of the death of Julius Caesar and the question of his deification; in the Virgilian depiction of Actium, it is as if Augustus is already a god (or at least virtually so); certainly he is under the protection of his deified father Caesar.[8] And these are the emblems of *pietas*, of that peculiarly Roman virtue of loyalty to one's family and state.

Agrippa is *parte alia*, 'in another part'. Agrippa has favourable gods too, and also winds. He is leading the battle line of ships, his own head marked by a naval crown as a special token of his leadership of the Roman fleet, the insignia that he had won on account of the defeat of the naval forces of Sextus Pompey. The brief, poetic description highlights both the leadership of Octavian's admiral, and his use of the winds in leading forth his ships.

On the other side is Antony, whose description highlights his foreign, indeed barbarian wealth and diverse forces.[9] He is the victor over the peoples of Aurora, the dawn goddess, and those from the red shore (that is, of the Red Sea). He brings Egypt with him, and even Bactria, the fabled land of Alexander's conquests in modern Afghanistan. And following him is his Egyptian wife, his *Aegyptia coniunx*, who is not accorded the privilege of a name.

Augustus and Agrippa, Antony and Cleopatra; Virgil preserves the detail that on the one side, the two men were part of the main battle line, while on the other, Cleopatra 'followed' (*sequitur* in Latin). We must consider the problem of where exactly Cleopatra was in the opening disposition of Antonian forces at Actium. It seems that Antony was then on the right, facing Octavian's commander Agrippa on the left; in other words, the place where one could rightly expect the main action of the battle. Antony's left was comparatively less significant; it opposed Octavian on the right. Antony's centre had Marcus

Octavius and Marcus Insteius according to Plutarch, again, comparative nobodies in the drama of political intrigue and military reputation. Octavian had Lucius Arruntius.

Cleopatra vs. Arruntius.

Was Cleopatra stationed directly behind Antony, *or was she in the middle, facing Arruntius* (albeit behind Octavius and Insteius)? She appears to have had her sixty Egyptian ships with her; it is not certain whether these vessels were in the back, as it were, or whether some of them were ostensibly part of the frontal line of attack. The former would seem likelier. Certainly in the ensuing chaos of her flight, it does not seem likely that she saved her entire fleet of sixty or so ships. Horace's *vix una sospes navis ab ignibus* (c. 1.37.13, where 'scarcely one vessel was saved from the flames') has been rightly taken to be poetic exaggeration, but in truth we have no definitive evidence about how many ships were rescued or escaped.[10] Nor can we be sure of what Antony managed to extricate from the difficult situation he faced on his wing; between fire, ramming, grappling, increasingly difficult sea conditions, retreat in the face of hazard, and even quite irritating fish (the *echeneis*), it might well have seemed that virtually any rescue was near miraculous.

One might think that Cleopatra's ultimate escape would have been easier had she been originally in the rear middle; Antony, of course, managed to make his own departure from battle despite his original posting on the right wing.

The shield artistically links Antony and Cleopatra in close sequence; no one else is mentioned from Antony's side, and the two lovers are presented as counterparts to Augustus and Agrippa. Antony is depicted as literally 'conveying Egypt' with him (8.687-688 *Aegyptum ... vehit*).

A striking feature of the Virgilian presentation of Actium is the relative equality of status it accords to Augustus and Agrippa; *parte alia* reserves different spheres of influence for the two men, as indeed was the case at the actual battle. Antony and Cleopatra, in contrast, are depicted as something of a unit; Antony is named first and clearly a 'guilty' party in the drama, and the presence of Cleopatra is labelled a *nefas*, literally an unspeakable thing (we might recall the hesitation of the poets even to use the woman's name).[11] The shared honour of Augustus and Agrippa is part of the point of propaganda and political practice; Augustus and Agrippa might as well be consuls in shared power, partners in rule and protectors of the Republic. And neither has control of, or needs, any foreign contingent. Neither man is *varius armis* or 'varied in his arms'.

There would seem to be no reinvention of history in the depiction of Augustus and Agrippa on their respective wings; they were in fact, on the two edges of their battle line. Virgil's Cleopatra is rather ambiguously said to be 'following' Antony, which might lead one to think that she was literally behind him, on his right wing. But as we shall see soon enough, in reality she may have been in the rear of the middle. There may also be a touch of humour; Antony, in the crucial moment, would be the one who was following his Egyptian bride.

The battle commences. It opens with a dramatic flourish; everyone rushed together at once (8.689 *una omnes ruere*). Poetic touches aside, it would seem that there was a great clash between the two battle lines; interestingly, this detail is followed by the note that 'they sought the deep', *alta petunt* (8.691). The subject of the verb would appear to be both sides in the contest; it is as if Aeneas' shield is a living, near cinematic panorama of the battle, and both the Augustans and the Antonians are rushing to the deep sea (in presumed contrast with the shallower waters near shore). Poetically (not to say hyperbolically), Virgil says that you would think that the very Cyclades had been uprooted and were now swimming on the deep, or that lofty mountains were crashing into mountains; with such force did men assault the 'towered decks' of the ships (8.693 *turritis puppibus*).

The scene is potentially crucial for an understanding of Virgil's conception of the battle; certainly it is not entirely clear what precisely Virgil meant to depict. The key may rest in the proper interpretation of verse 8.693, *tanta mole viri turritis puppibus instant*, which can be translated as 'with so mighty a mass the men attack the towered decks' (or perhaps better, 'press upon'). In this case, the 'mighty mass' refers to the ships of Antony, which were famous for their great size; the towered decks are then those of Octavian. The ancient Virgilian commentator Servius would agree; he in fact says that Virgil took this detail from history, *hoc de historia traxit*, crediting Agrippa with being the first to develop this feature of naval warfare.[12] And yet Plutarch noted that Antony's ships were equipped with towers, from which projectiles were to be hurled at opposing ships. Again, the picture is one of land warfare and siege works on water, of a dramatic contest in which the naval forces of the two sides were arrayed for the potential sacking of an enemy 'city' on the waves. Most of the men fighting at Actium had no sense whatsoever of the particulars of naval warfare; most of them were seasoned at nothing other than ground engagements, if that.

J.W. Mackail observes in his commentary on this passage[13] that both fleets were originally at anchorage, and that thus they could both be said to 'seek the deep'; further, he takes the detail about immense size (*tanta mole*) as closely coordinated with the towered decks; the latter are marked by their great height and impressive form. Karl Gransden's commentary[14] takes the 'seeking of the deep' of Antony and Cleopatra (as if they were seeking a breakout from the blockade), and the *tanta mole* of their huge ships, with the towers understood in the Servian manner as being Octavian's.

One could argue that the ships of both sides are dramatically depicted as being especially large; after all, the very Cyclades were said to have been torn out of the sea, and mountains were clashing against mountains. Some of this is poetic hyperbole; some of it may reflect Hellenistic ship building tactics and practices in particular.

An interpretation is offered here of what Virgil may have intended to depict in his rendition of the battle. We begin with Augustus and Agrippa on opposite sides of their line of ships; on the other side, we have a vast polyglot (indeed exclusively foreign) force, with Cleopatra somewhere in the rear (8.678-688); this much is reasonably clear.[15] Then, at line 689, we learn that 'together all rushed' (*una omnes ruere*). This must refer to both sides as they clash together. The battle commenced then, with a general melee; there was no preliminary missile attack designed either to soften the enemy or to goad them into an early clash. If *una omnes ruere* refers to both sides, then *alta petunt* likely does as well; it does not seem probable that Virgil intended the reader to understand that there was an unannounced change of subject mid-battle, as it were. They all sought the deep. No one after all, wanted to be caught fighting a naval battle too close to the shore batteries and fortifications of Antony's Actian naval base, or in the narrow confines of the strait. The 'torn up Cyclades' may well refer to the Antonian ships in particular, which are then the 'lofty mountains' that clash against other mountains; this allows one to imagine that both sides were noteworthy for impressively sized ships, while still preserving the idea that Antony's and Cleopatra's were much bigger. In this interpretation, both sides can be said to have ships of immense proportions (as befitting an epic rendition of the battle), and both sides have ships that are outfitted with towers and siege equipment.

Fire comes next (8.694-695); as the battle rages, missile weapons and incendiaries are now flung at close quarters. Virgil poetically says that the 'Neptunian fields became red with new slaughter' (8.695 *arva nova Neptunia caede rubescunt*), where the waters apparently grow red with the blood of naval slaughter. This may refer to a second stage in the battle, a phase where fire now joins ramming as the means of destruction and death.

The Queen in the Midst.

Crucially, at this point Virgil notes that the queen, still contemptuously unnamed, was in the midst: *regina in mediis*.[16] She is summoning her battle lines with the sistrum of her native land; Virgil notes that she does not yet see the twin snakes at her back, a reference to the stories of her eventual suicide in Alexandria. In several important respects, the present dramatic scene of Cleopatra in the midst of the carnage at Actium will be reborn in the beautiful horror of the equestrian battle ballet of *Aeneid* 11, an exercise in poetic ghoulish aestheticism if ever there were one.

Whatever we make of the towered ships and the exact referent of the action against them, what is certain is that in Virgil there is no account of cowardly flight on the part of the Cleopatra; indeed, she is depicted as actively charging in the midst of the fray, heedless of the fact that suicide might soon enough be a worthy course of action for her to pursue. Antony, in fact, is nowhere. Cleopatra is seen as the prime agent of military action on her side, and 'side' is in fact rather inaccurate; she is now firmly in the midst of the battle.

Indeed, Virgil dramatically notes that all the monsters of the Egyptian pantheon of gods, among them the barking Anubis (8.698 *latrator Anubis*), were fighting with Neptune, Venus, and Minerva; the ancient god Mavors (that is, Mars) was in the midst, and the grim Dirae or Furies from the upper air, and Discord and Bellona (the Roman war goddess). The war god Mars is of course an appropriate deity to have raging in the middle of a scene of battle, but he is also a pre-eminent patron god of Rome, the divine father of Romulus.[17] In the mention of Bellona we may think of the locus of the goddess' temple where war would have been officially declared against Cleopatra by Octavian.[18]

The assortment of gods is both interesting and insightful; this is no mere poetic catalogue of divine beings. The sea is Neptune's realm; he favours, naturally, the victor.[19] Venus was a patroness of the Trojans, and in particular of the Julian line that had adopted Octavian. Minerva was a pre-eminent Roman deity of battle. These three immortals are depicted as directly facing the Egyptian deities; with Venus in the middle, a possibly significant detail to which we shall return later.

Cleopatra is in the middle of the fray, and so is Mars; Mars, the Roman war god and lover of Venus, is in one sense with his paramour in the middle, but in a more important sense, he is literally in the middle in the sense that he is everywhere where the battle would seem to be the thickest and most dramatic, rather like the Dirae, Discord, and Bellona.

Actian Apollo.

Looming over it all is Actian Apollo (8.704). He draws his bow (presumably from his lofty temple. He is after all, the loftiest of them all on this day, towering far above any impressive ship). When he bends his bow, then all Egypt is afraid, and the men of India, every Arab and Sabaean now turns his back. This is the moment of flight; this is the moment of the beginning of Roman pursuit of the enemy. Only now does Virgil note that the queen was seen to set sail (8.707-708); the god Vulcan is said to have depicted her as pale amid the slaughter, her pallor caused by fear of her future death (which now, at last, she sees); she is carried by the wind of Iapyx, the northwest wind (another detail to which we shall return). The scene of the battle closes with the Nile's mournful reception of the conquered; if we are to imagine Antony at all, it is merely as one of the vanquished in the dramatic final word of the passage (8.713 *victos*).

The queen ran then, but only after a hard fought battle, and one in which there was apparently no initial plan to flee. The Virgilian description is clear enough; there was a difficult naval engagement, a strenuous battle that opened with a general clash and attempts at ramming, followed by a resorting to fire and flame; at last the Antonians were overwhelmed, and Cleopatra made her escape, an escape that came only after a phase of battle where her Egyptians were in the very thick of battle, a prominent force in the midst of battle.

The scene is dramatic and even romantic; the depiction is of Augustus as facing a worthy foe, indeed the combined powers of Asia, a mighty force that makes Antony look rather insignificant. From reading the passage, one would think that Cleopatra was Augustus' real foe, not Antony; this of course was the correct interpretation for someone reading the political language of declarations of foreign war (as opposed to the unpalatable nature of more civil strife), and if this was to be a foreign war, then Cleopatra needed to be the main combatant.[20]

As epilogue to the dramatic depiction of the battle on the shield of Aeneas, we can mention the brief account of the games observed *de facto* in celebration of Actium that are anachronistically celebrated by Aeneas and his Trojan exiles (3.278 ff.).[21] The context is the long journey westward to Hesperia and the new destiny in Italy; the place is Actium; the games actually Ilian or Trojan:

Actiaque Iliacis celebramus litora ludis (3.280). Virgil sets the scene with awe-inspiring geographical and divine markers; Leucas has a stormy peak, and the Apollo of Actium brings apprehension to navigators: *mox et Leucatae nimbosa cacumina montis / et formidatus nautis aperitur Apollo* (3.274-275).

There is an ominous quality to the scene, perhaps even a sense that this is not quite where the Trojans belong. It is in fact a scene that is marked by a contrast between Troy and Actium, of the old past and the Roman future, a destiny that is still very much in the temporal and even spatial distance for Aeneas and his men. The games are Trojan because Actium has not yet happened; the shore is to be celebrated because the Trojan wanderers have made another safe landing. The waters off Leucas and Actium are hazardous, but Apollo will protect the future fleet of Agrippa and Augustus; he will guard it so well in fact, that it would be centuries before there was another significant naval action in the Mediterranean (and it would be Lepanto in the sixteenth century that would see another conflict in the vicinity).

Chapter 12

Horace's *Epodes* – The Earliest Evidence?

The Mysterious Leftward Movement.

The poet Quintus Horatius Flaccus (65 B.C.E.-8 B.C.E.) may well have fought at Actium. His first and ninth *Epodes* are intimately concerned with the battle and the Augustan victory over Cleopatra; his book of verse was probably published in the year after Actium (30 B.C.E.). It may well be regarded as the earliest extant source of information about the engagement.[1]

The first epode in fact, opens on the eve of Actium, as it were. Horace is wondering about how he could possibly abandon his friend Maecenas; how could he possibly not share the hazard of joining the Actian expedition? *Ibis Liburnis inter alta navium, / amice, propugnacula*: 'You will go, my friend, on Liburnian vessel amid the lofty ramparts or "crenellations" of ships.'[2] At once we have a problem; are the massive vessels that are here contrasted with the light Liburnians, the ships of Antony, or those of Octavian? We might incline here to the latter interpretation, especially in light of our reading of Virgil's depiction of the shield of Aeneas; *both* sides at Actium had large ships, and it may well be misleading to draw a picture of a battle where Antony and Cleopatra had huge vessels and Octavian small ones; likely the real picture was rather more mixed and balanced. We cannot be sure if the first epode was written before the battle, indeed it may well have been written before and revised after, or entirely composed in the wake of Octavian's victory, but all things considered, we may do well to conclude that Horace (like Maecenas) is thinking of how he would be a potential member of Octavian's entourage in a swift, light vessel such as that in which Octavian visited his crews before the battle. The first epode does not lend anything to our understanding of what happened at the battle, but it does accord with Virgil's reading that both sides had large ships, and that both sides were impressive for the size of their vessels (even if Antony's were bigger). We should note here that the Liburnian galleys were the specific vessels that received the most credit for Octavian's victory at

Actium.[3] Fittingly enough, the very opening of Horace's poem pays tribute to a key element in Octavian's naval victory.

A word here on the use of poetry in the study of warfare. 'Virgil, for what his poetic version is worth...' comments John Carter on the question of the wind that aided Cleopatra's flight.[4] Our position is that poetic accounts can be of tremendous importance in the understanding of that happened in a military campaign, so long as the proper precautions are taken in evaluation of the poetry. In other words, the same approach that must be taken with any source.

The ninth epode is ostensibly written in the wake of the victory. Now the question posed by Horace is when he will be able to drink wine with his friend; the lyricist recalls the days when the victory at sea over Sextus Pompey had been celebrated. A Roman, Horace notes, had been enslaved to a woman (9.11-12); the first detail of the actual campaign is the description of Antony's soldiers as Cleopatra's virtual servants and playthings. Indeed, the Roman is a slave to wrinkled eunuchs (*spadonibus ... rugosis*); the language is deliberately harsh and critical of Cleopatra's retinue.[5] Interestingly, Horace also mentions the *conopium* that the sun is said to look down on with contempt; the word apparently means a 'mosquito net' of some sort, such as would be needed in such locales as Actium to ward off the threat of malaria. The implication would seem to be that 'real men' would have no need of such precautions and elements of luxury.[6]

Romans may be serving Cleopatra and her eunuchs, but 2,000 Galatian horsemen are noted to have defected to Octavian before the battle (9.17-18). The passage is of note for its description of how King Amnytas' men seem to have known better how they should behave, than Antony's Italians/Romans; these are noble foreigners.[7] We should note that it is quite possible that the 'Roman soldier' is none other than Antony; certainly he is the most prominent Roman in the enemy camp, and the one most in bondage to Cleopatra.[8] No mention of the 'Roman soldier' in Horace's work can be made without reference to the disgraced triumvir.

A Mysterious Leftward Motion.

Verses 19-20 of the epode present difficulties of interpretation that relate closely to our understanding of the battle. Horace notes that *hostiliumque navium portu latent / puppes sinistrorum citae*, 'in the harbour the decks of the enemy vessels hide, having swiftly moved to the left.' The main problem here is the precise meaning of *sinistrorsum*, a term that naturally would mean 'to the left' or 'leftward', a directional adverb that begs the question of what exactly Antony's fleet is doing, indeed of what Horace wanted to depict for his audience. Few passages in the Horatian corpus have received as much attention as these two verses; scholars cannot be certain even if these lines refer to something that happened during the actual Actian battle.

As we take Horace's words in sequence, first we find the mention of the enemy ships; next of the port/harbour where they hide; then ship decks that were at some point 'swift' or 'rapid' or 'swiftly put in motion' (*citae*) 'to the left' (*sinistrorsum*). Most of the commentators on this passage have focused on the paltry evidence of exactly what happened during the climactic battle, hoping to find some clue in these two verses as to some Antonian tactic. Do these lines reflect the retreat of some of Antony's navy after the battle, ships that now seek the comparative safety of the Ambracian Gulf after the defeat and flight of Cleopatra and Antony? Do the verses reference one of the less significant conflicts that occurred before Actium, skirmishes and invasions that made Octavian's position all the more secure along the shores of Greece?

We might consider that this description of Antony's ships comes immediately after the reference to Amyntas' defection; it is possible that the lines refer to some point in the campaign prior to 2 September. When next Horace refers to actual events of the campaign, the enemy (9.27 *hostis*) is defeated *on both land and sea* (*terra marique*), and has exchanged his scarlet cloak for a robe of mourning. Horace notes that he may reach Crete under unfavourable winds, or perhaps the Syrtes of Libya with the south wind, or indeed he may be carried off on an uncertain course (9.29-32). Even here the interpretation is fraught with difficulties; some have seen a reference not to Antony but to Hannibal in the description of the man conquered on land and sea.[9] David Mankin does well to note in his commentary that *hostilium* of the ships could be taken to imply that the vessels were manned by non-Romans; we might recall the question of Antony's exact status as a *hostis*, as well as questions about exactly what the Latin adjective can describe. On the matter of vocabulary, it does not help that *sinistorsum* is an exceedingly rare word in Latin, and thus prone to varied interpretations and a range of meanings (everything from technical seaward motion to notions of luck and fortune, to simple leftward direction).

It might seem reasonable to argue that the focus of the epode is more on the preliminaries to the battle of Actium than the 'final' engagement. We move from the defection of Antony's Galatian allies to a possible reference to a naval defeat *before* the main battle (Leucas? Patrae?), which might also allow a balanced picture of trouble on both land and sea before the interlude of verses 22 ff., where the victory is announced as it were, by triumphant language and the repeated *io Triumphe*; in other words, Horace passes over the actual engagement in almost reverential silence, returning to his 'narrative' with a picture of Antony (and not Cleopatra, we might note) in flight. Daniel Garrison may be correct in his commentary note[10] in seeing a balanced reference to defections both on land and sea. All that said, the lines may refer to the return of Antony's limping, surviving vessels to the relative safety of the harbour *after* their commander made his infamous dash after Cleopatra; in other words, not defection but retreat after the defection of the general. Horace notes that the personified 'Triumph' has surpassed the glory of the days of the Jugurthine War and the conquest of Carthage; the references are to Roman victories in Africa broadly conceived; in other words, victories like that over Cleopatra's Egypt. There is a strong foreign element to the characterisation of the achievement; this was not so much a civil war as a defeat of a dreaded foreign power, a potential new Hannibal or African threat. Antony is said to be in search of either Crete or the sandbars of Libya, the Syrtes (compare the modern Gulf of Sidra), or else he is lost on an uncertain sea (9.32 *aut fertur incerto mari*). Curiously, Alexandria is not listed among the possible destinations.[11]

We cannot be sure of the intended setting and compositional date of the epode; we cannot know if Horace is imagined as being in Rome, on ship, before or during some phase of the campaign. These questions cannot be definitively resolved. But what can be noted is that there is no record in Horace's epodic account of Actium, of the flight of Cleopatra, nothing about any sort of departure that changed the course of the battle; while the Virgilian shield of Aeneas depicts the queen in prominent relief, and also with no flight; the epode seems to present only Antony in defeat, with Horace in a position of uncertainty as to where the vanquished Roman will go (with possible fears of the resumption of civil war). If the tradition of the queen's flight had an origin in some earlier source, it is not to be found either in Virgil's eighth *Aeneid* or Horace's epodes; whatever mysteries abound as to the actual progress of the battle, we must look further for some explanation of how the Cleopatra tradition developed.

We may note too, that the ninth epode closes with an appeal for wine, in particular a Caecuban vintage that may serve to help with seasickness (9.35-36). The reference may well allude to Octavian's (and Horace's) having spent the night of the battle on board ship; it certainly seems to accord with the

Suetonian and Orosian narratives of the lateness of the hour and the fact that the night of 2-3 September was spent at sea.[12] If the reference is to the overnight sojourn on board ship, then we have not only the earliest allusion to this detail, but the only one until Suetonius (and, after him, the Christian Orosius), but the subtle hint may point circumstantially to a hard fought struggle that lasted well into the evening. All mentions of wine and feasting in Antonian/Cleopatran contexts recall the notorious party escapades of the two lovers.

But we are left with the mysterious detail about the 'leftward' propulsion of ships to harbour. Again, does Horace's epode preserve some evidence that at Actium, a significant portion of Antony's fleet surrendered as it were, either on the spot or in the course of the battle at some moment that would prove decisive? In other words, was the real victory at Actium sealed (if not achieved) when Antony lost support of some element of his navy, some group of vessels that decided to retreat into the gulf and to await coming to terms with Octavian (whom they clearly saw as the victor)? If this is what happened, it is problematic that there is no other evidence of such a major episode; Cleopatra's flight and Antony's pursuit of course, would be the more 'romantic' version than a mere surrender mid-battle (especially if it came before the struggle was particularly heated and contentious). Historians would rightly question however, the secure footing of any interpretation of the battle that rested too heavily on the difficult evidence of Horace, even if the ninth epode may well be our earliest surviving 'account' of what actually happened.

Chapter 13

Horace's Cleopatra Ode

Noble in Death.

Ode 1.37 of Horace's collection of lyrics is devoted to a depiction of Cleopatra in the wake of Actium.[1] Here there is less of a question as to setting; Cleopatra has committed suicide in late August of 30 B.C.E., and news of the ultimate defeat of Rome's storied enemy has arrived in Italy. The first three books of Horace's odes were published in 23 B.C.E.; it is difficult to date c. 1.37 more precisely than sometime between 30 B.C.E. and the release of the collection some seven years later. Equally difficult is any attempt to determine the relative chronology of Horace's ode with sections of the Virgilian *Aeneid*. What is certain is that the odes post-date the epodes.

The so-called Cleopatra ode opens with a famous call to wine: *nunc est bibendum*, 'now one must drink.'[2] There must be a dance and a feast; the poet references the Salii or priests of Mars, a significant mention of the father of Romulus and the great war god who rages in the midst of Virgil's Actium.[3] Cleopatra returns, and again with her retinue; and here she is depicted as preparing insane ruin for the Capitol of Rome, drunk on the sweetness of her own good fortune (6-12). This is what we might call the classic Cleopatra of Augustan propaganda; the queen is depicted as a real enough threat to Rome, as someone who aspired to hold power in Italy and to lord it over the Romans in their own capital. The image of drinking is important to the development of the poem; Horace's point is that now there is freedom to indulge in wine, given that the perils posed by Egypt have been put to rest; there is a time for everything, and Antony and Cleopatra did not know how to balance or moderate their consumption of alcohol. 'Drinking is also to be a keynote of the entire poem,' notes the critic, Roland Mayer, on the opening of the ode; there were models for Horace's description of bibulous, sympotic behaviour in his Greek lyric sources, but in the immediate political context, the drunken Antony is a key reference.

Ultimately, the queen's madness or *furor* (12) was diminished, however, by the salvation of scarcely one ship from the fires of battle. Octavian is depicted as pursuing her from Italy, *ab Italia* (16), a significant geographical descriptor that highlights the nature of the campaign from the Augustan perspective (it is arguably inaccurate from the point of view of the geography of the actual battle). Octavian is described as being like an accipiter or hawk, a bird of prey that chases down a soft dove; he is compared to a hunter that pursues a hare in the fields of snowy Thessaly.[4] The mention of Thessaly recalls great heroes like Achilles and Jason (indeed, the implicit reference to Achilles will prove important in our analysis of Virgil's allegorical depiction of Actium); we might note that the references to Italy and Greece allude also to Octavian's domination of both lands; there will be no rise of Antonian land forces in Greece that will threaten the new order of affairs. Actium was the effective end of Antonian resistance, despite the continuation of war for close to another year until the fall of Alexandria.[5] And in Thessaly, we also find an allusion to the clash of Caesar and Pompey at Pharsalus. Few places then, were as storied and full of the stuff of legend. Octavian has walked the path of giants.

Octavian's goal is said to have been to put chains on the *fatale monstrum*, the 'fatal monster' or portent of doom; in other words, to lead her to Rome as a captive in a triumphal procession. Horace observes that Cleopatra sought to die more nobly than this, and so she was not afraid of the sword, and did not seek to use her swift fleet to seek hidden shores (23-24 ... *nec latentis / classe cita reparavit oras*), a passage that directly recalls the earlier Horatian depiction of the enemy vessels that apparently returned to the Ambracian Gulf. Whatever those ships did, Cleopatra did not take advantage of any opportunity to sail off to Arabia or India via the Red Sea. She was calm and serene, *vultu sereno* (26), which would please some Epicurean reader of her actions, and she was willing to handle fierce serpents as part of her suicide ritual. Indeed, she was more ferocious precisely because of her deliberate death, *deliberata morte ferocior* (29); she would not allow the savage Liburnians to take her away as it were, to be paraded around in Rome as a humiliated captive.[6] In her final act she was anything but humble (32 *humilis*).[7]

Horace's Cleopatra ode is a virtual response to his ninth epode; the end of the present poem rings back to the start of its Actian predecessor. The battle is over; fire was used in the final stages (compare the Virgilian description on the shield), and Cleopatra barely escaped with her one ship. The emphasis is on a hard fought escape, not some easy and swift exit from the scene of battle. The scene then shifts to Alexandria, where the queen is contemplating suicide with bravery; the act of her suicide will deprive Octavian of the chance to have his wish to display her in his victory parade.

Cleopatra as Fierce Foe.

An argument could be made that we see in the Cleopatra ode an important element of Augustan propaganda: Cleopatra was so fierce and dangerous an enemy that she was hazardous to Rome even in death; she was *ferocior* even in the face of suicide. We cannot be sure if Octavian allowed Cleopatra to commit suicide; if he did, this could be used by him to great effect; the queen would thus appear to be all the more formidable (she managed to escape the Roman commander's attempts to capture her alive for his triumph), *and* Octavian would be spared any potential ill repute from the act of killing a woman (even one of Rome's greatest enemies). Interpreted in this way, the suicide of Cleopatra was exactly what Octavian needed and would want; Cleopatra's seeming escape from his grasp would be a calculated and deliberate piece of theatre.[8] The queen would indeed make her appearance in Octavian's triumph, and not just in an artistic depiction of the celebrated serpentine instrument of her suicide; she would be a defiant, worthy opponent of the new lord of the world.

Again, what is certain from any reading of Horace's ode is that there is nothing here of the tradition of shameful exit from war and cowardly flight; there is no hint of a battle-changing departure from the scene of Actium that altered the course of the war and history. Rather, Cleopatra is depicted in what some might term a positive light by the end of the ode; in her death she shows a nobility that is in striking contrast to the description of her court and attendants. And Antony, we might note, is nowhere to be found; he is as insignificant to the description as he is to the battle narrative on Virgil's shield of Aeneas.

Chapter 14

The Evidence of Elegy: Propertius

Couplets for a Quinquennium.

The Roman poet Propertius is among the more mysterious and enigmatic figures of the Augustan Age; his four (or five?) books of poetry are notoriously plagued with textual difficulties and interpretive problems. He may have been born around 50 B.C.E. (though we cannot be certain); death may have come sometime after around 16 B.C.E. The first book of his poems can more or less safely be dated to 30 or 29; like the epodes of Horace, it would have appeared more or less soon in the aftermath of Actium. What we call 'Book 2' of Propertius may well be what remains of an original Book 2 and Book 3; it seems to date from the early 20s. 'Book 3' comes a bit later in the 20s, and the fourth and last book around 16 or just thereafter, with the poet perhaps dying more or less soon in its wake.[1]

Propertius is a poet of love and romance; not surprisingly, a mention of Actium in his surviving work comes as an example of how, if everyone were a lover such as he, then bones would not be tossed about in the waves off Actium (c. 2.15.44 *nec nostra Actiacum verteret ossa mare*). A common theme in elegy is how it is better to engage in what is essentially the military life of the lover than the cold and pointlessly dangerous world of the 'actual' soldier. Indeed, poets of love are considered by some literary critics to be susceptible to a tendency to criticize the ruling regime, especially in matters of military conquest and political domination. Certainly it is easy to see a subversive tendency in such sentiments as c. 2.15.44, though one should not go too far in ascribing such intentions to the poet.

Propertius refers also to the triumphal aftermath of the Actian victory, to beaked prows of ships that were conveyed across the Sacred Way (c. 2.1.34 *Actiaque in Sacra currere rostra Via*), the scene of the rejoicing in celebration of the great achievement.

Of great interest is Propertius' elegy concerning a praetor back from Illyria who seems to pose a threat to his infatuation with Cynthia, his celebrated love interest. Here the poet makes reference to the departure of Antony and Cleopatra from battle in language that repays close study: *cerne ducem, modo qui fremitu complevit inani / Actia damnatis aequora militibus: / hunc infamis amor versis dare terga carinis / iussit et extremo quaerere in orbe fugam* (c. 2.16.37–40). Illyria, we might note, was just close enough within the general geographical orbit of Actium to make the connection appropriate in context.

Propertius asks us to behold the leader (that is, Antony) who only just now filled the waters of Actium with damned soldiers, all amid an empty seething or loud noise of fright.[2] The *fremitus* is 'empty' or 'vain' perhaps, because the cause is doomed; the soldiers are 'damned' because they will be drowned or otherwise killed in the conflict. Propertius proceeds to say that a base love ordered him to retreat, his ships turned back, and to seek flight at the very edge of the world. It may also be that the 'empty' anxiety and alarm refers to the decision of Antony to flee after Cleopatra; thus seriously affecting the course of battle, and was an unnecessary complication that did no good either to Antony or the men fighting bravely with him.

Unlike Horace and Virgil, Propertius focuses on Antony; it is Antony who is depicted as the commander of the disaster to his forces, and Antony who is ordered by love (of obvious interest to the elegiac poet) to flee and to seek refuge at the edge of the world. If one were concerned about the reliability of Propertian evidence because of the question of Augustan propaganda, one might also need to add concern about the poet's vested interest in matters amatory, especially in the element of recklessness that accompanies the infatuated, drunken lover. Notwithstanding all of this, it could be argued that this is the first extant source of information about any sort of Cleopatra-inspired flight from battle by Antony. If there is any mention of the effect of love and the like on Antonian flight in Virgil, as we shall see, it is entirely in the realm of allegory and oblique expression; Propertius is the earliest surviving account of the destruction of the lover in war.

Propertius also highlights the clemency of the victor in the aftermath of the battle (2.16.41–42 *Caesaris haec virtus et gloria Caesaria haec est: / illa, qua vicit, condidit arma manu*). This is the propaganda of the mercy shown in the wake of what was an uncomfortably civil engagement, though we should also note the clemency with which Octavian is said to have treated the Alexandrians. It is also worded in such a way as to remind the audience that Octavian/Augustus is Caesar. Velleius Paterculus made much of Octavian's clemency to the defeated; one can ponder Propertius' verse in light of the fate of the elegist Gallus (admittedly in a quite different context).

Hommage to the Aeneid.

At c. 2.34.61-64, Propertius alludes to the composition of the *Aeneid* by Virgil as a work in progress: *Actia Vergilio cordi sit litora Phoebi, / Caesaris et fortis dicere posse rates / qui nunc Aeneae Troiani suscitat arma / iactaque Lavinis moenia litoribus.* One might imagine from these verses that Propertius was familiar with the very opening lines of Virgil's epic, given the strong reminiscences in language; Actium is also taken to be the sort of theme that a Virgil would fittingly celebrate.[3] Actium is clearly enough envisaged as a major concern for the poet of the *Aeneid*; Aeneas will win his victory, and Augustus achieved his. Some might even say that Augustus was the more clement of the two storied figures; Aeneas after, killed his adversary Turnus in the final lines of the *Aeneid*, while Octavian/Augustus was conveniently aided by the suicides of his foes and rivals. Propertius' allusion to Actium comes as part of something of a literary history that commences with the *Aeneid* and proceeds to mention the Virgilian *Eclogues* and *Georgics*, the poetry of Varro, Catullus, and Cornelius Gallus, and crowning it all, the Cynthia of Propertius.[4]

The *Aeneid* is to be concerned with Actium then, and with the Apollonian victory; Propertius will be busy with poetry that is ostensibly under the name of the sibling of the sun god, archers both they.

Poem 11 of Book 3 is devoted to the question of women who have power over men, a theme that resonates with the general thrust of the elegist's recurring argument, as well as the specific case of the power of Cleopatra over Antony.[5] A miniature catalogue of mythological women is followed by the dramatic introduction of the Egyptian queen, who is described at once as having had sexual unions with her very slaves, and as having demanded the *Romana moenia* or walls of Rome as the price for her liaison with Antony.[6] 'A hard legacy indeed for a woman who probably had no more than two, consecutive, sexual relationships' says Joyce Tyldesley, but of course we cannot be certain.[7] The Propertian catalogue highlights Medea, the witch of Colchis who was entangled with Jason of Argonaut fame, another hero who had travelled to the East in search of fame and fortune, and who had found love and destruction.

Cleopatra is the disgrace of the line of Philip of Macedon; she is the harlot of the incestuous Canopus.[8] She dared to oppose the barking Anubis to the Jupiter of Rome: *ausa Iovi nostro latrantem opponere Anubim* (3.11.41), a clear reference to the description in the *Aeneid* of the queen at Actium. She blasted the Egyptian sistrum in the face of the Roman trumpet (another Virgilian allusion), and she pursued the beaks of Liburnian galleys with the poles of her barge (3.11.44). This is a dramatic description of the queen at war, of her vessel as an active combatant at Actium. Indeed, it stands out as a description of Cleopatra as a fighter, whether she was meant to be taken as an aggressive participant, or as someone in flight seeking to clear ships out of her way as they might have sought to block her path. And all of this has much in common with the Virgilian depiction of Actium on the shield of Aeneas.

The queen is said to have dared to stretch out *conopia* or mosquito nets on the Tarpeian Rock, a reference to Horace's description of the effeminate luxury accoutrements of the Egyptians and their retinue, not to mention the infamous traitor.

Flight and Suicide.

And Cleopatra fled, *fugisti tamen in timidi vaga flumina Nili, / nec cepere tuae Romana vincla manus* (3.11.51-52). She fled to the wandering rivers of the frightened Nile, and her hands did not receive Roman chains. The suicide with the asps is mentioned, and even a final acknowledgment of Octavian's greatness.[9] She said this, the poet notes, though her tongue was accustomed to regular drinking and indulgence in alcohol, a closing insult for the notorious hedonist, who perhaps still comes off better than Antony.

The elegy closes with an admonition to a sailor to remember Caesar over the Ionian Sea; the poet notes that Leucadian Apollo will tell of how battle lines were reversed (3.11.69 *Leucadius versas acies memorabit Apollo*), and of how one day bore a war of such immense labour.[10] In Propertius' elegiac vision, the defeat of Antony and Cleopatra has surpassed all of the previous victories for which Roman military history is celebrated; the gods founded Rome, and Rome will scarcely fear Jupiter himself so long as Augustus Caesar is safe (3.11.66 *vix timeat salvo Caesare Roma Iovem*). Strong language, and dramatic import that may even seem to border on the impious; if one wanted to point to what could be termed crass propaganda, this might serve as a good example. Even the drunken Cleopatra was able to gain her senses enough after all, to recognize that Octavian was the saviour of the Roman world. And yet the history of the next few decades might well impress on some the legitimacy of much of the praise of the *princeps*, given his tremendous accomplishments and ability to sustain more or less effectively the peaceful advance and progress of the reborn Republic (not to say Empire). Surely the thought would have occurred to many that Antony might have been a significantly less successful and accomplished leader, and Cleopatra no friend of the Capitol. Antony, perhaps like Caesar before him in his last years and months, had surrendered himself to an Eastern woman, and if Augustus had his poetic propaganda, much of it had been written by the lovers themselves.

In an important sense then, much of Propertius' concern in c. 3.11 is an expansion of the theme of the besotted lover, of the man who is a slave to his passion for a woman; there is also a clear indication of the queen's flight from battle, though nothing to make explicit that this was her intent all along. It is different from the depiction of Cleopatra in Horace and Virgil in that it emphasizes the negative, indeed deplorable qualities of the queen; some of this change in tone can be attributed to the different genre; the poet of love needs to make clear the hazards of devotion to an *amour*. And in Propertius as well as Horace, the queen manages to escape Roman chains, the key detail in the image of Cleopatra as worthy adversary.

Perhaps most significantly though, we have Propertius' poem for the quinquennial games of 16 B.C.E., c. 4.6.[11] The elegy is ostensibly an aetiological study of the temple of Apollo on the Palatine Hill in Rome that had been dedicated in 28 B.C.E.; the poem is overtly intended to praise Augustus Caesar (4.6.13 *Caesaris in nomen ducuntur carmina* …).

The 'Actian' part of the elegy opens with a geographical description of Actian Leucas (4.6.15 ff.). Interestingly, the journey there is referred to as one of no great difficulty for a seaman who travels under the protection of prayers (4.6.18 *nautarum votis non operosa via*); the emphasis is on the fated nature of Octavian's destiny. The forces of the world assembled here; a piny mass stood in the sea (4.6.19-20 … *stetit aequore moles / pinea*), perhaps in reference to the huge ships of Antony in particular that stood still at the harbour mouth.

Antony's fleet is said to be 'doomed by Trojan Quirinus';[12] the reference is to the deified Romulus, though the mention of Teucrian/Trojan does associate the Antonian side with the old, indeed dead city of Troy. And Cleopatra is there too, shamefully wielding javelins in her feminine or womanly hand; another active vignette of the queen at war. The deified Quirinus may make us think of the deified Julius; Augustus is a son of Caesar and a new Romulus, though the latter name would not be one he would accept (probably because of its monarchical connection).

On the other side of Actium we find Augustus. The commentators do well to note that the appellation is anachronistically applied, and his sails are filled with the omen of Jove, and his standards skilled at fighting for their *patria* or fatherland, a clear reference to the glories of Italy. Jupiter is the supreme god, a deity who is consistently on the side of destiny and fate. The god who had been victorious in the gigantomachy is the patron who looms over all the achievements of the righteous.

The sea god Nereus is said then to have curved both battle lines into twin crescents (4.6.25 *tandem aciem geminos Nereus lunarat in arcus*). This is a valuable reference to something strategic and tactical; it is an early citation of what we can be sure must have happened at the battle, or at least what no one would have questioned as being implausible. The god is given credit for the action, we should note; this may be poetic licence on the part of the elegist, or it may refer to some action of the wind and sea that prompted action on one or both sides. Is this a reference to any attempt by Agrippa to outflank Antony's ships? Does it refer to any initial move by Agrippa and Octavian to pull back their vessels and let Antony move in toward them? We may be reminded of the crescent formations mentioned in Dio; it may well be unlikely that Dio's source was Propertius, in which case we might look elsewhere for speculation whence the detail was derived.

Military strategy turns at once to poetic drama; the god Apollo is said to have left his native island of Delos and to have visited Augustus on ship (4.6.27 ff.); the crescent imagery that may be associated with bows and archery now leads to the pre-eminent archer god. The god urges Augustus to conquer on the sea; he notes that victory on land is already his (4.6.39), a perhaps significant detail. The Apollo of Actium is explicitly connected to the god of the first book of the *Iliad* (4.6.31 ff.) too; no god of poetry and music, of the lyre and the peaceful world of the arts. There will be a time for that soon enough, just as in Horace we might recall, there was a proper time and place for indulgence in wine and the dance. The Actian Apollo is also compared to the god when he slew the mighty Python; the point in part is to highlight the association of serpents (monstrous and venomous ones in particular) with the realm of Egypt. Apollo will now slay another serpentine horror (and Cleopatra will soon enough have a most appropriate suicide by snakebite).

Apollo addresses Augustus, and he compares him most favourably with the Trojans of yore, the hero of the battle is greater even than the mighty Hector and his other Trojan ancestors (4.6.38 *Hectoreis cognite maior avis*). This is the language of the rise of Rome in the wake of the fall of Troy; this is the triumph of the Italian rebirth. This rebirth is expressed in the god's note to Augustus that if he does not free Rome from her fear, then it was not only in vain, but also a bad thing that Romulus, augur saw his favourable birds on the Palatine (4.6.41-44). Rome in other words, might well have been better off not having been founded, were she to be conquered by the likes of Cleopatra. Augustus is the new Romulus, the new founder of Rome for a new age, the new saviour of the Republic.

In the ninth book of Virgil's *Aeneid*, Apollo appeared in disguise to the young Ascanius/Iulus, the son of Aeneas, and guided his first actions in the war in Italy, actions that would also be his last. In Virgil's conception of Aeneas' offspring, the key detail is the problem of succession. Ascanius must be removed from the fray of battle because he is too valuable to be risked; his life must be preserved at all costs. In Propertius, Apollo addresses Augustus, who is ready to fight and ready to win the day; the problem of his succession a stress, and source of anxiety for another day.

Amid his words of encouragement, Apollo describes something of the action of the battle; he notes that the enemy is daring much with their oars, *en, nimium remis audent* (4.6.45). The god comments that it would be a shameful thing for Latin waves to bear royal sails so long as Augustus is leader, a possible reference to particularly daring action on the part of Cleopatra's forces in particular, though of course 'royal sails' could be used (especially in verse) to describe Antony and Cleopatra's forces in general. Romulus, of course, was a king, but if Augustus is to be a *de facto* new Romulus, then he must be one without regal trappings and royal machinery. He must not be a Roman version of Cleopatra; the mistakes of Caesar must not be repeated by his adopted son. The genius of Roman religion and the practice of deification is that the honour and *pietas* reserved for the gods and one's ancestors, does not by necessity imply that one must do everything in the same way.

Augustus is urged not to fear that the enemy fleet has a hundred oars (a clear enough reference to the notorious vast size of the ships); the very sea is unwilling to receive them (with possible implications of the ethnic argument of Italian *versus* Eastern; the water and the implicit power of its patron deities will not accept the invasion of the gods of Egypt, of Anubis and the rest). The waters of the Mediterranean are quickly being pacified by a god like Virgil's Neptune or even the Roman Venus, the patroness of the Julian *gens*; there will be no place for the monstrous gods of Egypt.

Centaur Ships.

Curiously, Apollo also notes that ships of the enemy by the name of *Centaurs* were threatening to hurl rocks at Augustus' vessels (4.6.49). Ships were often named after mythological monsters, and in Virgil's *Aeneid* there is a Centaurus or 'Centaur' that is an Etruscan vessel allied with Aeneas.[13] We shall return soon enough to this striking image, but for the moment, we can observe that once again there is a strong emphasis on active combat and conflict (again, perhaps only in the interest of flight, some might think, but there is no indication given that flight was the original intention). Cleopatra's flagship was the *Antonius* or 'Antony', one of the rare instances where we know the name of an actual ancient vessel (as opposed to a mythological one).[14] The Centaurs were famous mythological beasts that had done battle with heroes; in the half-men, half-equine creature of legend and lore we see an obvious enough parallel to the animal gods of the Egyptians, Anubis and the like.[15]

Ethnic and political considerations are at the fore; we have noted how it is viewed as a shameful thing that the waters of Latium had to endure royal sails (4.6.46 *regia vela*) while Augustus is in charge (*principe te*); ultimately the point is that no matter how good a soldier is, what matters is the rightness of his cause, a carefully worded tribute to the honour of a Roman soldier, indeed to the Antonian veteran, with the blame placed on the leader who would contemplate bringing a foreign potentate into Roman waters. The old bugbear of a king is at the heart of the sentiment; Rome will tolerate no monarch.[16]

The time has come, Apollo states, 'Commit the ships' (4.6.53 *tempus adest, committe ratis*). The commentators do not make much of this sentiment; it could of course, simply have a general sense of a call to definitive, resolute action in the face of a battle that is already won (or at least eminently winnable, for the taking, as it were). Apollo notes that he is the 'author of time', the *temporis auctor*, and that he will conduct the Julian beaks with his laurel-bearing hand. The laurel (at least if we can believe narratives such as that of Ovid's *Metamorphoses* 1) was connected to the god's passion for Daphne; that infatuation however, did not ruin the deity, and the virginal maiden was actually preserved as it were, for all time in her arboreal metamorphosis; the god's possession extends only to the use of the laurel as his sacred tree (here the insignia of his victorious action).

Apollo is then depicted as firing arrows from his quiver; second only to him is the spear of Caesar. The woman, the again (as ever) unnamed Cleopatra, pays the penalty (4.6.57 ... *dat femina poenas*). Her sceptres are now broken, and the remnants are conveyed through the Ionian waves. This is the Apollo of the opening of the Homeric *Iliad*; this is the god of Actium in his full splendour, defeating his enemies with arrow and quiver. It is interesting that Propertius describes Julius Caesar himself as looking down on the scene from the 'Idalian star' or star of Venus (4.6.59 *at pater Idalio miratur Caesar ab astro*); this is the deified Julius, but the same individual we might say, who had an affair with the woman who has now been defeated, the father of the son who would soon enough be slain by Octavian's order. Caesar observes that he is a god, and that this victory is the proof or token that Octavian is of his blood, *sum deus; est nostri sanguinis ista fides.*[17] Significantly, when the victory is achieved and the sea gods celebrate, the marine goddesses gather around the standards of freedom, the *libera signa* (4.6.62); monarchy *versus* republicanism. This is Latium and the glory of central Italy, Latium in opposition to the old, dying kingdoms of the East, the Italy of the Senate even, against the Alexandria of the incestuous Ptolemies.[18] We do well to remember throughout that Antony is nowhere; this is a foreign war against a foreign foe.

Soon enough the queen makes her escape on a vessel that is deliberately called a *cumba* (4.6.63), the Latin word that is almost a technical term for Charon's death bark in the underworld.[19] Here we may see a poetic reference to the departure of Antony and Cleopatra for Taenarum, one of the so-called entrances to the underworld. Ultimately, Cleopatra seeks the hidden Nile, and there she is destined to die on a day that was not ordered, *iusso non moritura die.* The description reminds us of Horace and his ode; the emphasis is on how Cleopatra will escape enslavement in a triumphal procession.

And Propertius notes that this was for the better, *di melius*, since a woman would hardly make for a grand procession; a woman would be no Jugurtha.[20] Here we see something of the point of Horace's Cleopatra ode; it was in Augustus' best interests on several levels to have the queen commit suicide.

Roman Gods at War.

Lastly, Propertius credits 'Actian Phoebus' (4.6.67) with having sunk ten enemy ships with each arrow; in return he merited his temple on the Palatine. This is the Roman virtue of *pietas*, a concept that is impossible to translate effectively (English 'piety' will not do); the god was responsible for the victory, and in return his grateful servants will render him the homage that is his due. It is the economy of Roman religion, the fit honour and respect merited by a powerful deity, in implicit contrast to the hollow and empty rites of the Egyptians with their animal gods.[21] This is the stuff of proper expiation and propitiation for all manner of circumstances; this is the birth of the right relationship between men and gods. It is eminently Roman, and profoundly traditional. We might wonder if any other civil war in Rome ever had such able commentary; we can remember that the essentially *foreign* nature of the war made such poetic treatments possible.

As Hutchinson notes in his commentary on c. 4.6.63-64, the Cleopatra of this quinquennial elegy certainly does not flee from Actium in the middle of the contest, and at best, the mention of her flight at c. 2.16.39-40 is 'probably implied'. But in truth there is no real inconsistency between the narratives and references in Virgil, Horace, and Propertius; all three tell a more or less consistent story between direct narrative and allusive reference, even if (understandably enough) the elegiac poet is more concerned about the effects of Antony's romance with Cleopatra than anything else.

In light of the evidence of these three Augustan Age poets, we may note that there is a seemingly curious lack of reference to Actium in the surviving elegies of Albius Tibullus, the contemporary of the great aforementioned trio. Some scholars have found a reference to the battle at verse 80 of c. 2.5, where the Apollo is invited to 'submerge the prodigies under untamed waters' (*prodigia indomitis merge sub aequoribus*),[22] but this is as much as one will find with respect to the Apollonian/Augustan victory. *Prodigia* certainly reminds one of the language of monstrosity and the foreign that can be found in Virgil's description of the shield of Aeneas, for example, but Tibullus contributes precious little to the question of battle reconstruction.[23]

Chapter 15

An Allegorized Actium?

Camilla and Arruns, Cleopatra and Arruntius.

Book 11 of Virgil's *Aeneid* is probably not to be considered among the more popular sections of his epic; for a long time it languished more or less unstudied by the scholarly tradition. In the context of the epic, Book 11 is the penultimate book of the poem, a portion of the epic devoted to battle and war in Italy. The context is the war in Latium that erupts in the wake of the arrival of Aeneas and his Trojans to Italy and the question of whether or not Aeneas will marry the Latin princess Lavinia, a girl whose hand in marriage was already expected by the Rutulian hero, Turnus. In one sense the narrative is a reprisal of the Homeric *Iliad*; once again a Trojan will be involved in the question of the ownership of a woman; first Helen of Sparta, and now Latinus' royal daughter Lavinia.

Book 11 of the epic is never cited among those possible sources of information about the battle of Actium. We shall investigate now the question of whether or not in Virgil's penultimate book of his *magnum opus*, we have nothing other than the most extended account of the Battle of Actium in surviving Augustan poetry, an allegorical *tour de force* in which the major events of the naval engagement are presented in the context of a cavalry battle that ultimately hinges on the performance of the Volscian heroine Camilla, and her ultimate defeat by the Etruscan servant of Apollo Arruns. We shall consider the possibility that the eleventh book of Virgil's epic is a valuable source of information about Actium that supports the scholarly position that the battle was a hard fought contest in which the Egyptians acquitted themselves respectably before they were forced to retreat in the face of the assault of Lucius Arruntius' squadron.

Context matters. By the opening of Book 11, both Trojans and Italians have been severely discomfited in war; notably, Aeneas' young friend Pallas, the Patroclus of the *Aeneid*, has been slain in battle. Aeneas agrees to a burial truce with an embassy of Latin envoys, so as to allow time for requiems and the rites of the dead. The question of which side is doing better in the war at the start of Book 11 is a legitimate one; both Trojans and Latins have suffered appreciably, though arguably the Latins have had the worst of it and are in more dire straits.

Funerals are thus accompanied by debate in the Latin capital. Turnus faces significant criticism from the older Latin man, Drances, who argues essentially that Turnus has put all of Latium at risk, and that he should fight Aeneas in single combat and make the war truly his own; too many have died, as it were. There are more than a few people in Latium it would seem, who are eager to end the war and in some way to come to terms with Aeneas, especially if all that this really means is the surrender of the girl Lavinia to the Trojan hero.

Antony and Cicero?

As the commentators note here, some have seen an allegory in Drances and Turnus of the figure of the great Roman statesman Marcus Tullius Cicero in his conflict with Antony in the years after the Ides of March.[1] This conflict directly led to the death of Cicero in the proscriptions of the second triumvirate; for Antony, any extra-judicial execution was negotiable except that of the man who proved to be one of his greatest opponents in the period after the Ides of March.

At some point during the conflict at the war council debate, news arrives that the Trojans, at least Aeneas, were beginning to move both camp and battle line (11.446 … *castra Aeneas aciemque movebat*). A messenger rushes into Latinus' palace in a state of great trepidation and excitement; he notes that the Teucrians have moved down from the River Tiber in marshalled array.

The immediate reaction of the Latin assembly is one of both anxiety and anger; at once the young men demand arms and seethe for combat, all nerves notwithstanding (11.453 *arma manu trepidi poscunt, fremit arma iuventus*).

A question to be asked here is what exactly has happened; have the Latins been taken by surprise while occupied with their debate? Were the Latins so focused on their discussion that they had failed to take note of the expiration of the burial truce, if indeed the truce has expired? Have the Trojans broken the truce and prepared military manoeuvres that include more than a few elements of surprise? The news that reaches the Latin war council proves to be a turning point in the narrative; there is no further word about Drances and his position. He has been effectively silenced by whatever it is that the Trojans did here.

Turnus, for one, sarcastically comments on how the Latins have been calling a council and praising the notion of peace, while the Trojans are rushing into arms against the kingdom (11.460-461). And as Turnus prepares to respond to the threat, Virgil makes ready the reintroduction of his mysterious Volscian heroine Camilla, a character he had first briefly introduced as the final figure in his catalogue of Italian heroes in Book 7.[2] Indeed, during the debate with Drances and the others, Turnus had noted that the forces of Camilla were still intact and ready for combat (11.432-433, verses that recall the description of the girl from the end of Book 7). Virgil does not make clear where Camilla was during the war council (cf. the presence of Cleopatra in debates between Antony and his officers).

The Equestrian Heroine.

Camilla rides to the scene on her horse; as she dismounts, all of her contingent follows the example of their leader and do the same (11.498-501), a fine mark of respect and honour for their leader. Camilla promises to face Aeneas' cavalry with her own; she is willing to charge off alone against his Etruscan allied horse. Her plan is for Turnus to remain behind in defence of the city of his prospective father-in-law Latinus. This is an act of bravery and heroism, a bravery that some might call reckless; Camilla is perfectly willing to be the principal fighter in the ensuing conflict. Virgil does not record the reaction of the Latins/Italians to the Volscian girl's suggestion; only Turnus is given any sentiments of reaction, and he is clearly in awe of Camilla. She was on his mind in the war council as a potential source of continued reserves and resistance to Aeneas; now she has confirmed exactly what he predicted; the Latins can expect significant aid from this girl and her cavalry contingent, despite their having been absent from the war thus far (and Cleopatra had fought in no engagements with Antony until Actium).

Turnus now reveals to Camilla (and the audience learns this for the first time too) that he has intelligence on Aeneas' plan; scouts have confirmed the strategy of the Trojan leader. Aeneas has sent forth cavalry across the plains in what amounts to a diversionary attack; meanwhile he himself plans to proceed by a deserted mountain route to launch a surprise attack on the town. Turnus plans to ambush this (presumably mostly) infantry force, while Camilla will wait for the Etruscan cavalry to attack; she will be with Messapus and Tiburtus as co-captains (11.511-521).

Virgil describes the treacherous locale where Turnus will in effect seek to meet trickery with trickery. The general outline of strategy then, is clear enough; the Trojans have a ruse in mind that will conceal the main attack by which they hope to seize Latinus' city. Reconnaissance has allowed the Latins to learn of the plan; if Turnus has his way, Aeneas could be destroyed by the unexpected ambush. It is a bold plan, though sound. It is born out of a careful consideration of the available intelligence.

At this point, Virgil interrupts his complicated narrative for a long interlude in which the goddess Diana describes the early history of Camilla to her nymph, Opis (11.532 ff.). The story presents numerous difficulties of interpretation, but it is clear enough in its general outline: the infant Camilla and her father, Metabus, were driven from their home and forced into exile; Camilla lived an isolated, sylvan existence that was spent with adolescent hunting and the works of the goddess of the chase. She has devoted herself to virginity and the life of the forest; somehow (however incongruously), she has become the leader of the very people who had once exiled her father; she is now their commander in war, and they are by all accounts fiercely loyal to their heroine captain. We might have expected none of this back story when Camilla was first introduced in Book 7; given the lack of evidence that Virgil either invented Camilla or borrowed her from some pre-existing tradition, we have no idea how much of Diana's account of the girl's childhood and adolescence would come as a surprise. On one level, it certainly speaks to the impropriety of Camilla's involvement in war; she might well have been better off staying in the forest, preoccupied with the hunting of animals.

Diana has instructions for her nymph; Camilla cannot be saved, but Opis is to avenge the death of the girl by seeing to the destruction of whoever it is, Trojan or Italian, who kills her (11.592). Diana will see to the honourable burial of Camilla and the preservation of her body from desecration. Of all the enemies of Aeneas who fall in war, Camilla stands out as one who will be protected by divine favour in the matter of the potential stripping of armour and even desecration of the body of a casualty; she will not even require some man-made requiem, but will have Diana herself as the manager of her sacred funeral rites. Diana cannot intervene to the extent of rescuing her devotee; she can however, work her will in some aspects of the girl's inevitable death.

The Trojans and their Etruscan allies advance near the walls of the city; the time for battle has arrived (11.597 ff.). What follows can be interpreted as nothing less than an elaborate allegory of the Battle of Actium, a poetic trick by which the great naval victory of Octavian over the forces of Antony and Cleopatra is carefully re-imagined in the dactylic hexameter of epic poetry. Certainly there are not exact correspondences that run through the narrative. For one thing, it would have been difficult for Virgil to insert an actual naval battle in his poem of the arrival of Aeneas and the Trojans in central Italy, but we shall see that certain crucial aspects of the narrative do indeed point to an allegorized version of Actium, including something of a commentary on the part played by Camilla as Cleopatra.

The Trojans and Etruscans are described as appearing on one side, and Messapus, Coras and his brother (that is, Tiburtus), and then Camilla on the other; a triple arrangement of forces. The forces advance to within a spear's throw of a distance between the two fronts, and then they halt (11.608-609). Suddenly they charge together with a shout and in furious onslaught; no indication is given of which side advanced first; what they do, they do in unison. Weapons fly as if snow (11.611 ... *nivis ritu*); the sky is darkened by the onslaught of the first rush. Tyrrhenus and Aconteus are the first to clash; their horses are literally broken, even thoroughly so, as they clash (11.644 ... *perfracta*). Aconteus is killed as he is dislodged from his horse and shot forth like a lightning bolt or a catapult's weapon of siege.

The lines are at once thrown into disarray (11.618 *extemplo turbatae acies*). The Latins are routed, and they throw down their shields and flee to the walls of the city. The Trojans pursue, but as the Latins reach the gates, they turn around to face the pursuing enemy, and now it is the Trojans'/Etruscans' turn to flee.[3]

Naval Battles on Land.

A simile is employed to describe the action; it is as when the ocean moved with alternating flow of water, first rushing to the coast and striking the strand with its waves; then it flees back to the deep in turn (11.624-628), a marine comparison that may well be more than merely ornamental or picturesque in the present case. Twice the Etruscans drive the Trojans to the walls; twice they are themselves driven to retreat. This delicately balanced ballet of cavalry forces may reflect Agrippa's apparent move to back water so that his engagement with Antony's forces would occur deeper out to sea, safely away from the hazards of fighting too close to the Antonian shore.[4]

The third encounter is deadlier; now the two lines are joined in fierce combat. Here we find the inevitable tremendous slaughter of the clash of man and horse; Orsilochus kills Remulus, and Catillus Iollas and Herminius. Gore and grisly battle wounds are everywhere (11.631-647). Manoeuvres as it were, are now ended; practised battle tactics give way to general chaos and slaughter. Virgil now reintroduces his heroine to the drama, just as the chaos of the battlefield reaches its height.

The Amazon in the Midst of War.

At medias inter caedes exsultat Amazon: but amid the midst of the slaughter, the Amazon rejoices (11.648). Camilla makes her entrance at the centre of the struggle; if she had been arrayed on one of the wings, she now takes her place in the very heart of the fray. She has the traditional Amazon accoutrements of the one breast exposed for the battle; she wields a bow as well as javelins and an axe. It is difficult in fact, to reconcile the number of her weapons with her astonishing performance in battle. She has a somewhat strange group of female associates with her, fellow heroines named Larina, Tulla and Tarpeia, names that are redolent with the spirit of old Italy, though not entirely without problematic associations.[5] The advance of these women is compared to the charge of the Amazons over the icy Thermodon, to the galloping of such a one as Penthesilea, the daughter of Mars, or Hippolyta (11.659-663). Of course, the reader with knowledge of the tradition of the epic cycle and the lore surrounding the fall of Troy, knows that the new Penthesilea, the Italian Amazon, is doomed to destruction.[6]

Camilla begins her military aristeia, the performance of her deeds of valour. Euneus dies first, then Liris and Pagasus; Amastrus and Tereus, Harpalycus, Demophoon and Chromis. Ornytus the hunter is said to be riding on an Iapygian steed (11.678). Interestingly, leaving aside the matter of Aeneas' aged doctor Iapyx (12.391-431), the descriptor appears in Virgil only in Book 11 and on the shield of Aeneas. On the shield it refers to the northwest wind that blew from Italy as Cleopatra fled to Egypt after Actium. In Book 11, it describes the home of Diomedes in southern Italy, a locale founded by Daedalus' son Iapyx.[7] And too, it appears to be the home of the Etruscan Ornytus' horse. Is the reference to Iapygia a reminder of the significance of that wind in the success of Cleopatra's escape from Actium?

Orsilochus and Butes are slain next; soon Camilla finds the son of Aunus, a Ligurian whose gruesome death is not directly described, but who is accorded the perverse honour of a memorable simile (11.721-724). Camilla's assault on her victim is compared to the action of an accipiter when it pursues a dove; the dove is grasped by the talons of the predatory bird in the sky, and the gore and feathers drip down from the doomed victim bird.

The image is a reverse of that found in Horace's Cleopatra's ode (again, we cannot be sure of the priority of the picture). Certainly in Horace, the bird of prey is none other than Octavian; in Virgil's narrative of course, 'Augustus', if Aeneas, is safely removed from the field of equestrian battle, though at risk from the ambush that Turnus has planned for him.

Jupiter sees the battle unfold, and grows displeased; if his intention is for the Trojans and their allies to win, then Camilla's impressive victories cannot be allowed to continue unchecked. Jupiter spurs on the Etruscan Tarchon, and the captain marshals his men in turn; interestingly, Tarchon criticizes his men for being eager for the world of nocturnal revels and Bacchic feasting, but not for battle. We might well think of the allegations (true and exaggerated alike) that were levelled against Cleopatra and Antony. Tarchon charges against Venulus, and carries him off on his own horse; a shout goes up to the sky, and the Latins turn their attention to the scene of the now changed battle (11.745-746).

Lucius Arruntius Redux.

Rather suddenly and without any previous introduction, the Etruscan Arruns makes his appearance, literally at mid-line (11.759).[8] Arruns is stalking Camilla, carefully tracking her steps and following her course across the battlefield. He is presented clearly enough by the poet as finding Camilla an absolute disgrace, with what might be taken to be an implicit misogyny and serious problem with the presence of a young woman in battle. Arruns could not be clearer about his detestation of Camilla; he wants this girl dead.

Virgil offers very little introduction or backstory to his Arruns, despite the relative importance of the character to the narrative as the slayer of Camilla. He clearly evokes Lucius Arruntius, the commander of Octavian's centre at Actium.[9] Arruntius was a reasonably successful figure in a difficult age; he had been saved from the proscriptions, and would in turn plead for the life of his friend Sosius after Actium. He was born in Atina, a Volscian town, and he had connections to the Pompeians (indeed, it was Sextus Pompey who saved him from the proscriptions). Lucius Arruntius, in short, was one of those figures who was fortunate to have survived in the era in which he lived, a man who was on different sides of a complicated situation at different points in the complex history of an age of change and revolution.

Interestingly, Virgil's Arruns is depicted as something of a fanatic, a priest of the Apollo of Mount Soracte, a partisan of a cult of firewalkers who reverenced the god by an extreme act of devotion. (We might recall here the Senecan evidence that Arruntius was known for his great frugality and what we might call simplicity of life; cf. too the evidence of Velleius Paterculus.) Virgil's Arruns has every reason to believe that Apollo will listen to his prayer to aid in the death of Camilla, given that he has been a devoted servant of the deity in the fiery liturgies on Soracte. Arruns is himself doomed, however; he prays successfully that the god may aid him in his victory over Camilla, but his rather presumptuously worded sentiment about being willing to return home without glory will not reach the god and meet with his approval. We might note here that in Arruns' expression of his wishes, there is a sentiment that the killing of a woman would not bring him glory (even a woman, we might note, of the military stature of a Camilla). The issue of the propriety and glory to be derived from the killing of a female is an important consideration in an appreciation of both Virgil's depiction of Camilla *and* the problem Octavian faced with Cleopatra. Killing women is always a questionable course of action, even women who are at the heart of a military struggle.

Virgil does not entirely make clear the allegiances of his Arruns in the cavalry battle: is he an Etruscan fighting on Aeneas' side, or is he one of Mezentius' Etruscans on the side of Turnus? Certainly he managed successfully to stalk Camilla without much difficulty (admittedly, across an increasingly complicated field of battle).[10] His attack, in any case, comes as a complete surprise, both to Camilla and it would seem, to those around her (at least until they take note of the sound of his weapon). He is single-minded in his pursuit of Camilla; she is his only quarry, and he exists in the epic solely to be the one who will take her life and face divine retribution for the audacious act. According to Servius' commentary on the cult of the wolf priests of Apollo, those who wanted to destroy the predatory wolves that had once stolen sacrificial offerings, needed themselves to become wolves, that is, to live on plunder, and once Arruns kills Camilla, Virgil will compare the exhilarated, frightened warrior to a wolf.

Ghosts of Troy.

Famously, at this point in the Virgilian narrative, Camilla is distracted by the appearance of the Trojan Chloreus, a devotee of the goddess Cybele (11.768 ff.). When Camilla was first introduced in Book 7, she was described as resplendent in purple as well as gold (we might think of the significance of those two colours to Cleopatra at Actium); now she sees the purple and gold of the lavishly dressed Chloreus, and is momentarily in doubt as to what she should do, the question being whether the arms of Chloreus should be displayed in a temple as spoils of war, or worn by Camilla herself as part of a rich set of apparel.

And Virgil is clear enough that Camilla has a very feminine love of spoils and plunder, *femineo praedae et spoliorum ardebat amore* (11.782).

Here we may well see an evocation of the image of Cleopatra in her lust for wealth, indeed of Cleopatra's interest in treasure and the safeguarding thereof. Arruns makes his prayer to Apollo, and Camilla is fatally wounded. It is clear enough from the unfolding of the epic account that both Jupiter and Apollo are involved in the doom of Camilla, and her own confusion over what to do with the arms of Chloreus is part of the drama, indeed a key element. Chloreus is depicted as either a priest or a former priest of the goddess Cybele, a deity whose worshippers included castrated devotees, eunuch adorers of the immortal of the Trojan Mount Ida. The worship of Cybele and the fanatic rites of her followers stand rather in sharp contrast to the sober traditions of Italy and Roman religious practice. Camilla is distracted by a devotee of the Trojan mother goddess, and Apollo ultimately sees to her death, an appropriate blend of the old gods and the new in defence ultimately of the Troy that is destined to be reborn, after a fashion at least, as the new Rome. Camilla does not entirely understand what she is looking at as she sees the strangely attired Chloreus, but she does have an unquestionable attraction to, and fascination with his luxurious, splendid raiment. The precise meaning of such phrases as *femineo amore* has exercised the talents of Virgilian commentators, but the sentiment could just as easily be applied to Cleopatra as to her Volscian avatar.

For the larger Virgilian narrative, the main point behind the divine interventions in the matter of Camilla, the immortal actions of both Jupiter and Apollo (the latter god significant from the Actian perspective), is the effect her death has on Turnus. In a strict sense, if Turnus had maintained his ambush, Aeneas would have been severely handicapped, perhaps even killed. Camilla has final instructions for Turnus before she breathes her last; she conveys them to her trusted companion Acca (who is either the same as the aforementioned Larina, or a hitherto unmentioned character). She instructs Turnus, via Acca, that he should succeed her in the battle, and ward off the Trojans from the city (11.826 *succedat pugnae Troianosque arceat urbe*).

The exact point of these orders is perhaps elusive; one interpretation would be that Turnus is needed to stem the rout of Camilla's forces in the wake of her death, while another would be that he should now play *his* role in the battle. He should maintain his ambush and await Aeneas, thereby keeping the Trojans away from the city (this interpretation is given some weight by the fact that it has been mostly the Etruscans who have fought in the cavalry engagement, while Aeneas is leading Trojans for his surprise attack).[11] In one sense the question is academic, given what transpires in the wake of Acca's arrival in Turnus' presence.

For whatever the precise qualifications of Camilla's orders, Acca does not relay the message at all accurately. Rather, she reports that Camilla is dead and the situation before the walls of the city more or less a disaster (11.898-900). One imagines that she was understandably emotionally overwrought. Turnus' reaction is one of fury and rage, and Virgil makes it clear that it was no one less than Jupiter himself who demanded what Turnus now did; *he abandoned his ambush* (11.901-902 *ille furens (et saeva Iovis sic numina poscunt) / deserit obsessos collis*). Significantly, the poet describes how the report of Camilla's death was 'most savage' (11.896 *saevissimus*), and how it was the savage will of Jove that demanded Turnus' abandonment of his well arranged plan; lastly, Turnus recognizes savage Aeneas once the Trojans safely make it to the city. Aeneas cannot actually achieve his goal of capturing the town by surprise attack, but he has also survived to fight another day. Further battle would have taken place at once, but night intervened, thus ending the long and terrible day of martial strife. There is a final detail of Apollonian presence even, in the book. The horses of the god are referred to as part of a poetic description of the action of the sun as it dips into the western ocean; in this case the point is to recall not only the key role played by Apollo in the book, but also the nature of the equestrian battle.

Camilla as Cleopatra.

The Virgilian Camilla narrative is a complex amalgam of many different traditions, but in terms of what we might call the 'basic' outline of the story of Aeneas and his Trojans, it represents the death of a dreaded foe, the Volscian Camilla. Whatever the facts of her Virgilian rehabilitation and treatment, and in many aspects, she is presented as an intensely heroic figure, on a fundamental level, she is destroyed as an enemy of the Trojan destiny (a destiny that concerns ultimately nothing less than the settlement and foundation of the future Rome). There is no place for Camilla in the future Rome, at least not in the way in which she presents herself in battle, at least not as anything other than an example to spur others on to heroic deeds of valour. Indeed, the women of Latinus' city are inspired by the example of Camilla to risk their lives in defence of the capital; in death, Camilla serves as a model for heroism and love of country. The implied contrast to Arruns is clear; Camilla is remembered, and her Etruscan slayer forgotten. History would treat Cleopatra and Lucius Arruntius in much the same way.

In terms of battle strategy, the cavalry engagement of *Aeneid* 11 reveals a simple enough structure. Two sides meet in opposition. They advance against each other twice, and maintain battle lines as they both pull back and move forward in turn. In the third round however, the two sides clash and become enmeshed in a violent slaughter. In the midst of the mayhem and chaos of battle, Camilla exults, and she achieves significant victories over her enemy. Finally, she is defeated by Arruns. In the wake of her death, Turnus decides to give up his part in the battle in emotional disarray and disconcertion over the loss of Camilla.

An argument can be made that we move in *Aeneid* 11 from an evocation of the political conflict between Antony and Cicero to nothing less than the Battle of Actium, a battle in which both sides had every intention of achieving victory. In the Actium of *Aeneid* 11, we certainly see a strong element of the tradition that Cleopatra fled first as it were, and that Antony followed; in the Virgilian narrative, the death of Camilla is the direct cause of Turnus' decision to give up what could still have been a decisive victory. If one wanted to find evidence in the Augustan poets for the clearly expressed later tradition of Antony's fatal infatuation with Cleopatra, one need look no further than the drama of the equestrian battle before the gates of Latinus' city, a struggle that in several important respects reinvents the struggle at Actium.

We may note too, something of the image that Virgil wanted to craft for his Turnus on the cusp of battle. Before Turnus proceeds to meet Camilla, he is compared to a stallion that is made free of its stable, a horse that proceeds to an open plain and the joys of both mares and streams of water (11.492–497). The simile is borrowed from Homer's *Iliad* (6.506–511), where the picture depicts Paris as he departs for battle. Virgil thus compares his Rutulian commander to the infamous lover of Helen, the Trojan hero who is described consistently as more or less in thrall to his Greek lover. It is a telling comparison in terms of the intentional characterization of Turnus on the eve of battle; in the Virgilian context, it is especially appropriate given the cavalry battle that it immediately precedes; Turnus is the stallion, and Camilla and her companions the mares in the open field. If Helen was a destructive force for Paris, so too is Camilla for Turnus, and historically, so also Cleopatra for Antony.[12] We might note here that in Plutarch's comparison of Antony and Demetrius, he describes the departure of Antony from Actium as that of Paris to Helen, and he emphasizes the fact that when Paris fled to Helen, at least he had actually been defeated (i.e., in combat with Menelaus), whereas Antony's flight to Cleopatra is precisely what caused his defeat at Actium.[13]

Virgil's Camilla narrative serves an important function in the poet's larger conception of the war in Italy. *Aeneid* 11 describes a military engagement involving both infantry and cavalry, we might think (assuming that Turnus and Aeneas would find it difficult to use horses in the thick, dense terrain where the ambush is planned), but certainly an encounter where Turnus stood a reasonable chance of victory, absent divine disfavour and the immutable destiny of Aeneas to survive. The means by which Jupiter and Apollo worked their will in favour of Aeneas was the infatuation of Turnus with Camilla, an infatuation that proved fatal. Camilla performed splendidly in battle, her achievements of unquestionable valour and impressive scope and range, and her defeat was of a more complicated nature than simply the death of a girl who was entranced by the potential riches and loveliness of some Trojan's attire. Nor could Camilla in any way prevent Turnus' reaction to her death, and the catastrophic consequences for his cause.

Chapter 16

The Lost *Carmen de Bello Aegyptiaco/Actiaco*

Herculaneum papyrus 817 preserves something of a tantalizing verse treatment of events immediately after Actium, a work of uncertain authorship and date that may serve as something of a haunting 'final' word on the poetic tradition of the war in Latin verse.[1] Gaius Rabirius, Cornelius Severus, and Lucius Varius Rufus[2] have all been proposed and defended as the responsible poet; it is possible if not probable that the work was intended to glorify and amplify in some way the last phase of Octavian's victory over Antony and Cleopatra; the Alexandrian War.[3] The scope of the poem is quite uncertain; there is no way of knowing definitively if it were intended to include treatment of the Actium campaign as well as the Alexandrian.[4] It is also a challenge to determine if the poem did or did not mean to convey anti-Augustan sentiments.[5] In short, essentially we have all of the 'usual questions' about Latin fragmentary works, authorship, date, intended extent of composition, various problems of reconstruction; all are in dispute to greater or lesser extents.

The first column of the work seems to describe a siege conducted by Italian forces (*imminet opsessis Italus iam turribus [ho]stis*); as Courtney notes, '*Italus* insists on Octavian as a national champion.' *Italus* is followed by *[La]tius*; Caesar (i.e., Octavian) conquers Pelusium. The second column makes the narrative context reasonably clear; we are in the midst of the *Bellum Alexandrinum*, the Alexandrian War, but again, we have no sense of how the poem started. As Courtney notes, in 1466 a Renaissance humanist boasted that he possessed a manuscript of a poem *de bello nautico cum Antonio et Cleopatra quod incipit armatum cane, Musa, ducem, belloque cruentam Aegyptum*, a likely enough reference to Actium (as opposed to the relatively minor naval adventures in Egyptian waters). We have no idea what the humanist actually saw (or at least claimed to have seen); since his fifteenth century announcement, the closest we have come to anything remotely fitting his fine description is the papyrus on which our knowledge of the *Bellum Aegyptiacum* rests. The aforementioned opening verse, *armatum cane Musa*, etc., is suspiciously similar to the opening of Virgil's *Aeneid*, a fact that either points to learned forgery, or to the early influence of the great epic of Rome's founding on the poetic tradition.

Column III presents numerous difficulties of interpretation; it seems to describe how the goddess Isis mourned to see the misadventure at Actium, and how Cleopatra can be assured of a famous name in the annals of history and epic. Courtney observes that 'all explanations are provisional' and indeed it is perilous to base arguments on half-a-dozen contested and imperfectly preserved Latin verses, but it seems reasonably certain that Cleopatra is referenced as the *causa maxima belli*, 'the great cause of the war', and a sharer in command (*pars erat imperii*); it may be that Cleopatra was compared to Helen of Sparta/Troy. This topos is part of the background drama to the depiction of Aeneas with the Carthaginian Dido in the fourth book of Virgil's *Aeneid*; again, we cannot be sure how developed the idea would have been in the complete epic. There seems to be a reference to the bed chamber of Alexander; this could be the Alexander the Great of Alexandria and the Macedonian kingdom, but it could also conceivably refer to the name of the Trojan hero better known as Paris.

Column IV seems to represent the internal angst and emotional turmoil of Cleopatra as she ponders her fate and considers such alternatives as flight or suicide; there seems to be a reference to the courage of Antony in facing death for the name of her race, and to Antony's wish to join the Parthian and Pharian realms. Interestingly, Antony is referred to as Cleopatra's husband (*est mihi coniunx*), at least in the estimation of the Egyptian queen; this is one of the rare pieces of evidence in the matter of the disputed nuptial status of the doomed lovers. The third column would seem to have prepared the way for the suicide; there may have been strong influence from the depiction of Dido's death in Virgil's *Aeneid* 4, but again we are lost in a world of speculation and difficult argumentation from imperfect and incomplete evidence.

Column V describes the gathering of prisoners in Alexandria to test various poisons to determine which would be the most efficacious in procuring a swift and painless end; Column VI is devoted to details about the famous suicide by snakebite and venom. The seventh column presents an eerie image of Atropos, the Fate who was credited with the responsibility for snipping the thread of life, as she stands ready by the queen; the eighth and final section seems to depict the Roman forces outside Alexandria; we have no way of knowing what military episode is referenced, but it seems to be the final fall of the city; the Romans appear to be moving near the walls with impunity.

Very little then, can be gleaned from this nonetheless fascinating source of near contemporary information about the Actian and Alexandrian campaigns. We may have here the pitiful remains of a lengthy epic poem on the victory of Octavian over Antony and Cleopatra; it is impossible to determine what influence the work may have had on contemporary and later poets. Nor is it possible to know how an epic on an apparently large scale was lost; the surviving fragments do not allow much in the way of a fair judgment as to quality and interest.

Part Four

Analyzing the Evidence

Chapter 17

So What Really Happened?

W e are left then, with two fairly detailed accounts of the Battle of Actium; those of Plutarch and Dio, and a host of briefer references and allusions, including the possibility of a full scale allegorized version of the battle in the dactylic hexameter of epic verse. The evidence, as we have seen, is fraught with contradiction and enigma; we lack a definitive ancient account that is devoid of the twin perils of romance and propaganda, and which does not pose problems of interpretation in light of other surviving sources. In short, we have both too many and too few puzzle pieces; we would seem to have good literary and historical reasons to support quite different accounts of what took place (most especially in relation to the fundamental problem of whether or not Actium was even a 'battle' in the traditional sense).

We can begin the difficult process of attempting to reconstruct what might well have 'really' happened.

One is perhaps struck by the extreme paucity of details about what happened on land in Greece and Macedonia during the months leading up to 2 September. In simple terms, the fight had to take place somewhere, and the weight of Caesarian and Pompeian precedent, at least, was that the decisive military engagements would *not* take place in Italy proper. Antony was a phihellene (a 'Greekophile') who clearly considered Greece his personal preserve; certainly he was in a strong military position there, at least on land. He had also managed to assemble a significant fleet in the confines of the Ambracian Gulf; that fleet was clearly not merely intended to be maintained at great expense and for an indefinite time as a merely defensive patrol.

Politically, it must have been an easier task for Octavian and Agrippa to plan an invasion of the East, than for Antony to conceive of landing in Italy with Cleopatra in tow. And invade they did, given that the real story of Actium may well lie in the preliminary campaigns that saw Agrippa as the victor at Methone and eventually, Leucas and Patrae. Strategic considerations made it essential for Octavian to seize multiple bases that could both serve to protect Italy from any threat of invasion should it be contemplated, and to harass any supplies

Antony sought to send into Greece from Egypt in particular. However well Antony defended and fortified such locales as Methone, it was not sufficient in the face of Agrippa's assaults; by the day of Actium, Antony was in a far weaker position than Octavian in the matter of naval bases, and in the face of what we might call an island hopping strategy.

That said, Antony's tremendous fleet must have been intended to defend Greece and to menace Italy; the problem was that no matter how extensive his forces, the Greek coast is exceedingly difficult to defend. The fact that Octavian was able to cross over from Italy virtually unopposed is no real discredit to Antony; it would have been next to impossible to prevent a successful landing somewhere, whereas it is comparatively easier to defend the Italian coast, which has far fewer safe anchorages and harbours for a fleet. Actium is an ideal place to base a navy, but its defence requires the possession of such places as Leucas and Patrae, ideally Corcyra too, and for those whose trade routes depend heavily on Egypt, other bases become essential too.

The losses of those way stations and stopping points on the journey between Actium and Alexandria constituted a major blow to Antony and his strategic position; still, he had an undeniably formidable force, trapped or not in the Ambracian Gulf. Certainly a breakout would be a desirable course of action, particularly if disease and desertion were as afoot as our sources indicate (and we have no reason to distrust them on this point), but breakout would need to mean something more than simply escape to Egypt, particularly if the departure would mean the inevitable loss of Greece, which could not be effectively held without naval support. We should note however, that there is no evidence to support the idea that the bases that Agrippa captured were actually held and maintained as military outposts. Lange cites this point as part of his argument that Antony's position was not quite as bad as some might argue.[1] One could counter that it is hard to imagine that Agrippa waged his preliminary campaigns merely with the intent to abandon his conquests; on the other hand, depriving the enemy of bases would be attractive in and of itself. Methone, Leucas, and Patrae however, are the obvious places to take if you want to blockade someone in the Ambracian Gulf and to disrupt supply lines from the southeast, and any ships that were rounding the Peloponnesus. Agrippa took exactly the right places in other words, and it is reasonable to assume that Octavian was able and willing to spare the forces to hold them, even with a skeletal presence. These bases were essential to his strategy, and they would not be taken, only to be surrendered at the slightest counterattack.

The ideal course of events might well then be breakout with a successful naval engagement against the main body of Octavian's fleet; a catastrophic defeat of the enemy would allow for the security of Greece (at least for a while), and provide a tremendous boost to morale. Devastating losses to Octavian would mean a need to see to the defence of Italy, as Antony and Cleopatra were handed the initiative, even if in the end Octavian might have been able to rely on greater reserves of qualified manpower from Italy and the West. If there was any hesitation on the part of Octavian's supporters to back him in a war that was clearly against Mark Antony, then a victory at Actium would be a major step in the process of securing a change of mood in Rome in the matter of the rival triumvirs.

It seems likely then, that Antony did not envisage a simple escape in veritable shame from the site of Actium. To imagine that he intended to sacrifice a vast number of his ships, all for the purpose of saving Cleopatra and her treasure and monetary/treasure resources, is difficult to accept; the price would have been very high indeed for such a course of action.[2] One need only consider how quickly Antony's position collapsed in the wake of Actium; in many ways the civil war between Octavian and him was settled on that day. To be known to have planned to run away with Cleopatra, leaving his forces to death or surrender to Octavian, could not possibly have worked to his advantage; one may conclude therefore that it was not Antony's plan simply to run at the cost of a sizable portion of his fleet.

That said, there is little question that there did need to be an escape plan in case the battle went poorly, and an escape plan would have needed to prejudice the survival of Cleopatra's immense wealth. Certain elements of his fleet and force were indeed more expendable than others, and all romantic considerations aside, it was Cleopatra who was a key financial backer of the whole operation.

Flight however, planned or not, was not an easy thing to execute during a battle, especially in consideration of the prevailing winds. Timing was critical, and the early afternoon was indeed the best period in which to break away and sail for the general direction of Egypt. The crucial wind was indeed the Iapyx from the northwest, the name of the very man who in the last book of Virgil's epic would heal Aeneas of a serious wound in the period leading up to the decisive single combat of Aeneas and his enemy Turnus. We should also take note that winds cannot always be absolutely relied upon, especially for something as major as the question of breakout and withdrawal under fire. Winds can be predictable enough, especially for those who spend a sufficient amount of time in one place, but to depend on the winds doing exactly what you need in a critical moment can be an exercise in frustration if not folly.

And how exactly does one time a battle so as to allow for departure at the most opportune time, given the circumstances of a blockade? It would matter little that Cleopatra's vessels were stationed in the rear, strung out however much or little they were, if there was no way that could successfully take flight from the battle scene. It is also not entirely clear just what sort of military vessels Cleopatra had with her; it seems inconceivable that her entourage was entirely composed of merchant and transport ships.

No, the only way to secure Cleopatra's potential escape at the right time would be to have a battle in which the enemy was far too preoccupied with fighting for survival than with chasing down Cleopatra's departing force successfully; Antony needed to gain the upper hand, or at least to fight a hard won stalemate, at least long enough to permit the Egyptians to depart. It is absurd to think that Antony planned a virtual suicide stand to allow Cleopatra to escape unscathed; indeed, one might argue it was absurd to imagine that Antony planned *either* to run away or to die for his lover. He intended to do his utmost to win. It is reasonable to assume that Cleopatra intended to help him achieve his victory in every way she could. And even if everything went reasonably well for Antony, there were still significant risks for Cleopatra's contingent, as for everyone else in the water that day. It would be reasonable to conclude that if one were going to try something as daring as a running of the blockade, then one might as well fight the actual naval battle; the odds were likely against any chance of reasonably safe extrication, even if this were the desired goal. Antony may not have wanted to fight when he fought, and the terms of battle in general may not have been to his satisfaction, but once the war was thrust upon him, we might well judge that he responded as best as he could in the circumstances.

Did Cleopatra's forces fight at Actium? It is difficult to imagine that they did not, either as part of a serious attempt to win the day, or in the process of trying to extricate themselves at some point. There was no realistic way that her ships could have expected to be able to flee the blockade on the day of engagement without conflict and losses. She could remain in the rear for only so long; eventually she would either have to retreat into the Ambracian Gulf or make her way to Egypt. Managing to get out of the harbour and successfully round Leucas, all the while evading enemy ships, would have proven a significant challenge *even* for swifter vessels under sail, though of course once the ships had an open path, the combination of sails and wind might work to the favour even of more lumbering boats. And too, in a hard fought naval battle it would be inconceivable that her vessels would not assist in the struggle; there was pride at stake of course, and also the fact that the opposition to her in Antony's camp would have a much more difficult task in silencing her, should her Egyptian contingent prove to be of decisive help in securing victory.

Octavian's position was comparatively easier. He wanted of course, to destroy the enemy, especially Cleopatra, and he was in the far superior strategic position on the day of battle. Admittedly, the winds would work against him if someone were planning to flee in a generally southeasterly direction, but those fleeing ships, even under sail, would have some work to do to extricate themselves from Agrippa's cordon. Cleopatra's death and destruction was not necessarily a desirable goal either; the successful capture of her onboard riches was. It is not surprising to find evidence that fire was used sparingly, and perhaps not until the final stages of the battle; it would have posed a significant risk for Octavian's force as well, even if there was a concern about the preservation of merchant ships and wealth. And as we have seen, there was the question of experience. If this were Cleopatra's first taste of naval battle (as appears to be the case, we might note, for Virgil's Camilla in the matter of equestrian war), then Agrippa and Octavian had a tremendous advantage thanks to Sextus Pompey and Naulochus.

Most scholars who have written on Actium have contested one of two major arguments: Antony and Cleopatra always intended flight, or else they intended to fight a 'real' battle to win a victory; somewhere between these two opposing views is the idea that they intended to launch a fighting breakout that could of course, turn out for the better and lead to a total (or at least close to total) victory.

Carsten Lange is right to note that the withdrawal notion hinges on what he calls a 'fundamental perversity'.[3] Antony and Cleopatra, it could well be argued, lost the war precisely because they fled; the fact that all resistance truly seems to have collapsed fairly quickly after the battle is testament enough to that; one cannot blame Octavian's admittedly well-oiled propaganda machine for everything. It is difficult to believe that Antony (or his lover) thought that a strategic victory would be possible after a tactical withdrawal of this magnitude; it is hard to imagine that they had any hope of retaining the loyalty of the ground forces in Greece (and Syria, if any were actually left there in substantial numbers) after a less than glorious escapade off Actium. It strains credulity too, to imagine that the goal was to put on a show of a truly impressive naval battle, when all along the plan was to run, though of course a commitment to a 'serious' battle does not mean a commitment to a fight to the death. One problem we shall see, is that flight from battle almost inevitably brings with it the charge (especially long after the engagement, with eyewitnesses dead and gone) that those who left did so prematurely, without sufficient struggle. Sometimes only the dead are assured of a label of bravery.

We should note too, that Actium was fought more or less before the onset of autumn and winter; certainly a naval engagement could have taken place later than early September, but as the weeks wore on, it would be more and more risky to maintain either naval force in the vicinity. This need not be taken as evidence that Antony needed to make a breakout under dire pressure even from the calendar, but we should remember that neither commander could stay indefinitely in the area, sheltered harbours or not. Both sides were in something of a hurry to decide affairs on the water.

In every battle, there comes a time for surrender or continued resistance to the death. The only way Antony and Cleopatra might have escaped the charge of flight (whether a fighting breakout or not) would be if they had all been killed in battle, and even then some might question their 'true' intentions.

The Number of Ships Involved.

It is time to consider the evidence of how many ships each commander had to deploy at Actium. Plutarch's evidence is straightforward on initial numbers; 500 for Antony and 250 for Octavian, but it is complicated by the report that Antony burned some ships before the battle, possibly only Egyptian ones. Regrettably, there are no numbers in Dio's account, though he does agree with the Plutarchan view that Antony had more ships, possibly even post-burning.

Problems emerge when we consider the only other two sources that mention ship strengths: Florus and Orosius. Florus says that Antony had fewer than 200 vessels, and Orosius 170. Octavian has over 400 ships in Florus, while in Orosius he is said to have had 230 beaked ships, 30 without, and triremes that were of similar velocity to Liburnian galleys. The only way that the numbers can be reconciled is if the triremes numbered around 140, which may seem unlikely or even incredible.

What are we to make of the evident disagreement between our Greek and Latin sources? Does the figure of fewer than 200 vessels for Antony reflect a tally post-burning, so that something like 300 ships were destroyed before the engagement (which may seem implausible?). How do we move from 250 ships for Octavian in Plutarch to over 400 in Florus? Here we might note that Plutarch's 250 is tolerably close to Orosius' 230 beaked ships.

Lange concluded that Octavian must have had 250 vessels at Actium, all more or less ready for war. I suspect that the number '250' is reflective of what we might call his capital warships, and that he had a fairly sizable fleet of smaller vessels that could allow us to creep toward the Floran figure that is not so different from the Orosian when we begin to account for the non-beaked ships and triremes that the latter source cites. There seems to be no question that Agrippa's strategy involved heavy reliance on naval manoeuvrability and the ability to issue orders with relative flexibility. We might remember too, Horace's note about the experience of being on a small vessel amid larger, towering ships.

But what of Antony? We have seen that there is some evidence for the belief that Octavian captured 300 ships from his foe, a figure that may seem suspicious if we grant that Antony started with 500 and burned some portion of this fleet before the battle, but certainly a number that is plausible, especially if there were significant numbers that surrendered. Certainly we have no clear sense of how many ships on either side were destroyed during the engagement. The citation of 300 captured vessels however, would seem to be utterly at variance with the Floran evidence of 170 Antonian ships, and the similar figure of less than 200 in Orosius.

Did Antony really have 170 ships under his own command, with an additional 60 that were nominally under Cleopatra's, so that if we were to assume that Octavian had about 250 ships, then the two sides were reasonably matched in the numbers game at least, with say 250 facing 230? Does the figure of 300 captured ships refer not to 2 September alone, but to the entirety of the Actian campaign, including for example, whatever Agrippa captured at Methone, Leucas, and Patrae?[4] And if the Antonians had a total of 230, how did Plutarch arrive at a figure of 500, which requires us to imagine a massive operation to burn more than half a fleet? It is difficult if not impossible to twist all the surviving evidence into a picture that makes everyone somehow 'right'.

Should we trust Florus more than other sources on the question of numbers, using the argument that he may have epitomized Livy, the closest in time to the events of all our authors? Should we then also be suspicious of Orosius for being so far removed, or should we assume that all the historians involved read their Livy? Lange argues that we should perhaps dismiss Plutarch's figure of 500 Antonian ships as a 'mere doubling' of Octavian's.[5] Were Antony and Cleopatra not so much planning an escape as hoping for more ships to arrive in support in the months and weeks leading up to Actium, a hope that was no doubt increasingly dashed as the blockade became ever more secure?

Lange concludes that Octavian had about 250 ships, and Antony 170 of his own and 60 Egyptian. This is reasonable, though it does indeed involve rejection of Plutarch's figure for Antony, and the question of what exactly was intended by the pre-battle burning of ships is left unanswered. We should note here that the burning of the ships is recorded only in Plutarch and Dio; weighty sources to be sure, but not something we find corroborated elsewhere.

Councils of War.

It has been observed that only in Plutarch and Dio do we get any account of the pre-war deliberations in Antony's camp. There is not much evidence of what was contemplated and discussed before the battle between Octavian and Agrippa; given that the mystery of the battle has hinged on the question of Cleopatra, it is not surprising that there is less concern in our sources about Octavian's strategy; he intended to destroy Antony and his lover, while the plans on the other side may have been more complicated (especially if Antony despaired of achieving a victory at Actium).

Virgil however, does preserve an account of a pre-battle deliberation: the war council. Significantly, his Rutulian hero, Turnus, cites the support of Camilla and her Volscians as a potentially decisive factor in the war. One wonders if this reflects a tradition of Antonian defence of Cleopatra's Egyptian force as a weighty element in war against Octavian; certainly if we are to count 60 ships in a contingent of 230, we have a force that was both potentially significant and more or less in accord with Virgil's division of the cavalry battle between the commanders Camilla, Messapus, Tiburtus, and Coras; 60 x 4 giving us 240, as it were. In Virgil, there is evidence of gender bias against Camilla; interestingly, she does not appear in the war narrative at all between her arrival in Book 7 and her re-introduction in Book 11. Turnus praises her lavishly and without reserve; one wonders if there is anything in Virgil's account that reflects the actual situation of Antony and Cleopatra in the period leading up to Actium; in other words, resentment of a foreign woman as commander in an essentially Roman (civil) war. In Plutarch, we may remember, Canidius advised Antony to send Cleopatra away, and to prepare for a land struggle, not a naval battle; both Virgil's Camilla and the Cleopatra of the Actium tradition are eager for an active war role in their respective cavalry/naval battles. Did Cleopatra feel that the Egyptians were more skilled at naval engagements than the Romans?

Certainly, if she wanted any stake in the battle, it would be likeliest that she would seek it through naval power and prowess. Certainly Virgil's Camilla wants to take a leading role in the struggle, and this can be easily be associated with Cleopatra's wishes before Actium.

The Respective Captains.

If there is no agreement about the sizes of the fleets, there is certainly none about who was commanding what in the battle. Our sources here are Plutarch and Vellius. Plutarch has Antony on the right, with Publicola, Coelius on the left, and Marcus Octavius and Marcus Insteius in the middle; Cleopatra, as we have seen, somewhere in the rear. On the other side, Octavian was on the right, Agrippa on the left and Arruntius in the middle.

Velleius has Marcus Lurius on the right; this may be correct if Lurius was the actual responsible party for the right, with Octavian starting the battle there, but more or less able to move freely where he wished on a light galley. Arruntius is on the left, and Agrippa in supreme command. These discrepancies are harder to reconcile with Plutarch, who as we have seen, seems to have been wrong about Coelius in his Antonian array. Velleius is closer in time to the battle, and one might be tempted to agree with his arrangement, and one wonders if what actually happened was that Arruntius *was* on the left, and that he responded to Cleopatra's Egyptian advance on the centre (we might compare Arruns' shadowing of Camilla in Virgil). In the actual engagement, Arruntius may well have achieved his most noteworthy exploits against the Egyptians; if that battle raged in the centre, it is plausible that by Plutarch's account, he was thought always to have been there. But definitive resolution of the problems of who was where is impossible in the absence of more evidence.

Regarding Arruntius and Cleopatra, certainly there is evidence from Plutarch that the centre quickly became a mess. If Plutarch is correct, Agrippa tried to outflank Antony on Antony's right, and connection between the flank and the centre was lost. If you have more ships, you certainly want to outflank the enemy, but if your numbers are more closely matched, the tactic can prove exceedingly difficult to execute. Outflanking manoeuvres work best when one can hold one's centre, and conversely the navy that is in danger of encirclement strives to maintain its battle line. There is good evidence that the centre of Antony's fleet was quickly thrown into confusion, and this confusion might well have involved the Cleopatran contingents in the rear. For in the disposition of forces and commanders, it is Cleopatra's that prove the greatest mystery.

Politically, Antony had a Cleopatra problem, and it is not surprising that her Egyptians did not command a wing or other station at the battle. Those who would argue that the plan was always to escape do not find this at all suspicious; Cleopatra and Antony always intended to run, and so Cleopatra could certainly not be in command of anything, not to mention the problems posed by having her Alexandrians in charge of anything save themselves. We might note here an interesting facet of the problem of command and leadership. Octavian certainly broadcasted and advertised his war as a decidedly foreign one, against Cleopatra. If Cleopatra did not actually command a wing of the Antonian battle line, but *did* perform bravely and significantly in the campaign, then in effect she would have played into the hands of Octavian's desired propaganda.

Octavian of course, had painted the whole campaign as a war on Cleopatra, not Antony. One need not be cynical to think that this argument was not particularly persuasive to the majority of Romans at the battle, who may have clearly envisaged this as a civil, not foreign war, but the presence of Cleopatra and her Egyptians, not to mention the numerous other client and allied kings, is no mere bogey of Augustan propaganda.

Antony's problems may have included having too many commanders. Cleopatra's force clearly started the battle somewhere in the rear, almost certainly the centre. If the Antonian line broke, it is not inconceivable that the Egyptians moved to close the gap; Arruntius may well have responded to this attack. In other words, Cleopatra did not somehow magically or near magically break through from the rear and flee to safety. Rather, her forces responded in the centre to the thinning or threatened collapse there. This accords with the Virgilian allegory, where Camilla suddenly appears in the midst of the fray, but only after there have been preliminary engagements that reach a climax with the disruption of battle lines (11.618 ... *turbatae acies*). Cleopatra was not seeking a quick escape that had been more or less planned in advance, she was, in contrast, quite eager for the fight, ready to launch her contingent where it was most needed; the vulnerable centre that may have become dangerously overtaxed as a result of Agrippa's outflanking manoeuvres on the Antonian right. Lucius Arruntius would likely have been the opponent her forces would have encountered.

Cleopatra's Flight.

Critics of Cleopatra certainly raise the argument that she ran. Some of her defenders note that getting clear away from Actium was perhaps no easy feat, especially for someone who started in the rear of the battle line. Lange is correct to note that if Cleopatra poured through a gap in the centre to take advantage of the opportunity to escape, then her action could only have been opportunistic; no one could have foreseen that such a gap would open and allow for reasonably safe passage, and no one could possibly have timed it perfectly so that the gap would be open just when the winds would be most favourable for escape.

On the other hand, if a gap opened in the centre, it makes perfect sense that a rear reserve force would pour through in response. If Arruntius were in command of Octavian's centre (so Plutarch), then Cleopatra's forces would suddenly face him, and this may well be the likelier scenario than to imagine that Arruntius lent support to Octavian's centre. And Lange's point needs to be underscored that the Battle of Actium developed soon enough into a scene of absolute chaos; certainly the prevailing image in Virgil's narrative of his cavalry battle, and of the dramatic account in Dio.

No source argues that Antony fled before Cleopatra; the weight of the evidence is that the queen, or at least her forces, made the first move to flee the battlefield. Cleopatra's contingent could not possibly have had a definitive sense of what was happening to Antony's flank; certainly the Mankiewicz cinematic image of Cleopatra on a restful barge with painted ships being moved on a toy map in response to mirror signals is utterly fanciful. Still, if Antony's wing were in danger of encirclement and collapse, this could prove fatal, even if things were going moderately well in the centre, and some sense of what was happening on the right wing might well have become known.

Why exactly Cleopatra fled, for take flight she certainly did, is a mystery. Speculation, however, is quite possible. An obvious explanation is that she considered the war lost and was seeking to save her life; this consideration could come either from a sense of what was happening on the right wing, or from being too hard pressed herself in the centre. Whatever the precise reason for the departure, Antony seems to have followed her, somehow managing to extricate himself from whatever discomfiture he may have been enmeshed in on the right. Once Antony departed, resistance collapsed, though by no means in short order. Fire seems to have been involved in the latter stages of the engagement, and the ancient evidence does point to a struggle that may have lasted until late in the day, for a total of several hours of naval clashes and combat.

Lange dismisses the 'evidence' of Horace's epode about any possible desertion by Antony's men during the battle. Retreat however, is certainly possible without implication of desertion. Horace presents the parallel activity of Gallic cavalry and Antonian ships;[6] the implication for some would be that Antony suffered a fleet desertion that resulted in the leftward retreat to harbour of some of his contingent at Actium. But there is no reason that the Horatian description needs to point to what would be a fairly shameful act of treachery; it could simply refer to the collapse of Antony's right wing in the face of Agrippa's outflanking manoeuvres. Octavian's principal tactic at the battle would then have been to encircle the enemy on the wing that was led by his distinguished naval commander; if the tactic worked, Antony's forces would either need to fight to the death or retreat. Retreat it seems, they did.

Cleopatra, then, responded to what would prove in an important sense to be something of a sideshow, albeit a central sideshow. The 'real' conflict was between Antony and Agrippa, and here Agrippa won the day (we do well to remember that of all the commanders on the water that fateful day, Agrippa was likely by far the most qualified; simply in the matter of experience alone, Antony was no match for him). Agrippa was not able to press home his victory, because Antony ran. Whether he did so before or after a general collapse of his wing cannot be definitively ascertained. The combination of sails and wind would have been decisive in preventing an effective pursuit. Cleopatra had moved to defend the centre and to respond to a threatened collapse there, and we may compare here the Virgilian description of the planned attack of Aeneas to catch the Latins unaware, with the ambush laid by Turnus that failed when the Rutulian fled, and the part played by Camilla as she exulted in the midst of the slaughter, only to be defeated by Arruns.

What exactly happened in the middle of the battle line, where Cleopatra seems to have faced Arruntius? Here the struggle may well have been hard fought and difficult; the Antonian line seems to have given way, but we have no way of judging the relative skills of Arruntius and Cleopatra's contingent. What seems clear enough is that Arruntius won, and Cleopatra fled, quite possibly for her life. The flight, we must underscore, would not have been planned nor the original intention, but rather the understandable response of someone in serious discomfiture who did not want to die in battle, and who could not have been entranced with the idea of retreat to the Ambracian Gulf (in this regard the Egyptians were in a far more perilous position than the Antonians, who could have had a reasonable expectation of achieving mercy from a victorious Octavian, as indeed they did). Cleopatra's force may have done more than merely stabilize the centre after its initial collapse or threat thereof; she may well have managed to perform quite impressively in what was literally the centre of the battle. If anything, what we know next to nothing about was the activity on the other wing, where we can assume an equally hard fought struggle that was fairly evenly matched. The weight of the evidence points to a battle that was by no means quick and easy. And until the wind rose from the northwest, manoeuvres would likely have been even more difficult; both sides might have been rather limited in what they could do navigationally.

Christopher Pelling comments that 'Cleopatra's squadron of sixty ships rested behind [Antony's] centre, ready (it seems) for a concentrated strike on any weak point in Octavian's line, a sort of maritime Panzer-tactic, in fact.'[7] The description is reasonable enough, though the point of the planned pouncing was likely not merely to find a way to get away from the battle.

Antony's Fatal Decision.

But Cleopatra did flee, and Antony followed.[8] Perhaps only a fight to the finish and death would have satisfied critics; any sort of flight by Cleopatra would easily have come to be construed as sheepish cowardice, and it was an easy step from condemning the coward to arguing that the woman had planned her flight from the start. Antony, for his part, was in a worse position once *he* fled; it would have been an impossible task for an Antonian propagandist to excuse that.

Indeed, motivations here must be considered. Certainly in Virgil, the decision of Turnus to give up his planned ambush for Aeneas is presented as an emotionally overwrought reaction to the news of the death of Camilla. We cannot be certain of the exact sequence of events on Antony's wing. Was he more or less holding his own in a difficult engagement, until he abandoned the enterprise when he saw that Cleopatra was fleeing? Did his fleet indeed suffer significant losses that motivated a good portion of his vessels to seek the relative safety of the Ambracian Gulf, a retreat that he chose not to share? Was there a moment, and it could not have been so very long, when he realized that Cleopatra was fleeing, and concluded that flight in pursuit of her was preferable either to staying in the fight (possibly to the death), or trying somehow to retreat back to his base and Canidius' last force?

A sober appraisal of what happened might well conclude that it was nothing less than a fatal mistake on Antony's part to flee after Cleopatra. That decision in fact, could be taken to be the single critical moment where the war was lost. In other words, Antony was the greatest author of Augustan propaganda. Certainly the flight of Antony after his Egyptian lover was the perfect stroke of luck one might think, for Octavian. It spared him the potentially messier situation of having to deal with Antony still in Actium, ensconced with his land forces, and with Cleopatra alone in Egypt. It was far better to have both of them together in Alexandria, both of them having run away from the bloody, flaming waters of Actium.

Did Antony flee because of romantic infatuation with Cleopatra, or was there some strategic or tactical reason to do so? In one sense the question would not have mattered much, since flight would all too easily be defined as the action of a hopelessly enthralled lover in quest of his foreign paramour. Canidius had recommended that Cleopatra be sent away; one wonders if it occurred to Antony in the moment he realized that she was running, that his general's wish had been granted. Certainly it is difficult to imagine that Antony intended anything else by his dash than escape; it seems a foregone conclusion that his flight was in direct response to Cleopatra's. A potentially more important question is what exactly the queen was supposed to do in the course of battle; in other words, what had Antony and she decided would be her part in the engagement? It may be significant that in Virgil, Camilla asks initially for complete command of the battle; certainly this was the complaint of defectors from Antony's camp, a complaint that would already have been envisaged by Octavian's friends and allies. Cleopatra might well have been expected to be in charge of the maintenance and safeguarding (so far as possible in an actual battle) of the treasure and wealth of the expedition; this largely passive role may not have been sufficiently pleasing to an ambitious leader. Again, we must weigh the considerations of Augustan propaganda *versus* what 'actually' happened, but there is no good reason to believe that Cleopatra was not daring and brave, and no good reason to imagine that she did not desire to play an active part in the struggle.

Adrian Goldsworthy rightly concludes that Antony and Cleopatra were interested more in their own survival than in that of the men under their command.[9] We might well argue that Cleopatra however, deserves to come off the better in a comparison between the two; she may well have fled in response to a difficult situation and threat of collapse in the face of Arruntius' assault, while Antony's departure after his lover of some ten years[10] may have been motivated more for interest in Cleopatra than consideration of the possibly sounder plan to retreat back to the Ambracian Gulf and his land army.[11] Antony may have been fearful of treachery too, should he suffer a defeat and return to his base and land. Surely Egypt was a safer place to be in the immediate moment. We ought not to forget too, that whatever decisions were taken, they were likely taken quite quickly and without much chance of thought; even the most meticulous planning for battle could not possibly have taken into account every conceivable possibility.[12]

The Number of Dead.

Lange does well to consider the question of how many people died at Actium. He correctly notes that the problem is relevant to the larger issue of just how important the battle really was; in other words, was it really much of a battle at all? Here the conclusion is correct that Actium was indeed a major conflict, not just in terms of the story that emerged from history and propaganda, but in terms of the actual death and destruction wrought by the battle.

Plutarch's figure of total losses in manpower is 5,000, which as Lange observes, must refer to the dead Antonians and their allies. The only other source that cites a figure is the late Orosius, who claims that there were 12,000 dead, with 1,000 fatally wounded. As Lange notes, the Plutarchan numbers of 5,000 dead and 300 captured ships are credited to Augustus' own memoirs; we should note that the Orosian figure may be a total casualty list, though for 12,000 to be accurate alongside Plutarch's 5,000, we must conclude that Octavian lost 7,000 men. Lange's point in considering casualty figures is to conclude that what might seem to be a low number of dead is in fact no indication in itself of a less than strenuously fought battle; he compares Midway, where there were some 3,000 Japanese deaths and fewer than 1,000 American. We should note here that a casualty toll of 5,000 Antonians should be weighed in comparison to the relative populations involved (taking into account the number of foreigners present, and the problem of whether or not Plutarch's figure refers only to Roman casualties). A battle with a grand total of 6,000 deaths (counting the 1,000 fatally injured) would be a significant catastrophe in 31 B.C.E., more so, we might coldly reckon, than in 1942.

Lange notes that there is evidence for 5,000 dead as being the number needed to secure a triumph; he also observes that Augustus had reason to want to downplay the number of dead; the *princeps* would have needed to weigh the need for a sufficiently glorious battle for Augustan propaganda purposes with the wish not to give too many reminders of just how many Roman men died in the waters off northwestern Greece. Again, 5,000 deaths would have been a battle of great significance, *especially* if it were likely that the relative close shore could have provided the means to secure the rescue and salvation of at least some of those in jeopardy.

The Mysterious Burning of the Ships.

We must also consider more closely the question of the alleged burning of the ships that is reported by Plutarch and Dio. The scholar W.W. Tarn argued that it was Octavian, not Antony, who burned the ships; the vessels were thus destroyed in the wake of his victory with Agrippa. There is of course no ancient evidence for this theory, which is admittedly attractive and might make some sense in context, though some might wonder why Octavian would not seek to retain the ships for himself (though we should recall that standing navies were not exactly easy to maintain).[13] Ship-burning plays a prominent role in Virgil's *Aeneid*; in his fifth book, the poet describes how the goddess Juno inspires the women of Troy to seek to set fire to the Trojan fleet in Sicily, all in the hopes of forestalling and preventing any further sailing; in Book 9, Turnus has it in mind to launch his own incendiary attack on the vessels, which are then magically transformed into sea creatures at the behest of the Trojan Mother Goddess Cybele.

Fantastic narratives to be sure, and not of much help in understanding what may well seem the incredible extravagance of Antony's self-destruction of his precious warships. The episode of the burning of the vessels has been cited in support of the argument that Antony intended to break away; the obvious point would be to avoid having the ships fall into enemy hands. One wonders if there is any significance to the possibility that the ships that were burned were Egyptian and not Roman. As we have seen, the exact import of Plutarch's words in 64.1 is open to dispute; it is possible that the Egyptian fleet was destroyed except for sixty that were arguably the best of that squadron. Was the destruction of the Egyptian ships (we have no idea how many vessels are in question) somehow a reaction to some fear of treachery or deceit on the part of Cleopatra's force? Was it a response to criticisms and fears voiced by his own men? Just how worried about treachery was Antony in the lead up to Actium? Were Cleopatra's forces viewed with that great a degree of suspicion? Romans in the service of Antony (and, *de facto* in the eyes of some, Cleopatra) would easily have been suspected of treachery and pro-Octavian sympathies, especially as news of one disaster or setback after another arrived in camp.

Just before the mention of the burning, Plutarch offers an interesting sequence of events. First Cleopatra wins the argument about fighting on land or sea (63.5). We might note here that if there had been a land battle rather than a naval, Cleopatra's contribution in contingents and resultant glory might well have been less than noteworthy. Her desire to fight on water could well have been inspired by a quest for valour and praise in victory. Plutarch says that after her position won the day, she was planning flight, and had in fact disposed of her forces not where they would be most helpful, but where they could make the quickest getaway. This detail about the disposition of her forces may be of great significance. Even if Cleopatra herself had no intention, it would be more than enough to poison the waters as it were, if her enemies in Antony's camp began to spread the word. Every position of her vessels would be open to suspicious question and cavil. Her actions would be under intense scrutiny in an atmosphere rife with defections and a breakdown in unity among the varied contingents.

And just after this detail about Cleopatra's allegedly suspicious placement of her ships, Plutarch introduces the strange tale of how Antony was nearly abducted while passing between camp and harbour. A slave is credited with having warned Octavian of Antony's habits and route; if Plutarch can be believed, Antony barely escaped capture, a tale that may indeed have a basis in truth, a story that may well have been the inspiration for the Virgilian narrative of the ambush plan for Aeneas.

If there really was some treachery on the part of a slave, a treachery that could easily have led to the catastrophe of Antony's capture, we may well wonder whose slave the mysterious traitor was. After this briefly sketched tale, Plutarch returns to the question of sea battles by saying that once the decision was taken, the ships were burned; an act that may well have been inspired by fears of deception and treachery that were not so unreasonable, especially in a situation where there were likely not enough men available to man all of the boats adequately *and* maintain a credible land force. And by the time we come to Dio's narrative at 50.15.4, the game is quite different; Antony and Cleopatra are now co-collaborators in the treachery of planning to flee, and the burning of the ships is an expedient to get away as easily as possible without surrendering vast resources to the enemy.

The sails have been taken too, as evidence of the intention to flee. In point of fact they may have been intentional compromises to make up for any problem of speed and even maneuverability on the part of Antony's larger ships; they may also speak to a situation where the harbour in any case, was going to be abandoned. The Ambracian Gulf was a prime location for a navy, but its usefulness dwindled by the day so long as Agrippa and Octavian held the strategic points of (*inter alia*) Methone, Leucas, and Patrae. Especially in time of privation (and the mention of the *conopia* speaks well to the atmosphere that was rife with disease), the Actian base was a liability, and the sails would be needed both to manoeuvre and to advance where needed with reasonable speed. We should remember that we have no idea what forces had been left behind on Agrippa's newfound bases; a major campaign would have taken advantage of a defeat of Octavian to recapture lost strongholds, especially if resistance there could be expected to be less than robust.[14]

Why the Sea?

We ought to address too, the question of Cleopatra's encouragement for a naval battle in the first place. In Plutarch this is presented as if it were a matter of appealing to the queen's fancy and favour, some sort of toy; this is after all, the queen who lusted after power and ambition, and a sea engagement would seem to fit with a romantic ambition for heroic glory. If true, one motivation for Cleopatra's desire for a fight on the water may well have been that the sea was where she had more power than on land. This rationale could be explained then as both a desire for glory, and a practical consideration; the two would not be mutually exclusive possibilities. Certainly there was a struggle for power and influence in Antony's camp, and Cleopatra was resented as the one sharing the bed of the Roman commander.

But strategically, as we have seen, a naval battle did make sense. Victory on land would not ensure the end of trouble; if Greece were to be held, supply lines would need to be maintained, and Agrippa had already proven the vulnerability of Antony's trade routes. If Greece had been taxed to the limit by the privations of Antonian occupation and the draft of men and resources, then Antony would have had especially serious problems on land as well as on water. Put another way, Antony needed to win on *both* land and sea, and a good argument could be made that the sea was the more pressing concern, especially as winter drew closer.

Some Conclusions: A Possible Reconstruction.

The Battle of Actium was a difficult naval engagement that saw the combined navies of Antony, Cleopatra, and Octavian engaged in a vicious and violent struggle, with both sides seeking to destroy the enemy's capacity to wage war at sea. It would have taken some time for the vessels to assemble for the conflict; conceivably this was done at some point near eleven in the morning. There may have been two hours then, of more or less low intensity warfare.

The opening of the engagement was a stressful and anxious time of worry and waiting as both sides try to determine more or less definitely what they thought the enemy might be planning or trying to accomplish; wind conditions would also have had a significant effect on the seeming 'phoney war' that at first prevailed. Octavian's lines may have advanced first, almost as if to test the enemy; when the Antonians did not move, there may have been retreat and repeated efforts at what could be considered a virtual taunting action; something of this tactic may have been tried on the other side as well. If Antony had moved first, it was likely on his own wing, in anticipation of an attempted envelopment by Agrippa. This action, however sound in itself, may have helped to contribute to the thinning of an already dangerously overstretched line; before long there were gaps here and there in the cordon of ships, especially on the edges of the centre, and along the centre line that may even have been supplying what little resources it could *not* spare to the defence of the threatened wings. Battle lines were inexorably giving way to chaos; Antony had no reserve strategy to use for the desperate circumstances in which he soon found himself. Cleopatra acquitted herself quite well in the centre, and there was a serious contention for victory in the middle of the battle.[15]

At last Octavian launched a full blown crescent-shaped assault; Antony likely faced the most serious attack of this tactic at the hands of the expert Agrippa, and soon a significant contest had developed between the two men. A less intense shooting and ramming war likely erupted on the opposite wing too, as the other horn of the crescent was within range of the enemy. Throughout, Antony's large vessels were assailed by the swift Liburnian galleys that engaged in quick strikes, sometimes by the coordinated action of multiple vessels, as rapid action aimed to strike down the deadly assault towers and archery platforms of the lofty Antonian vessels. Vessels were rammed, with resultant onboard fighting between invading and defending marines. One might conclude that no high-ranking officers were killed; no record survives of the specific identities of the casualties. In many instances, multiple smaller Octavian vessels would seek to entrap large Antonian ships, careful to seek a swift crippling of the dangerous weaponry that threatened death from on high. The deployment of more swift ships meant that there could be an effective response to the rapidly changing circumstances of battle by means of quick communication between different elements of Agrippa's navy.

The main goal of the Agrippan strategy was envelopment. The resultant battle on the wings contributed to a situation where the centre was already weakened and dangerously thin for the outnumbered Antonians. As the

Antonian centre (under Marcus Octavius and Marcus Insteius) was increasingly discomfited, Cleopatra's Egyptians responded in the middle and clashed dramatically with the warships of Lucius Arruntius. The ensuing struggle saw some of the fiercest fighting of the conflict, or at least some of the most memorable. Suddenly, the centre theatre of the engagement constituted the most fluid and active situation on the map. Cleopatra was eventually seriously discomfited and forced to choose between destruction or flight; she opted to escape under the favouring aid of a timely wind from the northwest that may well have helped to determine when she made her escape. At some point in the worsening conditions of the battle, fire was employed, perhaps first by Agrippa's vessels, and the rising wind conditions contributed to a greater sea plain of destruction. Any avoidance of fire in the early stages of the battle (so as to avoid any risk of submerging the queen's treasure or other wealth) might have been dismissed as impractical in the face of more intensely fought ship-to-ship engagements. The very winds that aided in navigation and eventual escape were agents of even worse destruction than had taken place thus far. It was perhaps after two in the afternoon now, maybe a bit later.

Once aware of her departure, Antony, who was meanwhile engaged in his own serious mess of a battle on his own wing, took the fateful decision to choose flight with Cleopatra over death in an increasingly untenable position, a position possibly made worse by the flight of much of his force in desperate efforts to save their lives. Having transferred his flag from his own warship (which may well have been disabled by this point), he escaped on a swift vessel and was eventually picked up by Cleopatra's flagship, which appropriately enough bore the name of the disgraced commander it now rescued. The struggle continued for several more hours, and possibly well into the night; certainly Octavian's forces would have approached the *sinus Ambracius* with extreme care and trepidation for land-based defences, and some if not the majority of his navy may have eventually returned to its own base. Night descended as fires continued to burn from wreckage, and the sky filled with smoke. Thousands had been killed in a matter of several hours.[16]

But under the aid of wind and sails, the two lovers successfully fled the carnage that they had helped to set in motion, and the struggle continued for some time, until finally Octavian's victory was readily apparent to all, though it was a victory in which the two enemy captains would live to see yet more defeats before death came as their end.

Chapter 18

The Birth of a Romantic Legend

O ctavian faced more than a few problems on the night of Actium and on the morning after; one might well wonder just how anxious he was for what awaited him on land in Greece, let alone in Egypt. He had outperformed his adversaries: he had crossed the Adriatic before Antony, thus seizing and ensuring the strategic initiative, and he had successfully won the minor but important engagements that would prove preliminary to the main conflict. His opponents had fled in defeat, Antony quite possibly to a shame and infamy that he more than merited. And yet we should remember that Octavian's intelligence reports were not omniscient in the immediate aftermath of the battle; even the very destination of Antony might have been in some question, at least at first. Octavian had more than enough to occupy himself on 3 September, and his situation was by no means free of hazard and care. Once Horace recovered from any nausea on board ship, he may have already been composing verses in his head about what had happened, but Octavian likely had a quite long list of tasks that demanded attention and concern.

But a story was developing even as the wreckage was all too visible on the bloodstained waters. By the time of Propertius' c. 2.16.37-40, it might seem that the idea was already *au courant* and well established that Antony had run away for love, and thereby had ruined his good reputation and his standing with his valiant men, the sort of soldiers who later would be said to have waited a week for word of their departed commander before they would so much as talk to Octavian.[1] The charge may have been legitimate indeed. We do well to remember that there must have been some audience in Rome that was all too well aware of what happened at Actium, an audience that would be something of a check on the more exuberant claims of propaganda-minded hyperbole or outright mendacity. Countering this audience would be the difficulty in news reports and messages; the information network would not have been foolproof or comprehensive. But we have no reason to believe that the general thread of the story of the Augustan poets is false; it may in fact, be more reliable than the accounts of Plutarch and Dio. Whatever had happened in the centre, and however fierce the fighting, Antony had chased after the defeated queen in her moment of setback and withdrawal, and with no evident concern for the battle that was raging on his wing (a battle that may, admittedly, have already devolved into a clear enough losing situation for Antony).

The narrative of the poets is on the whole respectful if not complimentary to Cleopatra (Horace most of all, Virgil quite arguably so, with Propertius the most condemnatory), at least in comparison to Antony, who is given no credit or respect for much of anything. Compliment of Cleopatra, of course, was crucial to an Augustan mythology; the queen needed to be condemned for any number of vices, but she also needed to be a formidable foe for Octavian. It was also necessary to emphasize how she was a sufficiently seductive and attractive force that one as great as Antony could indeed have succumbed to her, as Caesar before him, thus proving that Octavian was the greatest of them all, the only Roman of his age who mattered who was able to resist the wiles of the Ptolemaic Siren.

Octavian could not have predicted what actually happened at Actium; he certainly could not have planned for it or nursed any serious hopes. No one could have counted on Cleopatra's departure from the battle as the impetus or instigation of Antony's *de facto* abandonment of the sea battle and his land army. Arguably, Cleopatra's action saved Octavian from numerous problems (and at a time when he had more than enough to keep him occupied, together with Agrippa and Maecenas). Affairs would have been significantly more complicated for Octavian if Antony had pursued the wiser course and retreated with his men into the *sinus Ambracius*; the winter of 31–30 might well have been very different for all parties.

Camilla and Cleopatra.

Virgil's Camilla narrative is more complicated than a mere one-to-one correspondence of Camilla to Cleopatra would demand. Indeed, we do well to remember that in the poet's description of Aeneas with Dido in Carthage, we see a strong evocation of the tradition of Antony at repose with Cleopatra in the East; Aeneas of course, escapes the clutches of *his* foreign would-be bride. Camilla in many ways *saves* Aeneas, however inadvertently, given that her death is the direct inspiration for Turnus to give up his best chance to destroy his enemy and deal his victory. Cleopatra, in her own unwilling way, did something of the same for Octavian; small wonder in fact, that one looking at the situation from Octavian's perspective might well credit divine favour for the whole affair. Truly, the patron deities of Rome were guarding their favourite Roman.

The evidentiary models for Virgil's Camilla are lacking; the Volscian heroine certainly evokes certain aspects of the Pentheilea of the cyclic epic tradition, of the Amazon who came late to the aid of Troy, but she is not mentioned elsewhere in surviving literature. There is evidence in the Servian commentary tradition on Arruns and his slaying of Camilla for the folkloric world of the Hirpini or wolf priests of the Sabines, men who were charged with the task of responding to lupine marauding. Apollo was himself venerated as a wolf slayer. The wolf was a predatory animal that posed significant risk to unlucky wayfarers, but it was also central to the imagery of Rome's early mytho-history, to the stories of Romulus and Remus and the suckling by the celebrated she-wolf.[2]

Virgil's Camilla fits exactly into this lore and tradition. She is herself arguably lupine in nature, if not lycanthropic; her companion(s) Acca/Larina recall(s) the Acca Larentia of Roman lore of the rescue of the infants Romulus and Remus, the bastard children of Mars (a paternity they share with the Penthesilea of epic lore, whom Virgil explicitly associates with the god).[3] We do well to remember that the goddess Roma herself, the personified city of Romulus, was sometimes depicted as having affinities with Amazons.

If Camilla is the product of traditions of animal-like, indeed quite possibly anthropomorphic creatures, then it is a small step indeed to draw a connection between her and the barking Anubis and fantastic animal-headed gods of the Egyptians. The Centaurs of mythology are also recalled, especially in the context of a cavalry battle like Virgil's, and we may recall the Propertian evidence of the *Centaures* vessels on Antony's side at Actium, and the *Centaur* of Aeneas' Etruscan adventure.[4] The Virgilian rehabilitation of Camilla then, is exactly a reflection of the fact that Egypt's queen managed to save Octavian/Aeneas, though in the final analysis both Camilla and Cleopatra must be destroyed as part of the coming of the new order (as must Turnus/Antony).

In an important sense, the Virgilian narrative not only offers a reimaging of Actium, it also rehabilitates the Cleopatra image by developing the thesis that the 'enemy' Camilla is actually a saviour of Rome. And too, there is the key detail that in the final ethnic analysis of the future Rome as depicted in Virgil's epic, Camilla is on the right side of history; she is Italian and not Trojan. For the future Rome will indeed be the Italy of Camilla and her Volscians, not that of Chloreus, the Trojan priest, or any of the denizens of the dead city in the Troad.

The Augustan tradition was more than willing to depict Camilla/Cleopatra as a fierce combatant in battle, a more than equal foe for an opposing enemy. At Actium of course, there was no clash between Octavian and Cleopatra, any more than there was a clash between Octavian and Antony. While Agrippa seems to have faced the great Marcus Antonius, it was the comparative second stringer (if not virtual nobody?) Lucius Arruntius who faced Cleopatra.[5] In Virgil, Aeneas proceeds to march against Latinus' capital, and Turnus waits for him; the slaying of Camilla is the work of the Etrucan Arruns, a figure who appears in the *Aeneid* only for the sake of the vanquishing of Camilla. Arruntius had something of a chequered career in the period of the civil wars, and one wonders if there is not a bit of learned humour in Virgil's description of how Arruns wins an Apollonian victory over Camilla, only to be killed by the nymph Opis and left in obscurity by his friends (he remains unburied). Were both sides at Actium surprised by the performance of Cleopatra in the centre? Was Arruntius expecting a particularly difficult engagement with Antony's middle?

But of great importance in all of this is that Virgil's Aeneas is not associated with the killing of a woman, just as Octavian neither faced Cleopatra at Actium, nor was responsible for any post-triumph execution. If image mattered, then it was certainly to Octavian's advantage to have no entanglement with 'his' Camilla at Actium, and no part in seeming directly to orchestrate her death, even if in the end, her suicide was exactly what he most wanted. Suicide, as we have seen, would allow for the mythology that the formidable opponent of Octavian's Rome was actually successfully defiant even on the cusp of total defeat; she was able to choose the time and manner of her death. If there is propaganda and embellishment in the story of the last days of Egypt's queen, it is likely to be found in the narrative of her alleged cheating of Octavian of a triumphal victim he might well have been quite content to leave behind in Egypt; a convenient corpse as it were. On this matter of the killing of a female, even in war, we might compare the somewhat similar situation of the celebrated 'Helen Episode' of Virgil's *Aeneid* 2 (567–588), a passage whose authenticity has been seriously questioned by Virgilian scholars. The Helen episode represents Aeneas on the last night of Troy, ready to kill Helen as the guilty and responsible party for the suffering and death of so many. His divine mother Venus appears just in time to save her favourite; the hero after all, has much work left to be done on this fateful night. Helen will not be killed, and Aeneas will not have any taint from the slaying of an unarmed woman in battle.

If the Helen episode is authentic, then both the second and the second to last books of the *Aeneid* have vignettes that are concerned with the problem of the violent death of women in the context of war. The question may have been of particular interest in light of the Cleopatra drama.

As we have seen, if legends were to be crafted to help to support a nascent Augustan mythology, then Cleopatra may well have done much of the work to engender the romance. Octavian, unlike Caesar and Antony before him, did not fall prey to the seductive charms of the Egyptian queen; apparently he also needed no god Mercury to urge his departure from a paramour in the manner of Virgil's Aeneas with Dido. The Augustan image in the matter of Cleopatra was one of the honour and moral supremacy (both implicit and explicit), and Cleopatra, for all her faults, needed still to be a valiant and formidable foe. For it would be better by far if the *Roman* Antony could be the coward and the fool; civil war would then seem more tolerable.

A Cinematic Queen.

Joseph Mankiewicz's 1963 *Cleopatra* offers an excellent opportunity for consideration of how a legend can be constructed in diverse ways and to varied ends. Mankiewicz's Actium narrative is on one level nonsensical. Cleopatra takes no part in the strategic or tactical formulation of the battle plan; she remains on her barge in harbour, watching and waiting anxiously and nervously for news. Antony, for his part, has a straightforward plan; he intends to rush directly at Octavian's flagship and to have some sort of single combat with his adversary after the successful ramming of his vessel. For Antony, there is but one consideration; the death of Octavian. Richard Burton's Antony makes no other plan for battle; he has one goal, one intention and one hope.[6]

Octavian for his part has somehow learned of Antony's plan. This is perhaps a reflection of the evidence of defections that were rather one-sided, and he devises a ludicrous plan to fly his insignia of command on the wrong ship, assuming (correctly) that Richard Burton's character will chase down and destroy the insignificant vessel. Given the intelligence he has on Antony's plans, and with the film's Agrippa expressing the hope that the gods grant that Antony does not change his intentions, one can almost understand why Roddy MacDowell's Octavian is caught napping during the battle; he really did have nothing to do, given the strategic ineptitude displayed by Antony.[7]

This fictionalized plan was likely derived from a detail that is rooted in the historical tradition; Agrippa's ships retreat strategically and allow Antony's vessels to approach. We have seen that there is reason to believe that Octavian's own idea may have been for his fleet to retreat far enough back to allow for some kind of encirclement that would permit a rear attack by Agrippa and the utter destruction of the enemy fleet; Agrippa seems to have argued (reasonably enough) that this would be extremely risky, certainly unnecessarily so. In the film version, Agrippa's ships allow the enemy to draw closer and closer, all with the intention of welcoming Antony in his pursuit of the wrong ship; there is reference to how Antony's ships are bulkier and slower, but this comes from the all too wise Canidius who watches the battle from his post on land and makes anti-Cleopatra comments to his entourage (comments that certainly find some basis for truth in the historical record, if only in terms of Canidius' antipathy for Egypt's queen).

Burton's Antony captures the wrong vessel, and he finds himself fatally trapped deep within the Roman fleet. Cleopatra's naval advisor notes that perhaps Antony destroyed a vessel bearing Octavian's insignia; somehow he divines that it is possible that the ship did not actually carry the Roman leader. But he also observes that Antony is surrounded by the enemy, and that he has no help to send. Cleopatra's pleas for aid for her lover are dismissed as impossible. Canidius, less alert to the possibility of a trick, notes that both Antony and Octavian are dead, with Cleopatra as the victor. This is the same Canidius whose comment on Antony's first action of the battle was that Antony was going straight against Octavian's centre, just as was his usual practice in battle. The entire picture was perhaps thought easy for an audience to follow, but beyond its historical inaccuracy it strains credulity to imagine that Antony would view a naval battle as nothing more than a chance for single combat. By the time Burton's Antony boards Octavian's ship and admonishes 'Octavian' (conveniently disguised in a face-concealing golden helmet) that 'now is his chance to *be* a Caesar', the audience may well be tempted to laugh more than to sit in respectful awe. Burton's character is once again disappointed and frustrated, and not for the last time.

When Cleopatra assumes that Antony has died, she asks if the winds are favourable for a departure to Egypt, as indeed they were on the afternoon of the battle. She makes her escape in her golden barge, and Antony sees the flight. Once he becomes aware that his lover is leaving, he commandeers a smaller vessel, abandoning the desperate fight his men are waging deep within the Roman fleet. He chases after her, his shame and degradation profound. Antony coldly sails through the waters that are filled with the dying and desperate, focused utterly and only on the pursuit of Elizabeth Taylor's Cleopatra. Some might say it is neither good history, nor good cinema.

One of the striking elements of Mankiewicz's version is its refusal to present Cleopatra as taking any active part in the battle. Even her departure is remarkably free from risk and peril; there is absolutely no danger as she leaves the scene. The most activity that any Egyptian takes part in is the single case of one of her officers who announces before the battle that he 'would consider it an honour' to join with Antony in battle, and Antony promptly rewards the man with a subcommand on his flagship that will prove his undoing; the man ends up being a voice that tries in vain to reason with Antony when the latter decides to chase after his paramour.

It may well be that the only thing the film version actually captures accurately is the decision of Antony to chase after Cleopatra, admittedly the crucial point. We may well wonder why Horace's epodes do not preserve any tradition of this crucial element of the story, and why even his Cleopatra ode does not reference the episode. Certainly the latter highlights a rather hard fought escape; if Horace can be trusted as a source on the matter, Cleopatra fled with barely one ship amid a fiery sea of ruin.[8] Of course neither the epodes nor the odes offer anything in the way of a systematic or detailed narrative of the battle; one gleans impressions, but no more. The ninth epode focuses on the collapse of Antony's right wing it would seem, either before or after any flight by Antony himself. Indeed, perhaps the most important question in interpreting Horace's evidence is asking about the exact sequence of events with respect to Antony's departure; did some of his vessels begin to fall back to the harbour even before their commander had made his dash for Cleopatra?

The ode focuses on the queen, and as we have seen, in language that does her a fair amount of credit. Octavian, significantly, is pictured in pursuit. True enough for someone who chooses to ignore such things as calendar and chronology. The description of the hawk and the dove, and the hunter and hare, points to a mopping up operation (however protracted, in part by the approach of winter) on both sea and land. Octavian would be the conqueror of Achilles' homeland of Thessaly, but he would face little in the way of opposition. Through it all, the prevailing image of Cleopatra from the Augustan poets is one of active engagement in the fray, and in the end, a markedly better treatment in verse history than her Roman lover.

The Creation of a Story.

And yet, at some point, history became confused, at least the record thereof. Let us imagine that what 'really' took place was that Cleopatra's Egyptians fought bravely, some might say manfully, in the centre, where a thinned line had led to a serious threat of collapse and the danger of a catastrophic enfolding of the Antonian right wing. The struggle is hard fought, but eventually Cleopatra is in serious discomfiture, or at least she sees that defeat is a very real possibility, at least from her vantage point and in her judgment. We cannot of course discount the possibility of anxiety (not to say panic).

Cleopatra flees the battle scene, and Antony follows. We have argued that it was Antony's pursuit of Cleopatra that utterly ruined him; by that point, not only was the immediate engagement imperilled, but also his reputation and honour were irretrievably lost.

How do we advance from this scenario to one where either Cleopatra's flight was always premeditated, or to one where Cleopatra and Antony together intended to flee the harbour of Antony, to run the blockade as it were, and to escape with as many ships as they could?

One element of this resultant mythology may have been nothing more than stereotypical sexism, not without a healthy dose of ethnic prejudice. Cleopatra was a woman and an Egyptian, and she was in consequence a coward and a pusillanimous foe. This narrative would not work well with Augustan propaganda or imagery, but as the need and importance for that faded, deeply held prejudices against the performance of women in battle may well have taken a toll on the evolution of the tale.

One of the most savage indictments of Cleopatra, as we have seen, comes from Propertius.[9] Propertius is angry over the role of Egypt in the death of Pompey, and he attacks Cleopatra viciously for all manner of personal immorality and debauched living. Rage and anger directed at Egypt would be prominent in Lucan's poetic account of the murder of Pompey and its aftermath, too; by the time of the Neronian poet, Egypt had more than once showed its faithlessness toward Rome.[10]

But Propertius also notes that evidently Cleopatra also dared to oppose the barking Anubis to the Roman Jove; in other words, she fought (Virgil's Turnus is made to state that Jupiter is his enemy). Despite all her valiant boasting and threats to the Capitol, the queen fled.[11] Her decision to flee is, as we have seen, linked to the shame of Antony her lover, who followed her. There is no evidence though, that the intention had been to run away and escape an intolerable blockade.

To run away from battle is always to incur the possible stigma of having not done one's best or performed the utmost acts of heroism and martial valour. In the case of Actium, the flight of Antony is clearly what prompted the wholesale surrender of significant numbers of his forces, both on sea and land. The running away is the crown of the action; running away is what pricks all the more sharply than the courageous fighting that preceded it.

For the Augustan poets, the flight of Cleopatra was worthy of note because it engendered (pun intended) the far more important flight of Antony. Adrian Goldsworthy observes in his treatment of their lives that Antony was the more important one, given the realities of Roman political life and the place of foreign women in the Roman estimation. This is true enough; Antony's departure from Actium is what sealed the mythology of the Augustan poets. Cleopatra was the cause of that flight, and thus both a formidable foe, not to mention however well or at least respectably her contingent performed in battle, and Cleopatra was the one who did the great service to Octavian. And too, Cleopatra's bravery in battle would, in Augustan times, as now, arouse different feelings in different minds. Propertius refers to Cleopatra's holding of javelins in war as a shameful thing, a *pilaque femineae turpiter apta manu,*[12] where we might recall Virgil's own use of the adjective *femineus* to describe Camilla's love for spoils. The service of women in the works of war arouses certain emotions and feelings, unless, we might think, the woman in question is a Minerva or a Bellona. The matter is complicated by the uneasy coexistence of admiration for bravery under fire from anyone, male or female, and the discomfort felt by many about the appearance of women in combat, especially women as instigators of military strife.

The fourteenth-century, writer Giovanni Boccaccio, includes Cleopatra (and Camilla for that matter) in his encyclopedic *De mulieribus claris* or lives of famous women.[13] Cleopatra is presented in a highly negative light (as is Antony). One night at dinner she asks her lover for the Roman Empire, and he grants it. War soon enough follows, and the two lovers proceed to Epirus with their purple and gold. There is a land battle, where they are defeated and retreat. At Actium, the Antonians exercise their fortunes in a naval battle, where Octavian and Agrippa are said to have struck against them with 'marvellous audacity' (*mira audacia*) with their huge fleet. The battle remained in doubt for some time; the Antonians appeared on the verge of surrender or flight (*tandem cum subcumbere viderentur Antoniani,* where the verb is somewhat ambiguous as to its precise meaning). Insolent Cleopatra, though, was first to flee, *prima omnium insolens Cleopatra ... fugam cepit*). She departs on her golden vessel with sixty other ships, and Antony immediately follows; the moral implications crystal clear.

We cannot be certain of the extent of Boccaccio's sources, but we find here an account of a difficult engagement, even after the stunning assault credited to Octavian's force, and interestingly, the Antonians as the first to succumb. It is possible that the *Antoniani* are all of Antony's and Cleopatra's forces, and indeed, Cleopatra is clearly the first to flee. The passage is by no means complimentary to her (or her lover, for that matter).

Part Five

The Aftermath

Chapter 19

'Death Comes as the End'[1]

Events after Actium.

A ntony and Cleopatra had a little less than a year to live after the defeat at Actium. It would be an eventful year, though there would be no grand battle to rival 2 September. We shall offer a consideration of the evidence for those crucial months in Roman history, not with an eye to a major reconsideration of problems that have been studied countless times, (the suicide of Cleopatra most prominently, with its story of asps and venom) but as part of a look at the reception of Actium, of the military and strategic situation that led to the final stages of Octavian's victory.

When we paused our analysis of Plutarch's *Life of Antony*, the commander's abandoned men were said to have held out for a week in the hope that there would be some word from their military father. Octavian is said to have made overtures that were soundly ignored during those no doubt tense days for both sides. Plutarch observes that only a few knew that Antony had fled, and that others found it difficult to believe; it may well be that the latter detail is certainly true, though it strains credulity to imagine that word did not spread rapidly (Plutarch of course, held that the escape was always planned). Canidius abandons the camp in the night, and soon enough the land army defects to Caesar. The 'ground war' had lasted all of a week.[2]

Octavian is said to have proceeded to Athens, where he handled affairs with the representatives of the Greeks; paragraph 68 of *The Life* offers a personal story of Plutarch's great-grandfather and the question of the privations that the Greeks had been suffering under Antony. Indeed, it is not difficult to imagine that Octavian was viewed as a munificent conqueror, especially if Plutarch is accurate in his account of the distribution of grain that now took place.

Antony reaches Paraetonium and sends Cleopatra ahead; this is preparation for the famous episode of the once great general's isolation and depressive misery.[3] Blithely, Plutarch notes that Antony's commander in Libya also defected at this point, and that Antony contemplated suicide. He was rescued by friends and brought to the queen in Alexandria, where he found Cleopatra planning a great venture to transport her fleet across the Suez to escape in the Red Sea to Arabia and beyond.[4] We see here something of the resilience of the queen, indeed something of the spirit that makes it believable that she was an active combatant at Actium; she is thinking vigorously of a challenging enterprise and undertaking to ensure her survival, while Antony frets in isolation and depressive pallor.

Plutarch notes that Cleopatra was foiled by the burning of her vessels by the Arabians, a believable enough further episode of incendiary assault on naval ships, while Antony is said to have thought that his land forces at Actium were still intact, so that preparations were commenced to fortify and hold Egypt. This narrative is difficult to believe; if Libya had defected, why would the ground forces closest to Octavian at Actium be holding out for their leader in flight? Interestingly, Antony again goes into seclusion, this time at Pharos. Here he said that he was imitating the life of the misanthrope Timon of Athens. The depression here certainly does not at all accord with the idea that he thought that the main body of his land force was intact.

Canidius arrives in Alexandria with definitive news of the loss of Antony's contingents (71.1). This news is accompanied by the word that there are no longer any allied kings (the burning of the ships in Arabia might have underscored this point), and that Herod of Judea in particular had defected to Octavian. These dire reports inspire Plutarch's Antony to retreat into a life of libidinous revels with Cleopatra; they even rename a club they had founded, 'Partners in Death' (71.3). Cleopatra is said to have tested out poisons on various prisoners who were condemned to death; this is cited in the *Carmen de Bello Aegyptiaco*.[5] All of the tests mentioned in Plutarch have but one goal: the ease of Cleopatra's own suicide.[6]

Plutarch relates that word was sent to Octavian, who is now said to be in Asia, the queen asked for Egypt for her children (the identities are not specified, but Caesarion must be implied as the key offspring), while Antony requested a private life in Athens if not Egypt. It is perhaps telling that this detail seems to imply suicide for the queen, or at least a fall from power, while Antony's request involves the preservation of his own life. One wonders about the mention of Athens. Did Antony envisage this as a life with Cleopatra in exile (unlikely), or was he seeking survival either in a post-Cleopatran world, or with his lover as a private couple in Egypt (albeit, with a blood connection to the ruling sovereign).

Valuable information is preserved in Plutarch about the composition of the embassy to Octavian. Euphronius was sent, the teacher of Cleopatra's children, since it was difficult to find anyone who could be trusted. Plutarch notes that Alexas of Laodicea had already been killed; he had been sent to Herod and had betrayed Antony, only then to lose his life when he went to Octavian and was immediately arrested as a vile traitor. This Alexas, the biographer notes, had been Cleopatra's ally in the matter of convincing Antony to forget any sort of sign of favour for his wife Octavia; additional clear evidence, if we needed it, of the troubles and difficulties in the royal enclosure in Egypt.

Plutarch states that Octavian would not listen to anything with respect to Antony, but that he did invite Cleopatra either to kill or to exile Antony; a clear case of the Roman leader dealing with her as an independent monarch who was now in a position to hand over the traitorous Roman to justice, or even to take matters into her own hands. Octavian is said to have sent a freedman by the name of Thyrsus, the Greek word for the wand of Dionysus that was a typical accoutrement of the god, and likely a deliberate play of Octavian on the Dionysiac, Bacchic revels of Antony and his lover. Thyrsus seems to have instigated such dissension in Alexandria that he was whipped and expelled by Antony; again, the evidence points to a breakdown of relations between the lovers. There is a soap operatic quality to the report that Cleopatra subsequently tried to mollify Antony's suspicions by ignoring her own birthday in comparison to the lavish celebration of his; the fact that Octavian was now summoned, Plutarch notes, back to Rome by Agrippa is testament enough to the fact that there was no real concern about what either Cleopatra or Antony was likely to do.

The resumption of the 'war', *Sitzkrieg* though it might seem to have been, came after the winter of 31-30 B.C.E. The attack now was two-pronged; Octavian is said to have advanced through Syria, and another force into Libya. Pelusium fell (84.1), and Plutarch notes that there was a report that Cleopatra had allowed for its commander, Seleucus, to surrender it without a fight, but she permitted Antony to kill the man's wife and children all the same as an example.[7]

At this stage, the queen is presented as being focused on her tomb, and Octavian on her treasure; messages seem to travel back and forth between the Roman and his 'quarry,' messages on Octavian's part that are said to have been full of unspecified guarantees of kindly treatment of the queen.

The military advance continues however, and at last we find an account of some sort of military encounter. Octavian was near the hippodrome, or horse and chariot racing stadium, and Antony attacked (74.3). The sally was successful, and Octavian's cavalry was driven back to his camp; no details are provided of what may have been a minor engagement with reconnaissance forces. The key detail about the whole enterprise may be the aftermath; Antony is said to have returned to Cleopatra in glory, presenting for her consideration the man who had fought most bravely and splendidly; a candidate indeed for high decoration and honour.[8] The man receives the high honour (a golden breastplate and helmet), and defected that night to Octavian's camp.

Plutarch records another challenge by Antony for single combat; we have no good reason to disbelieve the report. The recorded answer of Octavian, that Antony had many ways to die, is vintage Caesar. Antony decides to try for one last doomed gamble, a joint attack on land and sea. There are shades here of the situation at Actium; in theory, and we must emphasize theory, Antony still had at least rump naval and land forces. His position was of course hopeless, and again we have no reason to disbelieve the brief account and tradition of his last meal. The detail that he would not lead his friends out to battle, given that he sought death and not victory, has a poignant quality that may be embellishment, but it has a ring of truth. The account of the sounds of revelry in the night and the interpretation that the god Bacchus, the Dionysus to whom Antony was always compared, was somehow leaving the city as if in a sort of *evocatio* whereby Octavian was calling on the gods of Alexandria to depart the doomed city, may well reflect an early interpretation of carefree banqueting and feasting that may have occurred on the last night of the city. At the end, the god to whom Antony had most compared himself, Father Liber, was making his own escape from the doomed city.

At dawn, Antony is said to have posted infantry on hill positions outside the city, and to have watched his ships move out of harbour to attack the enemy, and at just the right moment, Antony's vessels saluted the ships of Octavian with their oars, and received the return salute of surrender and welcome home to Rome. This great defection of ships deserves closer scrutiny. Plutarch gives no account of how many vessels were in the harbour, or of their provenance; we should remember the tradition of the Arabian burning of some of the presumably Egyptian vessels that Cleopatra sought to deploy in the Red Sea. In Plutarch, the defection of the ships (we might recall too, the evidence of Horace about the leftward retreat of Antonian vessels at Actium) was followed at once by the desertion of Antony's cavalry.

If Plutarch can be believed, there *was* a military engagement, despite these massive losses; Antony's infantry was defeated. Frustratingly, there are no details in *The Life* as to the exact disposition of events. Perhaps there were core loyalists who were willing to fight at least for the sake of making a show of honour and allegiance to their commander. Of greatest interest may be the fact that Plutarch reports that when Antony returned to the city, he complained that Cleopatra had betrayed him, though he was fighting at her behest and for her sake.

This detail accords with the rest of the Plutarchan tradition that there was tension in the city between the two lovers, and the air was rife with the fear of treachery and deceit. It is at this point that Plutarch relates the now famous story that Cleopatra had word sent to Antony that she was already dead. Antony's reaction is to announce that he would soon be joining her in death, and that he was grieved and embarrassed as it were, to be shamed by a woman of such eminently greater courage.

The Death of Mark Antony.

If Plutarch's account can be at all trusted, witnesses to Antony's subsequent botched suicide attempt brought news to the queen, who at last ordered that he be brought to her chamber. Plutarch does not make it at all clear why Egypt's queen had wanted Antony to think that she was dead (Dio will offer his own explanation); in the context of the story, clearly she was already resolute and determined to kill herself. Did she in any way fear Antony's anger in the wake of what she must have known was his pointless efforts at military resistance? The pathetic scene of the queen at the ropes as Antony was hoisted into the tomb certainly reflects a fear on Cleopatra's part that if her tomb were opened, she might be captured alive by partisans of Octavian, but this does not entirely explain her desire to have Antony think that she was dead. One has the impression that if Antony had either been killed in battle or had successfully committed suicide, that his body would not have been elaborately welcomed into Cleopatra's tomb for burial.

The whole scene of course seems staged; Antony dies with words of encouragement to the queen to look after her own fortune; he seems not to think that suicide is her plan and option. He urges her to use Proculeius as her best avenue of Roman access to Octavian, and Proculeius thoughtfully appears on the scene as soon as Antony breathes his last. The timely arrival of the emissary from Caesar's camp is credited to a believable enough story of how one Dercetaeus, a bodyguard of Antony, had brought his master's bloody sword to Octavian with news of the suicide. The report that Octavian wept is not as interesting as the detail that he carefully read his correspondence with Antony to his companions, detailing for them 'with evidence', how he had always been so reasonable in his dealings with his adversary, and Antony so impossible. A legalistic and carefully constructed narrative was already well under development. Pelling considers the tears of Octavian to have been 'crocodile', and this may well be true. Certainly it was good political theatre to be able to show a lachrymose demeanour before his men about the death of a fellow Roman, especially if anyone wanted to note that another great Roman had now died in Egypt (after Pompey). Again, Octavian had every reason to be scrupulous in his performance of Roman niceties and polite behaviour in the aftermath of Antony's death; the situation was very different in some regards from what Caesar had experienced with the murder of Pompey, a murder that in some sense did, after all, do Caesar a favour.

Proculeius is sent, and his supreme order is to capture Cleopatra alive.[9] Here we have the 'traditional' tale of the concern of Octavian both for the queen and her treasure, and the seemingly strangely languid account of how Proculeius has his initial interview through the door of the tomb. And then of how Gallus was sent for a second meeting, one in which Proculeius was secretly assigned to procure a ladder to try to enter the structure while Gallus distracted Cleopatra. Cleopatra tries to commit suicide with a dagger as soon as one of her women shouts that Gallus is upon her; soon enough the queen is both deprived of her weapon and searched for poison, and yet even now, with suicide clearly on her mind, she is merely put under the guard of the freedman Epaphroditus, a man whose name evokes the idea that he was put 'in charge over Aphrodite'.[10]

Events seem leisurely enough. Octavian is described as being concerned about the survival of the queen (and her treasure), but he has plenty of time it would seem, for attending to various matters (not least the death of Antony's son by Fulvia, the unfortunate Antyllus). Antony's body is said to have been buried by Cleopatra in her tomb with Octavian's permission; there is a report that she had intended to use a timely fever as an excuse to stop eating, but that the queen revealed her suicidal intentions to the physician Olympus, who reported it to Octavian.[11] At this point, Cleopatra was forced to eat after Octavian threatened the lives of her children.[12] We have no clear sense of where exactly all the children were at this point. But it is still a few days that transpire before Octavian visits Cleopatra in her tomb. The scene is one of Plutarch's best, replete with fine rhetorical touches and dramatic narrative power. Of particular interest may be the report that Octavian calmly refuted Cleopatra on every point where the queen tried to justify her actions; Plutarch presents a Cleopatra who was willing to try to blame Antony for everything, a ploy that Octavian would not tolerate. Cleopatra is said to have been caught in a lie about the size of her treasure and wealth by her steward, Seleucus, and to have bitterly attacked him in Octavian's presence; the Roman is reported to have been pleased at this apparent proof that the queen was interested in prolonged life. It is impossible to know for certain whether the whole business with Seleucus was a theatrical contrivance; many scholars agree that in Octavian, Cleopatra may well have met an intellectual and rhetorical equal, someone she could not manipulate so easily with argumentation (not to say wiles).

Octavian leaves, and Plutarch notes that he was pleased to have deceived her by his pledges of generous support and kind favour, but that in reality he was the one who had been tricked.[13] The implication of this statement was that Cleopatra was resolved to die, and that she had successfully convinced Octavian that she intended to live, and so Octavian could expect that he had a prime specimen for his triumphal procession in Rome.

The glaring problem with this narrative is that it compels us to believe that Octavian, despite his alleged great concern for the survival of Cleopatra for display as a presumably condemned captive in Rome, was in no great hurry to take her under firm guard and control, and that he was more than willing to accord her significant independence of action and relative privacy. Again, it requires the Octavian who had done everything right thus far in the story suddenly to take leave of his senses and logic, and to leave things essentially in Cleopatra's hands.

The Plutarchan story becomes stranger still when we learn of the odd goings-on between Cleopatra and Cornelius Dolabella.[14] Dolabella is said to have been somewhat infatuated with Cleopatra, or at least gently disposed to her, and we hear that he was now somehow contacted for the 'real' story about Octavian's intentions (we may remember the story in the Elder Seneca about the obscene letters that Dolabella had written to the queen). He is recorded as having reported to Cleopatra that Octavian intended to advance through Syria within three days, and that in the same triduum Cleopatra and her children would be sent off (presumably to Italy). It is now that the queen puts into motion her plan for suicide; it would seem that she had few if any options left.

Pelling notes here that we have very little evidence for what happened next to Dolabella; he speculates that the present scene may well have spelled ruin for his future career in Octavian's service. The problem is that the scene does not at all accord neatly with what preceded it; it implies that Cleopatra decided to kill herself *only* after Dolabella had warned her of Octavian's plans. So why would Plutarch report that Octavian had left the queen's presence deceived rather than deceiving?

The Suicide of Cleopatra.

Cleopatra makes ready her suicide, and she has time for a message for Octavian. The message is sent; the contents make a request for burial with Antony; and we might recall the dramatic story of the Antonian will and the request for burial in Egypt. Now Octavian is said to realize that she was set on suicide; he thinks at first that he should go to the tomb, but then he reconsiders and sends emissaries. Here is the celebrated death *tableau*, the famous scene that Mankiewicz did well to choose as his final composition and shot. Cleopatra is attended by Iras and Charmion; the former already dying at her mistress' feet, the other arranging the diadem on Cleopatra's head.[15] Plutarch does not specify who was sent by Octavian to the tomb; in the film version, it is Agrippa (perhaps fittingly enough, historical accuracy aside), together with Octavian (who storms out in frustrated anger once he realizes what has happened). The Mankiewicz account takes Plutarch as its source for the dramatic final dialogue between the Roman and the servant, which is repeated by the narrator: 'Was this well done of your lady?' 'Extremely well...as befitting the last of so many noble rulers.'

Plutarch appends to his dramatic scene the inconclusive reports about the asp and other poisons; he notes that no one actually claimed to have seen the reptile.[16] Aelian, in his work on the nature of animals, notes that Cleopatra had enquired after the various types of death in dinner conversation before Octavian's arrival at Alexandria, and also that there was a certain riddle or enigma to the death of the queen, until the telltale marks of the bite of an asp were detected on the body.[17]

Octavian is said to have been irritated by the suicide, but also to have admired the queen's noble spirit.[18] He orders that she be granted her last request, and she and Antony are buried together in noble fashion; her women too, accorded the same treatment. And perhaps most interestingly, we are told that while the statues of Antony were ordered to be torn down, those of Cleopatra were left standing, because her friend Archibius paid Octavian 2,000 talents so they could remain. The recurring theme of rapacity and greed ends the narrative; Cleopatra was a condemned enemy, but her statues can remain in Alexandria for the right price. No one it seems, was interested in paying for monuments to Mark Antony. Some of this too, may reflect the victor's intentions to be as respectful as possible to the Alexandrians.[19]

There are numerous problems of interpretation and analysis that are presented by this lengthy and richly complex account in Plutarch. In some ways the narrative is more challenging to explicate than his Actium story. One problem is why Cleopatra was allowed to remain alive for more than a week after the fall of Alexandria; here the most plausible explanation would seem to be that this was exactly what was needed to permit the passage of time that would be required to make it seem as if the 'imprisoned' Cleopatra had managed to escape her new master even in her moment of defeat. In other words, the last week and two days of her life was a stage play that was directed and cast by Octavian himself. There was never any intention of bringing her to Rome in chains; she needed to be made to kill herself, and her suicide needed to be conducted in a manner and at a time that was most in accord with Octavian's own wish to appear deceived if not defeated by his great enemy.

Dio's Evidence.

We may turn to Dio Cassius' account of the aftermath (51.1.4 ff.). After Actium, events move quickly. Antony's land army is said to have been retreating into Macedonia; it is overtaken and surrenders without a fight. Some Antonians did escape; the Romans made it to Antony, and the allied forces to their respective homes. None of the latter fought any further against Octavian. Lengthy narrative describes the dealings and resolutions of Octavian with respect to his now former enemies, both foreign and domestic. Agrippa and Maecenas are presented as having been key figures in the administration of Octavian's will in Italy and Rome.

In Greece, Octavian participated in the Eleusinian Mysteries in honour of Demeter and Persephone.[20] He proceeded into Asia, careful to seek intelligence about where exactly Antony had gone and what he was doing. In the middle of the winter of 31-30 B.C.E., he returned to Italy to quell disturbances and trouble on the home front; others were assigned the responsibility of tracking down Antony and his movements. After a month (thirty days) in Italy, Octavian returned to Greece and then to Asia; Dio reports that Antony and Cleopatra learned of the departure and the return on the same day, so quickly did Octavian manage to conduct his business and his journeys. Dio records that after Actium the queen and her lover had fled to the Peloponnesus, where potentially suspect friends and associates were dismissed, an occasion where it appears there were defections even from among those who were not under suspicion. Cleopatra proceeded to Egypt quickly, afraid she would be overthrown if the Alexandrians learned of the disaster at Actium before she could arrive. She pretends to have conquered, arriving with a victorious sound of celebration, and at once moves to order the execution of leading officials in Alexandria, a purge that may well have taken place. We learn that Antony actually travelled to Africa to visit his troops there under Pinarius Scarpus; the latter is said to have refused to receive Antony, and even to have killed both Antony's emissaries and those soldiers in his camp who were displeased with his blatant show of support for Octavian's cause; one of the most dramatic shows of support for Octavian by a defector in the history of the war.

Dio preserves the detail that Antony and Cleopatra sealed the fate of their sons Caesarion and Antyllus when they proceeded to present them as *de facto* successors to the cause of their perhaps doomed parents; there is a record that Caesarion was thought of as a more pleasing potential monarch because of his gender. The Red Sea is mentioned, as is a possible diversion to Spain to raise a revolt there; all indications are that continued war was fully under consideration. Messages from both the queen and her lover to Caesar are presented as delaying tactics; this is certainly true. The Plutarchan detail is found about how Antony received no real response to his overtures, while Cleopatra was made the offer that she should kill Antony to retain her crown. Killing Antony of course, would be the new version of what had happened at the court of her brother in the matter of the death of Pompey; Cleopatra would indeed have done a great service to Octavian, who could then blame the Egyptians for yet another death of a noble Roman, and who could then employ a new chapter in his propaganda: the queen was a faithless lover who would even go so far as to kill her paramour to save herself.

The Arabians burn the ships; Dio credits the instigation of the incendiary strike to Quintus Didius, the governor of Syria. If there was military action in this period, Dio would have us believe that it was under the impetus of the gladiators of Cyzicus who fought bravely for Antony; they are credited with strikes against Amyntas of Galatia, Tarcondimotus in Cilicia, and even Quintus Didius in Syria.[21] They were finally cornered and offered terms of surrender; they sent for Antony, who neither came nor even responded to their message, and so they concluded that he must be dead. Dio records that they were more or less deceived by Octavian's men and eventually all killed.

Cleopatra is depicted as promising vast sums of money to Octavian; Antony rather pitifully is presented as recalling their youthful adventures together, the times when both men were given to reckless and questionable behaviour. He does send one of the assassins of Caesar, Publius Turullius, who is promptly killed; Antyllus is sent too, with a sum of gold that is promptly taken. The boy returned to Egypt with no answer for his father. Cleopatra is said to have received numerous threats as well as pledges, the threats likely aimed at both her and her children. The gist of the threats and pledges must have been to try to secure the death of Antony as quickly and conveniently as possible, though it is interesting that Octavian seems to have been willing to have accepted the possibility of *another* Egyptian murder of a noble and defeated Roman. Pompey had been treacherously slain in Egypt after his defeat in Greece by Caesar; it must have seemed that there was an opportunity for history to repeat itself, and of course to have the blood of Antony on the hands of his lover. All in all, it would have been a masterful stroke of luck if Octavian had been able to achieve it.

Dio's Octavian is reported as having been concerned about Cleopatra's treasure, and also about the possibility of an uprising that they might engender in Spain or Gaul. The embassy of Thyrsus is related; in Dio, the freedman is sent to tell Cleopatra that Octavian was in love with her, and Dio reports the reason for the plan: Cleopatra considered herself worthy to be passionately loved by everyone, and so she would now kill Antony and allow herself to become Octavian's paramour. Modern readers are rightly, critically sceptical of the description of Cleopatra as planning to enter into an amorous entanglement with yet another powerful Roman, but history is full of stranger tales, and there is no reason to dismiss the notion entirely.[22] Some scholars make note of the fact that the now close to 40-year old Cleopatra may not have been able to expect success in the seduction of a third Roman.

Dio continues to provide more details about military manoeuvres in these crucial months. Antony learns that Cornelius Gallus had taken over Scarpus' command and was moving against Paraetonium; this is blamed for the non-answer of Antony to the Syrian gladiators. Antony pins his hopes on either the successful winning over of Gallus' men, or of battle by sea and land with a reasonable chance of victory. He fails to be able to talk to them (Gallus is said to have drowned out his voice with trumpets), and he soon enough suffers defeat in a quick attempt at a land sortie, and defeat on the water. The latter setback is credited to Gallus' ingenious use of chains to trap the Antonian ships as they were allowed to sail into harbour; soon the vessels are set on fire. Whatever hopes Antony had in Africa seem to be gone.

Octavian takes Pelusium; Dio agrees with Plutarch that Cleopatra allowed it to be taken without a fight. Dio's Cleopatra is presented as being more aware of the reality of the situation than Antony; she is depicted as both convinced that the cause was doomed, *and* seriously in contention to win the heart of Octavian, just as she had successfully seduced both Caesar and Antony before him. In Dio, this confidence in her ability to persuade Octavian to take her as a lover, especially in light of Thyrsus' lies, convinces her that she might attain power over Rome as the paramour of its new greatest man.

In consequence, she surrenders Pelusium, and orders no response from the Alexandrians to his approach to her capital. Antony learns of the former loss and proceeds to Alexandria, where he clashes with Octavian and wins a cavalry engagement; Dio, unlike Plutarch, explains the victory as being the result of Octavian's men's fatigue from a long march. Antony sends propaganda pamphlets into Octavian's camp, and thinks that he has a chance for success, but he is soon defeated in an infantry engagement. Antony retreats to his navy (one wonders if the capital were becoming a treacherous place for him) and considers either another naval fight, or the repeated strategy of retreat to Spain. Cleopatra is somehow credited with causing the desertion of the ships; the defection of the navy is mentioned in Plutarch, but only Dio records that the queen was the instigation, which makes one wonder if the ships in question were Egyptian (at least in part). It would fit with Dio's narrative of Cleopatra's unwillingness to fight Octavian that she ordered the surrender of her navy to him (at least as a token of her good faith). We are quite uncertain of what exactly Antony's 'legal' status was in the eyes of the Alexandrians at this point; there is every reason to think that Cleopatra's word was the law that was respected and obeyed.

Interestingly, Dio claims that Cleopatra at this point makes a sudden (and unexpected?) departure for her tomb, claiming as a ruse that she was afraid of Octavian and wanted to commit suicide.[23] The real reason, Dio notes, was that she wanted Antony to join her there, and Antony suspected that it was a trick and an act of treachery. But he felt emotionally overwrought and could not face the possibility that she intended to do him harm, and he felt more anxious and concerned for the queen than for himself. It is a final declaration of the abiding servility of the lover; a final worry for his paramour and her safety as the net drew tighter on them both.

Dio's Cleopatra plays on these emotions of her 'husband,' and thus sends the word that she is dead, hoping by this stratagem to secure the suicide of Antony. It is unclear if this analysis is Dio's own, or if Plutarch shared it and merely refrained from making it explicit; perhaps it was stated clearly in other sources. The Antonian suicide, botched and all, is more or less the same in Dio as in Plutarch; once the queen receives word that Antony is actually alive (however barely), she has him brought into the enclosure of the tomb. Her shrewdness is highlighted; she assumed that now she had a real chance for survival, but she was not entirely convinced that her fate was secure, and she (no doubt correctly) felt that the best guarantee of her survival would be to remain near her vast riches.

There is a quality of the pathetic to the suicide scene of Antony; the man who had failed at so much in recent months is unable even to secure his own speedy release from life.

Dio's Octavian certainly wants Cleopatra's money and her living body for his triumph, but he is presented as having been stymied in the matter of how to take her without appearing to have tricked or deceived her. The key detail here is that Octavian is said to have wanted to appear to have treated her as a captive, as one who involuntarily submitted to his will.[24] Proculeius and Epaphroditus make appearances in this account too; in Dio's version, she is seized in the midst of negotiations with them both (the Plutarchan story of the ladder and the dramatic entrance into the tomb is omitted). She is deprived of any ready means to commit suicide, but she is also allowed days to spend in the preparation of the burial of Antony. She was then taken to her palace and allowed to retain the company of her attendants; she requested a meeting with Octavian, and Dio records that he tricked her by saying that he would come to her in person.

Octavian does visit her (as in Plutarch), and we may well wonder what exactly the deceit encompassed. Presumably it refers to Octavian's wish to appear to be magnanimous and to keep her appeased and at peace, the apparent willingness, in short, of the conqueror to be victorious. Octavian, as elsewhere in the tradition, seems interested in delaying and securing more and more time in which to mollify Cleopatra and to put to rest her concerns. Dio's Cleopatra is more seductive than Plutarch's; she is ready with letters from Julius Caesar, and expressions of how Octavian is now Caesar for her again. Interestingly, Dio notes that Octavian was not immune to her charms, *but that he pretended to be.*[25]

The picture in Dio is a stunning psychological portrait of the conqueror with his vanquished, noble foe. He refuses to look at her, well aware of her seductive charms, and he certainly does not offer any words of affection or enchantment to her. His cold reception of her causes fear and anxiety, apprehension and frustration; soon enough she begs that she might at least be buried with Antony, all in the hopes of arousing some sort of commiseration or pity for her on his part. She fails, but Octavian is described as becoming concerned that she might really kill herself after all, and so he urges her to remain calm. But he also displays special concern and care for her wellbeing, and Cleopatra comes to the realization that he wants her to look especially lovely for her triumph and ultimate degradation. She is now said to have been resolutely set on dying, and to have communicated with Octavian with pleas that she might be destroyed in this or that fashion. Nothing works, and so she now lies and says that she will indeed sail to Italy, and that she planned to select treasures that she might present as gifts to Octavian's wife Livia. Her strategy was to buy herself both more time (as if she has not already had quite a bit of that), and to secure a less vigilant guard. The stratagem and ruse works, and the guard is relaxed now that it appears that the queen is ready to depart for Italy.

One is tempted to say that the narrative is unbelievable, even if one can keep track of how often one party is said to have been deceiving the other. It strains credulity to imagine that Octavian would permit such a delay and the climactic surrendering of his close watch over her. Dio would have us believe that Epaphroditus was given a sealed letter for Octavian that was allegedly about some trivial matter, but which in fact conveyed her wish to be buried with Antony. The queen is able thereby to secure the departure of Epaphroditus and yet more time unguarded and unobserved; she prepares her dramatic suicide, and soon enough Octavian is informed and rendered stunned.

The Aftermath: A Very Different Alexandrian War.

There are attempts at revival and resuscitation in Dio that are not recorded in Plutarch.[26] At last, Octavian is said both to admire and to feel mercy toward Cleopatra, and grief and misery for himself as having been cheated of his victory. The romance has been composed; the mighty queen was able in death to secure some modicum of a victory over her conqueror, and the serpentine imagery of Isis was seen to have been wielded effectively in the face of the efforts of Octavian to secure a chained captive for his chariot. The stage was set for the eventual depiction of the queen in the triumphal processions of August, 29 B.C.E.; a mythology had been set in motion for how the end of the Alexandrian War would be remembered. Its finish was most different from the conclusion of the *Bellum Alexandrinum* of Octavian's adoptive father Caesar; he had left Egypt with a new girlfriend and a potential liability and handicap for his final years of power and life, while his son and heir would leave Egypt and the city of Alexander having conquered a world.

Dio also notes, interestingly, that there was some measure of continued resistance in Egypt to the resultant direct Roman rule that followed the death of Cleopatra and the end of Ptolemaic control (there may have been those who clamoured for the reign of her children now as the successors of the Ptolemaic line).[27] No details are given of whatever conflicts or guerrilla actions persisted. Instead there are more portents: blood fell from the sky in place of water, and in fact water rained down in desert places; there was even a great serpent that appeared and uttered a terrible hiss. Comets and ghosts alike were everywhere; it was a scene of portentous horror and dramatic terror, a perfect ring composition with the portents that preceded Actium. Octavian departed for Syria and Asia, where he spent the winter of 30–29 B.C.E.

The basic outline of the Dio story is the same then, as what we find in Plutarch (as it was, more or less, with the Actium narrative). The emphasis throughout is on deception and stratagems of ruse and mendacious plotting. Some observations can be made. In the final months before the fall of Alexandria, it is Antony who takes whatever lead there is to be taken in the matter of the defence of his position and the continued prosecution of war against Octavian. There is every indication that Cleopatra had abandoned any hope of further conflict. If Spain was a serious plan for Antony, it strains credulity to imagine that it was Cleopatra's desire or intention to join him. There is good reason to believe that relations between the lovers utterly collapsed in the last months of their lives, and that Antony at least, did not feel entirely secure in Cleopatra's capital and even presence, at least not at certain points in the course of their final year. It may well be that Cleopatra came to hope for the suicide of Antony just as much as Octavian did, and that Octavian in turn, hoped for the suicide of Cleopatra, a suicide that would in the end prove to be an attractive option for her as well.

In the tradition of the epic cycle, the Amazon Penthesilea came to the defence of the beleaguered city of Troy, and was slain by Achilles in battle. The great Greek hero is said to have felt enormous regret and sorrow on the loss of Penthesilea, and even to have been struck by love for her as she appeared lovely and beautiful even in defeat and death. Both Plutarch and Dio record that Octavian felt genuine admiration for Cleopatra in death; Plutarch reports that there were tears and words of praise for Antony as well, while Dio is silent on the reaction of Octavian to the death of his Roman adversary. Again, there is consistent evidence in our sources that the attention of the last days was mainly focused on the queen (who, we do well to recall, controlled the purse strings of the enterprise).

As we have noted in our consideration of the evidence for Actium, Plutarch and Dio are relatively late sources. Horace's Cleopatra ode is a contemporary work, and it offers an early glimpse of the extant record on the suicide. We have seen how Horace's account is one of respectful homage, even for the dead queen; Cleopatra is presented as being *ferocior* or 'fierce' by the death that she planned. It is interesting that in Dio the queen is depicted as having sent communications to Octavian about the different ways in which she could meet her end; all to no avail. Was there in reality active discussion between Octavian and Cleopatra about her fate? Was the queen aware that Octavian wanted her to commit suicide, and that the only question to be resolved was how and when?

Another interesting detail in Dio is of how Cleopatra had gathered all the riches of Alexandria into one rather convenient place.[28] The result of this was that the Romans were able all the more easily to seize the treasures of Egypt without any scruples about the invasion of temple sanctuaries and other sacred places; the loot was all ready for the taking. Of course, Cleopatra needed to use the wealth as a bargaining tool with Octavian, but it reminds us of the relatively lengthy period of negotiations between the Roman and the Egyptian. One might conclude that if Octavian were indeed utterly deceived in the matter of Cleopatra's suicide, then the man who had successfully accomplished thus far what many might have thought impossible, was utterly unable to secure the custody of a single woman, queen or Isis notwithstanding.

We do well to remember that the discussion of the fate of Cleopatra's children is another element of the mysterious puzzle. Plutarch reminds us of the use of the children as a threat against the queen, and indeed Caesarion would be killed as an inconvenient survivor and potential future threat.[29] We cannot know exactly what was said to Cleopatra about Octavian's intentions for her children, but surely the queen could not expect the best, at least not for all of them. Caesarion was now some sixteen years old, old enough to be considered more than a threat to the new regime.[30] In the end, the younger children would all be spared; there was arguably no need to eliminate them too, and their salvation would make Octavian look all the more magnanimous. The fact that Octavia would take them into her own care is another element of the picture; brother and sister appear all the more honourable and reasonable, and their vanquished foes all the more selfish and narcissistic.

The last days of Cleopatra are indeed fraught with even more mystery and enigma than the events surrounding Actium. There is no surviving evidence of any real military combat between the forces of Antony and Octavian in Greece. In the final months of their lives, an argument could be made that Antony was in a far more precarious position than Cleopatra. He had no real chance of survival, while his queen might have nurtured some small hope of retaining some rump monarchy that was in clear alliance, if not *de facto* servitude to Rome. While it is reasonable to conclude that neither of the defeated survivors of Actium had any realistic chance of long-term safety, in the hierarchy of despair a case could be made that Cleopatra was in a better position than Antony; indeed, he may well have faced perils both from his Roman conqueror and pursuer, and from treachery in Alexandria at the hands of Cleopatra and her court. In short, if there needed to be a narrative of embellishment and romanticized episodes of adventure and intrigue, it would need to come from Alexandria more than Actium. And surely there would be fewer witnesses to whatever really happened.

Dramatic and romantic tales of loyal gladiators aside, it appears that resistance to Octavian in Syria and Africa was also less than significant. A realistic assessment of Octavian's situation after Actium might conclude that his most serious risks were in Italy, not in the East, though obviously enough, he needed to settle affairs in Alexandria with reasonable haste. The apparent payment of the Arabians to burn Cleopatra's fleet before it could manoeuvre in the Red Sea speaks to some concern that this was a viable option for the queen; Spain is likely to have been a less serious threat as a potential Antonian base. What we do not have is any clear sense of what forces Antony had left in his final months (either Egyptian or Roman); we have no indication of how many of his men chose to make their stand in Alexandria; only in the end, in many if not most cases, to defect to Octavian.

Horace, as we have seen, highlights the image of Octavian in pursuit from Italy, and of Thessaly as the locus of the hunter's pursuit of the hare that represents Cleopatra and not Antony. The simile imagery of the hawk and the dove, which he shares with Virgil, ultimately derives from Homer's description of Achilles' pursuit of Hector.[31] In Virgil, Camilla is cast in the Achilles role, as the accipiter, or bird of prey, that pursues its dove. In Horace, the part of Achilles is reserved for Octavian, and the hunter in quest for his hare is located in Achilles' homeland of Thessaly. The Horatian ode speaks to a wish to have some acknowledgment of Greece as the locus of combat (or at least pursuit); it harks back to the epic tradition, even as it plays somewhat fast and loose with the historical record. Certainly there was no clear intelligence in the immediate aftermath of Actium as to where Antony and Cleopatra were headed, though Alexandria must have seemed an obvious destination for at least one of them. The situation in Greece would have been in some doubt at first as well; Antony still had appreciable forces, not to mention a population whose loyalties could not simply be counted on without question. But if there is any lesson to be derived from the Horatian ode, it is the insignificance of Antony, and we might note that in the reports of correspondence and emissary messages in Plutarch and Dio, it is the queen who merits Octavian's attention, not Antony. The war after all, had officially been declared against her and not him; perhaps a convenient legal fiction, but a fiction that was more than firmly rooted in reality.

Velleius.

Velleius offers nothing of the extended details of Plutarch and Dio in his account of the close of the story. Octavian proceeds to Alexandria, and Antony promptly commits suicide.[32] Cleopatra manages to frustrate her watchmen, *frustratis custodibus*, and an asp is brought to her for her serpentine suicide. Velleius thus records a story of trickery, one in which the queen was able to kill herself against the implicit will of her conqueror; the focus is more on the mercy and clemency of Octavian, who behaves in a manner unlike that of Antony with Decimus Brutus and Sextus Pompey. Canidius' fate is recorded; he is said to have been more frightened by the approach of death than he had boasted in life. As Woodman notes *ad loc.*, there is no other evidence of his alleged proclamation of fearlessness in the face of death, and no clear indication in Velleius of how he met his end (either a suicide or an execution in the wake of the defeat at Actium). Suicide may be implied by his comparison with the suicidal pairs Brutus and Cassius and Antony and Cleopatra, but we have very little evidence for Canidius' end. Cassius of Parma is cited as the last of Caesar's assassins to meet his end; we may compare the story of Publius Turullius in Dio, the assassin who was killed in the closing days of the Alexandrian War.[33] Those hoping for some sort of clue as to the actual sequence of events in the last months of Antony and Cleopatra, let alone some clue as to the military situation in the last year of the civil wars, will find Velleius a disappointing source. The details about the deaths of the last of the surviving conspirators against Julius Caesar are likely true, they certainly had run out of places of relative safety, and they provide an effective rounding off to the narrative of the civil wars. Octavian had set out to avenge the death of his adoptive father; all those involved in the assassination had now been accounted for in some way or other, and the debts to the deified Julius had been paid in full.

Orosius.

Orosius focuses his attention on the post-Actian dealings of Antony and Cleopatra on the question of their children.[34] He states that they decided to send their *communos liberos* or 'common children' to the Red Sea together with part of the royal treasure; the language is ambiguous as to whether the *communos* refers to the children they had in common, or to all of their offspring combined; the former may be likelier. They fortified Pelusium and Paraetonium as the two entries to their realm, with both infantry and naval forces. Octavian's return to Italy is noted, as is his advance to Syria; he proceeds to Pelusium, where he is received voluntarily by Antony's guard. Cornelius Gallus was sent to Paraetonium, and he received four Antonian legions that were defending Cyrenaica and the western approaches to Egypt, a rare clue as to just how much force Antony had left. There is a breezy reference to fighting at Paraetonium, or at least to Antony's defeat there (*victo Antonio*); soon enough Gallus is victorious at Pharos. Orosius provides valuable details here of the activity on the western front of the Alexandrian campaign, details that fill in a picture where other sources are silent; the western front may in fact have been where more danger lurked from Antonian ground forces. Whatever happened later, it seems that at least in late summer of 30 B.C.E., Gallus performed well for Octavian and more than merited the conqueror's trust and support; a performance of course, that may have engendered a certain degree of arrogance on the part of Gallus. Antony meanwhile, initiates an equestrian battle against Octavian;[35] he flees after having been 'miserably defeated' (*miserabiliter victus*). On 1 August (Orosius is a key source for the date) at dawn, Antony proceeds to the harbour of Alexandria to his vessels, which at once all go over to Octavian; Orosius makes clear that this was his last hope, so that now he retreated to the royal palace with but a few companions.[36] Octavian entered the city, which was thrown into disarray; Antony promptly commits suicide and is brought to Cleopatra's tomb half alive (*semianimis*), the tomb where Orosius notes that Cleopatra was 'resolved to die (*mori certa*).

Cleopatra is said to have understood that she was to be preserved alive for a triumph, and so she sought a voluntary death, and was found dead with a serpent's bite on her left arm. There is a reference to how Octavian tried in vain to have her healed of the injury, but to no avail; *frustra*. But what could easily have given rise to a lurid and extended moralistic account, is eschewed for a brief, business-like narration. Caesar was the victor, and at last he took the rich and opulent city of Alexandria.

Orosius offers little of exceptional note in the description of the last year then, though he does highlight Antony's failed cavalry action.[37] The story is set though, of Cleopatra's cheating Octavian of his plans for a triumph; it is perhaps noteworthy that both Orosius and Dio mention Octavian's use of the Psylli in the hope of saving Cleopatra; they were celebrated experts in herpetology and the treatment of snakebite who figure in Lucan's great narrative of the snakes in Africa that assail Cato's men in gory and unforgettable fashion in *Bellum Civile* 9. Octavian may have been well aware that there was no point in trying to resuscitate the dead, but the effort, and the story, would go a long way toward making it seem as if he had been cheated of the prize display at his triumph the following August.

Octavian had won, and one imagines that there was not much of an appetite for renewed internecine or foreign strife anywhere in the Mediterranean basin. As ever, given the magnitude of the task, there was much to be done to safeguard and to advance the cause of the Republic, a Republic that was unalterably changed. Octavian would soon become Augustus, and Augustus would soon enough become a god. He would have his critics both in life and in death. And yet the author of the Gospel of Luke had ample reason to note that the birth of Christ came under Caesar Augustus, *when the whole world was at peace.*

It would be for his successors to unravel much of what the first emperor of Rome had woven.[38]

Actium and Roman Naval Practice

T he student of Roman naval history does not have many engagements to study from the late republican and early imperial period. William Ledyard Rodgers observes that 'the business of a navy is to throttle the enemy's supplies,'[1] and throttle Antony's is what Agrippa did with Octavian's ships.

Actium was in one sense the beginning of a marked decline in Roman naval power, simply because ships were less necessary for military engagements; Octavian's victory and consolidation were such that further naval conflict in the Mediterranean was not necessary for many an age to come.[2] On the other hand, Actium was arguably the dawn of the permanent Roman navy, the battle after which fleets were maintained at established naval bases to guard commerce and to serve as what we might call a coast guard.[3]

The naval scholar Rodgers thought that the innovation at Actium was Agrippa's departure from the 'traditional' naval tactic of pretending as quickly as possible that a sea battle was a land one, of seeking as quickly as possible to land one's troops on an enemy vessel and to engage in a 'ground' campaign on planks of wood floating on the water. Agrippa, so the theory goes, practised the art of using such expedients as fire to eliminate enemy vessels before they might ever need to be boarded; Agrippa achieved mastery over the development of the art of what we might call a 'hit and run' tactic by sleek and swift vessels against larger and more sluggish targets.

Certainly Agrippa might deserve the title of first 'professional' admiral of the Roman navy. We can be sure that Agrippa trained for naval conflict to a degree that far outpaced the efforts of his enemies (both Roman and Egyptian). Fire had been used before in Roman naval history, but Agrippa would make pyrotechnics a centrepiece of his strategy; likely, the high towers that held both artillery and archery contingents would make inviting targets for missile fire from a safe distance.

The trireme was perhaps the basic workhorse of the Roman navy, literally a ship that was 'three-oared' (i.e., three banks of oars).[4] Latin historical texts refer to the *navis longa* or 'long ship,' i.e., a warship that was propelled by oars.[5] Unfortunately, no surviving ancient source gives a comprehensive account of exactly how the ships were manned, or how the oars were arranged; what matters was not only the number of banks of oars, but also the number of men per oar. Ships larger (in overall size or number of rowers) than triremes were employed both for tactical advantage and to create an impressive display that would instill both fear and respect in potential rivals. Quadriremes and quinqueremes were by no means unusual; hexaremes would have been especially noteworthy, hence the '6s' and '10s' of Antony's fleet were certainly meant to engender serious respect at Actium. Roman warships did not exceed 6s typically; the fantastic polyremes that are mentioned in the sources are part of the eager ship development and competition of the Hellenistic kingdoms (including Ptolemaic Alexandria), and no doubt there was a price to pay for their immense size. We have seen how Vegetius credited the light Liburnian for the victory of Octavian; again, there is probably good reason for the mention of that vessel at the opening of Horace's *Epodes*. Actium essentially spelled the end of the Hellenistic craze for ever more sizable ships; Agrippa showed exactly what the weaknesses of the passion for 'bigger is better' were. Of course the question of larger *versus* smaller ships is exactly part of the reason for Agrippa's victory over Sextus Pompey; at Actium, Antony was in an important sense fighting yesterday's naval war. The Hollywood film *Ben-Hur* has contributed to the impression that the rowers on Roman warships were slaves; in reality they were freeborn, though of course a given crew might consist of freeborn citizens from foreign lands and not Roman citizens. In times of crisis of course, certainly local populations would have been pressed into service in ways that we might think come close to approximating 'slavery', but from bireme to decareme/decere, Roman warships were manned by the nominally free.

To get some idea of naval warfare and technology in the Age of Agrippa, we may consider the evidence of Appian's account of one of Agrippa's clashes with the Pompeians.[6] The breakage of oar blades and ship rudders is described as boats collided in war; Agrippa's ships are said to have tried to use their beaks to ram the enemy, or to use missiles at close distance as well as grappling hooks. And Appian describes the invention of the so-called *harpax* by Agrippa, a device that was first used against the Pompeians at Naulochus in 36 B.C.E. Essentially, the *harpax* was a more efficient way to disable enemy vessels than the famous *harpago* or *corvus* (Latin for 'raven' or 'crow') that dated back to Roman naval engagements against Carthage in the First Punic War (the war about which Lucius Arruntius probably composed a history). The *harpax* was fired by a catapult; it consisted of a piece of wood and iron that was armed with a grappling hook. The innovations were a tremendous success and the main cause of the Octavian victory over Sextus Pompey;[7] Agrippa more than earned his naval crown both by research and practical application of his discoveries and improvements.[8]

The victory of Octavian and Agrippa at Actium was of so profound a significance and so great a magnitude, that neither they nor their immediate successors in the business of managing Roman governmental and military affairs, would have a chance to learn from and adapt in accord with the lessons of 2 September, 31 B.C.E. In the history of naval warfare, Actium surely ranks high among those conflicts of immeasurably great import that were not followed for quite some time by any further battles at sea of any significance or repute.

Endnotes

Preface and Acknowledgments

1 Cf. the excellent survey of R. Allston, *Death of the Republic & Birth of the Empire*, Oxford, 2015, with a chapter on Antony and Cleopatra.

Introduction

1 For a detailed consideration of the life of Agrippa, see now L. Powell, *Marcus Agrippa: Right-hand Man of Caesar Augustus*, South Yorkshire: Pen & Sword Military, 2015. Powell provides a detailed appraisal of the battle in his Chapter 4, 'Mastermind of the Victory at Actium,' 75-99.

2 Actium and Alexandria would receive separate triumphs in the summer of 29 B.C.E. (13-15 August, with Dalmatia first) – Alexandria was, after all, the occasion of the death of the greatest public enemy of the Augustan regime.

3 A note on Roman names. The 'first' name of a Roman man was his *praenomen*, literally in Latin the 'name in front.' There was a rather limited repertoire of such names – perhaps eighteen in fact, of which a few were fairly rare. The name that mattered more was the family name or simply *nomen* (i.e., 'name'), which was the appellation of the individual's *gens* or clan. So Gaius was 'Caesar's' *praenomen* or personal, first name – and Julius was the name of his clan – the Julian that marked its descent from Iulus, the son of Aeneas and grandson of Venus. Some – though by no means all – had a third name, the so-called *cognomen*, a name that originated as the nominal defining quality or characteristic of a given person. The poet, Publius Ovidius Naso for example, likely had an ancestor with a prominent nose. Some men had yet another name, which could technically be called an *agnomen* (literally, 'add-on' or additional 'name'), and some such *agnomina* were the result of the particularly greatest accomplishments of famous men of war (*Africanus* or *Germanicus*, for example). In theory a man could be referred to by any of these names, though usually someone named Gaius Julius Caesar would be named by the name that in theory mattered the most – his *nomen* (thus 'Caesar'). The name *Octavian* that is commonly applied to Caesar's heir comes the adoption practice of using an adjectival form of the *nomen* to distinguish the identity of someone post-inheritance. Conceivably, of course, someone who wanted to emphasize the act of adoption might not want to use an adjectival form that highlighted the *original* family line; hence when our

sources refer to 'Octavian' as 'Caesar,' they are in fact using the name that was both his legally and by personal preference – in fact only those who personally disliked or wished to insult him would have called him 'Octavian.' We can note here, too, that the original Latin alphabet did not distinguish between the letters 'C' and 'G' (cf. the third letter of the Latin alphabet and the third of the Greek, gamma or 'G') – and so both Gaius and Caius would be more or less correct – and the abbreviation 'C' was always retained (Romans were inveterate traditionalists). An additional problem for 'Octavian' is the awarding of the title 'Augustus' in 27 B.C.E. Adrian Goldsworthy observes well that '… using the name Octavian gives a posthumous victory to Mark Antony' – I can only plead for indulgence for my own choice to follow 'convention' in the matter of referring to the man I consider the hero of our story with a name he would have detested.

4 Cf. Suetonius, *Vita Augusti* 3.1.

5 Caesarion was born in 47 B.C.E.; it seems that he was referred to as 'Ptolemy Caesar' in Egypt – a hazardous title, as it would be. We cannot be certain of Caesar's paternity, though there is no good reason at all to doubt it; the son of the great military and political mastermind would not live long enough to make any real mark on history.

6 In his life of Antony, Plutarch introduces Octavian in the aftermath of the assassination of Caesar simply as the heir to the property (16.1); Octavian is depicted as being quick to remind Antony of his obligations with respect to Caesar's money. As Suetonius notes in his Augustan life (7.2), he received the name of Caesar in accord with the provisions of Caesar's will; Antony is said to have insulted him with the name 'Thurinus' later in life, with the new Caesar responding that it seemed strange that he should be attacked for what had, after all, been his name – a calm response in the face of Antony's attempt to provoke him. Augustus would come later, apparently in lieu of a suggestion that Romulus would be appropriate. On Caesar see especially Adrian Goldsworthy's *Caesar: Life of a Colossus* (New Haven, Connecticut: Yale University Press, 2006), the first volume in his trilogy on Caesar, Antony/Cleopatra, and Augustus.

7 Caesar had helped to make sure that her brother Ptolemy would be no threat to her; what Caesar started with what sibling, Antony finished with the death of his lover's sister Arsinoe.

8 As Adrian Goldsworthy rightly observes in his *Augustus: First Emperor of Rome* (New Haven, Connecticut: Yale University Press, 2014, 187), no ancient evidence survives to assert the claim that the Antonian will was a forgery, and there is no reason to believe that it was.

9 We know very little about Roman warships, relatively speaking; a good introduction to the subject may be found in Adrian Goldsworthy's *The Complete Roman Army* (London: Thames & Hudson Ltd., 2003), 34 ff. Goldsworthy notes that ancient warships were packed with men relative to the size of the vessel, all so that as soon as possible a naval battle could be transformed into a ground engagement. The whole enterprise was incredibly risky given the likelihood that both ships in a clash would

be seriously damaged in the fighting. Ships had very little room for carrying even such essentials as potable water, so that those vessels that carried treasure and other riches on the day of Actium must have had a significantly smaller complement of men. There is a surviving brazen prow from a vessel that was located off Actium; 'The medallion bust has damage to the breasts of the female figure, and the sides of the prow are torn…From a tondo at the tip of the prow emerges a bust of a figure wearing a helmet and an aegis strapped under the arms and over the shoulders. Both the sex and the identity of the subject are unclear, but it is usually thought to be female and either Athena or Roma… It has always been assumed that the prow comes from a sunken ship that participated in the battle of Actium. Its date is perhaps applicable, but there are few prows to compare with it.' (S. Walker and P. Higgs, eds., *Cleopatra of Egypt: From History to Myth*, Princeton, 2001, 264-265). The prow is preserved in the British Museum.

10 Upon his very return to Italy after his victories in the East, Octavian was apparently ill before he could even return to Rome for his triple triumph.

11 A useful brief study here is Kenneth Scott's 'Octavian's Propaganda and Antony's *De Sua Ebrietate*,' in *Classical Philology* 24.2 (1929), 133-141. Scott considers the rival propaganda of how Octavian was accused of playing Apollo, and Antony Dionysus, and the place of Dionysian comparisons in the Roman political settlement of the East. For the propaganda of the Antonian side, see M. Charlesworth, 'Some Fragments of the Propaganda of Mark Antony,' in *The Classical Quarterly* 27.3/4 (1933), 172-177. The main targets of Antony's pen seem to have been Octavian's less than impressive family lineage, and the question of his cowardice; there were also accusations of immorality, though this would have been the standard fare of any invective. Charlesworth concludes about these fragments of propaganda that 'Examination of them reveals that many charges often accepted as gospel-true about Octavian – *e.g.* the immorality of his early years, or his personal cowardice – or statements regarded as historical fact – *e.g.* the betrothal of Iulia to the Dacian Cotiso – have no surer foundation than the allegations of Antony and his supporters, and cannot be accepted. But the influence of this propaganda was tremendous and it has survived Antony's defeat and death … and finally a glance at *Annals*, I.10, where the principate and person of Augustus are damned, will show how deep an effect this and other propaganda exerted upon Tacitus, and through Tacitus upon the world.' Charlesworth's general conclusion is a good corrective for the oft-held view that the effective propaganda of the last of the republican civil wars only went in one direction.

12 See here John F. Miller's magisterial *Apollo, Augustus, and the Poets* (Oxford, 2011).

13 The bibliography on the battle is extensive, and the notes will make frequent reference to various works. One of the most influential works is the study of J. Kromayer, 'Kleine Forschungen zur Geschichte des zweiten Triumvirats VII: der Feldzug von Actium und der sogenannte Verrath der Cleopatra,' in *Hermes* 34 (1899), 1-54. Kromayer argued that the entire point of the Antonian and Cleopatran strategy at Actium was flight. Anglophone readers are likeliest to consult J. M. Carter's excellent *The Battle of Actium: The Rise and Triumph of Augustus Caesar* (London,

1970), which more or less follows in the steps of Kromayer. Carter's volume provides a good background to the conflict; in effect it is a history of the period of transition from the Republic to the Empire rather than a specialized study of Actium. The famous article of W.W. Tarn in *The Journal of Roman Studies* (21, 1931, 173-199), 'The Battle of Actium,' argued that the most important event during the battle was the defection of much of Antony's fleet. Kromayer's thesis (as distilled through Carter) is accepted by Eleanor Huzar in her *Mark Antony: A Biography*, Minnesota, 1978. Sheppard's 2009 Osprey title in their campaigns series (cf. the bibliography) devotes about a third of its space to the events leading up to Actium; most of the conclusions about the motivation of Antony and Cleopatra with Kromayer. Better for a good overview (with copious citation of the surviving evidence) is Robert Sandmann's *Die Schlacht von Actium – Vorbereitungen – Ablauf – Ergebnisse der entscheidenden Auseinandersetzung zwischen Octavian und Marcus Antonius* (Examensarbeit), Norderstedt: GRIN Verlag, 2007.

Chapter 1 The Evidence of Plutarch

1 There is a convenient volume of all the major sources in translation by Prudence Jones: *Cleopatra: A Sourcebook*, Norman: The University of Oklahoma Press, 2006.
2 There is a University of Victoria master's thesis by David Anthony Smulders, 'Poetic Responses to the Battle of Actium: A Study of Horace, Vergil, and Propertius' (1992).
3 The most useful edition of the life is the Cambridge 'green and yellow' of Christopher Pelling (*Plutarch: Life of Antony*, Cambridge, 1989, reprinted 1994), which offers a fine introduction both to Plutarch and to Antony, as well as an annotated edition of the Greek text. Pelling has also revised and updated the Penguin Classics translation of *Antony* by Ian Scott-Kilvert (*Makers of Rome*, 1965), as part of a new Penguin Plutarch project (*Rome in Crisis*, 2010), with significantly expanded notes and introductions. The Loeb edition of Bernadotte Perrin (Cambridge, Massachusetts: Harvard University Press, 1920) is convenient, especially for those with some Greek. The standard Greek text is that of Konrat Ziegler in the Teubner series (Volume III, Fascicle I of the *Vitae Parallelae*).
4 Elsewhere in surviving Plutarch there is but one stray reference to Actium at *Moralia* 322B, where the author notes how the gates of the temple of Janus were closed after the victory.
5 Dio Cassius 50.1.2.
6 This king is listed by Plutarch among those who were not actually present before the battle; see further Pelling's note *ad loc.*
7 62.1. The problem of the question of fighting at sea is arguably the most important in Actian analysis.
8 Plutarch comments on both the need to impress sailors for service on the 500-odd vessels, and the fact that even after the naval draft, the crews were both insufficient and undertrained. We have no idea what the practice was in terms of staffing

Egyptian vessels, but the Roman practice was to use the freeborn (even of foreigners or *peregrini*); we cannot be certain how exactly locals may have been pressed into service. In general, for much of Roman history regular service on board ship was considered distinctly inferior to tenure in the legions; in some respects Agrippa and the victories over first Sextus Pompey and then Antony and Cleopatra made naval warfare more honoured than it had been for some time; a sea battle would be the defining hour of the Augustan military triumph and establishment of order in the Mediterranean.

9 Plutarch makes clear that Octavian's ships were both better manned and more manoeuvreable given their smaller size.

10 Though in this case, arguably it would be Antony in the place of Pompey, and Octavian in that of his adoptive father Caesar.

11 A classic situation, then, of naval defence *versus* naval offence; the defender can hope to extract a tremendous toll from the attacker, but the patient attacker can wear down the enemy by delay in much the way a town or city can be put under effective siege. Time was not on the side of either man at Actium, but if it favoured anyone, it was Octavian.

12 1.29.

13 The most helpful map of the relevant sites is to be found on page 54 of Richard Talbert's monumental *Barrington Atlas of the Greek and Roman World* (Princeton, 2000).

14 'Torune' is Greek for a 'stirrer' or 'ladle,' and seems to have been a slang word for the *membrum virile*. The joke – if true – may illustrate Cleopatra's lowbrow, bawdy sense of humour (cf. Plutarch's observation at 27.1 that Cleopatra saw in Antony the classic common soldier and man of the street, a persona that she adopted when she dealt with him – attractively mimicking his own manner and presenting herself to him as one like him) – and certainly something of her knowledge of Greek *double entendres*, perhaps with a hint of arrogance. Certainly Octavian's presence in Torune should have been a source of concern; on the other hand, one can be concerned and still resort to humour. Shakespeare's Cleopatra is rather different here; Antony observes that it seems strange that Octavian could have crossed the sea so quickly – and the queen retorts that 'Celerity is never more admired than by the negligent' (Antony later expressed surprise and disbelief when a messenger arrives with the news that Octavian really is at Torune). Shakespeare's Scarus soon enough has the unforgettable description of how Cleopatra – the *nag of Egypt* – left the battle, *the breeze upon her, like a cow in June*.

15 63.1.

16 63.5.

17 63.5.

18 Recall that Canidius however, was more than willing to accept lavish bribes from Cleopatra to agree to argue her case with Antony (Plutarch, *Vita Ant.* 56.2). Plutarch makes clear that that period was one of both lavish celebration as well as jealous political manoeuvring in the matter of Cleopatra's rivalry with Octavia

(the description of the queen's jealousy at how the Athenians honoured Octavia is especially petty); we may well smile wearily at the anonymous observation the biographer records that someone asked how the victory would be celebrated, if so much revelry and extravagant spending marked the mere preparation.

19 In other words, the opposite of Cleopatra's advice. It may well be that the queen's strategy was sounder, but that she was hardly in a position to sway the Roman officer corps and rank and file.

20 63.8.

21 This may well explain why the queen would not have taken Canidius' advice, if indeed she were intent on departure; there may also have been a fair amount of arrogance on her part and contemptuous resentment of Canidius. One imagines that most of Antony's officer corps had problems with the queen, especially when she tried to take a leading role in military debates.

22 Trickery and deceit are also central to the narrative of Virgil's eleventh *Aeneid*, the book of his epic in which, as we shall see, the Battle of Actium is allegorized; Turnus prepares an ambush for Aeneas that fails to come to fruition.

23 64.1. The Greek here offers a number of possible interpretations (on which see Pelling *ad loc.*). Cleopatra had provided Antony with 200 ships (56.2), but it remains unclear exactly which vessels were set on fire. The consensus of the evidence is that she fled the battle with some 60 vessels – in which case 140 would have been burned.

24 A reasonable enough precaution, even if the story has led many to believe that Antony was also contemplating flight – let alone the question of whether the entire point of the operation was a breakout from the blockaded gulf.

25 It seems that it was Gaius Sosius; cf. Pelling's note here *ad loc.*; it is a reminder of the difficulty of interpreting our sources to have such a major detail be in dispute and error.

26 It was Lucius Arruntius; 66.5.

27 65.5.

28 A stade was approximately 600 'Greek' feet.

29 66.1-2.

30 66.3.

31 66.5.

32 We shall see a parallel to this in the decision of Virgil's Turnus to abandon his battle plans after the death of Camilla at the hands of Arruns – a decision that arguably costs him the war.

33 67.1.

34 Apparently a pirate or brigand of some sort who had been decapitated on Antony's orders; see further Pelling *ad* 67.2-3.

35 No doubt with ominous implications as Plutarch rounds off his Actian narrative.

36 68.1.

37 Cf. Pelling *ad* 68.1.

38 68.2.

39 The nineteen legions were the land forces that were not involved in the shipboard combat (the four less fortune legions, we might argue); if we can trust Appian (5.167), Octavian had a total of forty-five legions, of which perhaps a bit more than half were available for the Actian campaign. Dessau's collection of selected Latin inscriptions (*ILS* 2443) is our source for how *Actiacus* was awarded as an agnomen to one Marcus Billienus, who had served under Octavian at Actium. For the evidence (numismatic and other) for the legions on both sides, see N. Fields, *The Roman Army: The Civil Wars, 88-31 B.C.*, Oxford: Osprey Publishing Ltd., 2008, 60.

40 6.1.

41 Cf. the appraisal of Dio (51.15.2 ff.), where Antony is noted for brave, audacious daring and cowardice, as well as a combination of both greatness and the willingness and ability to be a slave to others. He is a picture of contradiction, capable of both mercy and cruelty.

42 One might also consider that the end of Plutarch's *Life of Antony* gives a brief genealogical record of the descendants of Antony and the fortunes of his family; the concluding note is of how Claudius ended up adopting the son of Agrippina, to whom he gave the name Nero. Plutarch observes that Nero was emperor in his own day, and that he murdered his mother and nearly destroyed the Roman Empire by his insanity. As Bernadotte Perrin translates the final words of the life, 'He was the fifth in descent from Antony' – a clear enough final insult against the ill-fated triumvir, who was damnable even in his more distant descendants.

Chapter 2: The Lost Appian

1 Volumes 2-5 of the Loeb Classical Library contain the complete surviving Appian; there is a Penguin by John Carter (1996) that contains the *Civil War* books (with brief notes).

Chapter 3: The Evidence of Dio Cassius

1 120 C.E.

2 The most convenient edition is probably the Loeb Classical Library edition in seven volumes; the French Budé series has an ongoing edition with accompanying annotations. There is a 1987 Penguin Classics edition of *The Roman History: The Reign of Augustus* by Ian Scott-Kilvert (introduction by John Carter), which contains the Actian material. Cf. also Peter Michael Swan's *The Augustan Succession: An Historical Commentary on Cassius Dio's Roman History, Books 55-56* (Oxford, 2004), with an especially rich and helpful introduction. Fergus Millar's classic *A Study of Cassius Dio* (Oxford, 1964) is an excellent introduction to a sometimes underappreciated historical source.

3 50.3.1-2.

4 A recurring theme in our sources; Plutarch gives the specific detail that they had been opposed to Cleopatra's accompaniment of Antony's expedition to Greece.

5 50.7.2-3.

6 50.8.1-2.

7 We may be reminded of the tradition of the *lusus Troiae* or 'game of Troy', in which young men re-enacted the fall of the great city.

8 60.9.1 ff.

9 The scene points both to Antony's perceived wish to take the crown of Caesar, as it were (complete with Cleopatra and Caesarion), and to Antony's fondness for the world of Dionysius, the theatre, and mimes.

10 We shall return to this portent below as part of our consideration of the evidence of Virgil.

11 50.11.1.

12 W.W. Tarn argued that 'Pictures of Antony meeting Octavian at the head of a motley half-Asiastic army do not belong to history' ('Antony's Legions,' in *The Classical Quarterly* 26.2 (1932), 75-81). But in truth we have no clear sense of how many foreigners were in service as rowers in Antony's fleet, and good reason to believe that Octavian's crews were more Italian than not – and Octavian had no foreign contingent plunging through the midst of the battle lines.

13 50.12.1-2.

14 50.13.4-5.

15 The latter with detail about his apparent dislike of Cleopatra.

16 By whom or what is not specified.

17 50.14.1-2.

18 But he appears later even in Dio's narrative, let alone Plutarch's account of Actium.

19 See, e.g., Michael Grant's account at 206-207 of his *Cleopatra: A Biography*, New York: Simon and Schuster, 1972. One cannot be certain of the exact referent of Horace's poetic claims about Antony's losses. Grant believes that Antony had no realistic chance of success in a naval battle, and that at most he could dream of a successful escape for a sizable portion of his fleet. 'Moreover, even now, in spite of desertions, he still had great regions of the wealthy east to fall back upon' (208).

20 Carsten Hjort Lange notes in his article 'The Battle of Actium: A Reconsideration' (*The Classical Quarterly*, N.S. 61.2, 2011, 608-623) that despite this apparent plan, when the moment of flight actually comes, the fleeing is marked by panic, not by any sort of calm intention to carry out a prearranged plan. One could of course be panicked by the unfolding of events (which in a naval battle would always be especially unpredictable), but the detail is important to note. Grant argues (211) that a significant problem for Antony was that once *he* departed, he had hoped that his other capital warships would follow his example and chase after him (as he had pursued Cleopatra). This would seem to be have been an incredible expectation had he not told many if any captains of his plans.

21 Dio notes that death and desertion had reduced their crews appreciably.

22 When we consider Virgil's allegorized version of Actium in *Aeneid* 11, we shall find that the cavalry battle there is also something of a ruse, a diversion intended on the one hand to provide cover for Aeneas' planned assault on the Latin capital, and on the other a response to the leaked news of the Trojan plan.

23 Cf. especially 50.18.2-3.

24 50.23.1.

25 50.29.1-2.

26 They would realize, after all, that their leaders had intended more or less to abandon them.

27 In contrast to Antony's fear of mutiny from the leading men he took with him.

28 50.31.5-6.

29 50.31.7. The comparison to a cavalry battle is perhaps natural enough, though we might note that Virgil seems have recreated the engagement at Actium in a description of a *proelium equestre*. Dio's description of attack and retreat is exactly how Virgil describes the cavalry engagement in *Aeneid* 11 (it is a typical enough manoeuvre in such a battle); one wonders how difficult this would have been given conditions of wind and sail.

30 Surely one of the most significant winds in history.

31 50.34.1.

32 50.35.4.

33 William Ledyard Rodgers concluded that 'With soldiers of the same nation, accustomed to the same method of fighting and with the same fleet organization, it was the unexpected weapon, the flames, which decided the victory in Agrippa's favour. By four in the afternoon the battle was finished and the remains of Antony's fleet escaped and entered the harbour before a fresh breeze.' (*op. cit.*, 534). Rodgers – who we should remember was a navy man of some experience – agrees with the contention that Kromayer's thesis could not be correct 'that the battle was purely a measure for escape'.

34 Diana Preston makes the good observation that 'While the conditions that day were not recorded, by noon at that time of year the temperature can easily exceed 90° Fahrenheit (33° Celsius) and the difference in the temperature of the air over the sea produces an onshore breeze that starts to rise at about this time and strengthens as the afternoon wears on' (*Cleopatra and Antony: Power, Love, and Politics in the Ancient World*, New York: Walker Publishing Company, Inc., 2009, 254). The situation must have become increasingly uncomfortable in the tight quarters of the vessels, especially if there were a slow process of assembly of the warships through the tight mouth of the harbour mouth.

Chapter 4: Strabo's Geography

1 There is an eight-volume Loeb Classical Library edition of the entire work, with lavish cartographical aids.

2   8.4.3.

3   On the controversial question of whether or not Antony and Cleopatra had some sort of marriage ceremony in Egypt, see S. Ager, 'Marriage or Mirage? The Phantom Wedding of Cleopatra and Antony,' in *Classical Philology* 108.2 (2013), 139-155. Ager is correct that no ancient evidence survives to attest to any such actual ceremony; clearly enough they were living in what some today would call a 'common law' marriage, and in the end, the question of whether or not there was a ceremony (which would have been according to Egyptian rites) may be immaterial to the final outcome: Antony fled a battle (and many Roman legionaries) in pursuit of the queen with whom he had willingly taken up arms against another Roman. Octavian could not have written a better script. We might note that the often adduced letter of Antony to Octavian (preserved in Suetonius' life of Augustus at 69.2, where Antony either states that Cleopatra is his wife, or (with interrogative mark) rhetorically asks a question that expects the answer 'no', is probably to be considered in light of Roman marital law – in other words, Antony could not marry Cleopatra under the *ius* or law of the Romans, and therefore the question of his nuptial status is simply answered – he is not married. I would agree in general with Ager's conclusions, though I would hold that even if Antony denied that he could be held liable for *affectio maritalis*, there would still be more than enough for Octavian to use against him in propaganda (indeed, as Ager concludes, '... very little prevented Octavian from accusing Antony of anything.' In any case, while we may not have any definitive evidence of a wedding, we also have far less evidence than we would like about arguably weighty matters – and what mattered in the end was that it was all too easy to depict the relationship in a negative light to a Roman audience, and this is exactly what happened.

4   Though historical events are of great interest and concern to him. The evidence of the Elder Seneca (*Suasoriae* 1.6-7) is interesting; there we find a reference to an insult written on the base of a statue that mocks Antony for bigamy, complete with reference to the Roman divorce formula (*res tuas tibi habe*, 'take your things with you'). Susan Treggiari does not consider the question in her monumental study of Roman nuptials, but she does address the fact that after the death of Antony and Cleopatra, it was Octavia (the repudiated wife) who took in their children (*Roman Marriage: Iusti Coniuges from the Time of Cicero to the Time of Ulpian*, Oxford, 1991, 468-469).

5   With no particular note that it was the queen who fled first.

Chapter 5: The Evidence of Josephus

1   The Loeb Classical Library has a thirteen-volume set that includes both of the major works as well as the *Vita* and the *Contra Apionem*, with the usual complete Greek and facing English translation format of the series.

2   2.59.

3   1.364, 370.

4 1.386, 388.
5 Cf. *Jewish Antiquities* 18.26, where Josephus dates the census of Quirinius from the date of Actium.
6 15.109, 121, 161-162, 190-193. The evident detestation of Herod for Cleopatra drips through the pages of Josephus' work.
7 16.147.
8 On Nicolaus (especially his relationship to Josephus), see Ben Zion Wacholder, 'Josephus and Nicolaus of Damascus,' in L. Feldman and G. Hata, eds., *Josephus, the Bible, and History*, Tokyo: Yamamoto Shoten Publishing House, 1988, 147-172.
9 See here the indispensable edition of Edith Parmentier and Francesca Prometea Barone, *Nicolas de Damas. Histoires; Recueil de coutumes; Vie d'Auguste; Autobiographie; Fragments*. Paris: Les Belles Lettres, 2011. This masterful edition has a detailed introduction, a reprint of the edition of the *testimonia* and fragments from Felix Jacoby's *Fragmente der griechischen Historiker* (no. 90, vol. II, 324-430), French translation and extensive notes. The longest surviving fragment of the Augustan life concerns the assassination of Caesar and the aftermath; it is, in fact, a priceless source of information about the period.

Chapter 6: Velleius Paterculus

1 The claim that he was killed in the aftermath of the fall of Sejanus is a speculation without sound evidentiary backing; the truth is that we have no real knowledge of what happened to the author of the compendium.
2 This Vinicius' grandfather was a friend of Augustus and suffect consul in 19 B.C.E.; his father Publius was consul in 2 C.E. The name was appropriated for the hero of Henryk Sienkiewicz's *Quo Vadis*.
3 Here the two *Cambridge Classical Texts and Commentaries* volumes of A.J. Woodman are essential for detailed commentary: *The Tiberian Narrative (2.94-131)* and *The Caesarian and Augustan Narrative (2.41-93)* (1977 and 1983 respectively). There is a Loeb edition that combines Velleius with the *Res Gestae Divi Augusti*.
4 2.82.3 ff.
5 We shall return to some of this imagery in our consideration of the evidence of Virgil's *Aeneid* 11.
6 2.84.1.
7 Domitius Ahenobarbus is given the special credit for being the only Antonian courtier who refused to greet Cleopatra except by name – somehow a fittingly Roman way to treat Egypt's queen.
8 Velleius' account is reasonably tolerably in agreement.
9 The only clear evidence for having Arruntius on the left is Velleius; a reading of Plutarch alone would lead one to think he was in the centre, though it is strange, as we have seen, that the biographer does not seem to have made this entirely clear at 65.2. Cornell's edition of the fragments of the Roman historians takes it as certain

that he was on the left (siding with Velleius); the mention of the Arruntius of the
proscriptions in Appian does not offer any indication of what the man did at Actium.
Cornell rightly notes that Arruntius was, in any case, a well qualified man to compose
a history of the First Punic War; he had naval experience both under Sextus Pompey
and Octavian – and for all we know, he was truly a key player at Actium. We have no
idea when Arruntius' historical work was lost; Cornell speculates that it may have
suffered from the obvious popularity of Livy.

10 2.85.3 *Prima occupant fugam Cleopatra. Antonius fugientis reginae quam pugnantis
militis sui comes esse maluit* …

11 2.85.6 … *qui ad eius arbitrium direxerit fugam*, where *arbitrium* recalls the same word
used of Agrippa's command over the marine battlefield.

12 Indeed, at the end of his narrative of the civil wars Velleius composes a rousing
veritable panegyric to Octavian Augustus: *nihil deinde optare a dis homines, nihil
dii hominibus praestare possunt, nihil voto concipi, nihil felicitate consummari, quod
non Augustus post reditum in urbem rei publicae populoque Romano terrarumque
orbi repraensentavit* (2.89.1-2). For Velleius, the return of Octavian after the wars
was nothing less than the restoration of the old form of the Republic: *prisca illa et
antiqua rei publicae forma revocata*, 'that ancient and old form of the Republic was
called back'. This is propaganda at its finest, but it may well reflect the sentiments
of many in Italy – though not all; just before this laudation of Augustus, Velleius
narrates the nefarious plans of Marcus Lepidus that were suppressed by none other
than Maecenas (acting as not only Octavian's literary agent, but also his manager
for maintaining urban order in Rome). And there would be other crises in the years
to come – but not all that many, or of that great a level of severity, when one matches
them against four decades of largely stable Augustan rule.

Chapter 7: Lost Roman Sources

1 We know from the so-called Oxyrhynchus Summary where Actium would have
been narrated; the only fragment that survives is a citation from a commentary on
the poet Horace that when Cleopatra was being held captive by Octavian and was
being treated well, she noted that she would not be led in triumph – an interesting
comment to which we shall return.

2 1.19.3.

3 And as for Tacitus, the other 'great' Roman historian, there is but one mention of
Actium (*Historiae* 1.1.5 *postquam bellatum apud Actium atque omnem potentiam unum
conferri pacis interfuit*). Interestingly, Tacitus dates the decline of Roman noteworthy
historical composition to the period just after Actium; for Tacitus, Actium was the
beginning of the empire and the dawn of a system on which he would offer historical
commentary and reflection. Tacitus appears never to have turned to his planned work
on Augustus.

4 Servius' commentary on Virgil's *Georgics* 2.162 cites the *vita* composed by Agrippa; on this and the remaining fragmentary sources noted in this chapter, see the three volumes of *The Fragments of the Roman Historians* (Oxford, 2013) under the general editorship of T.J. Cornell (with extensive introductions, texts, translations, and exhaustive commentaries). There are no convenient smaller scale editions of these works.

5 What we have fills fourteen Loeb volumes (and includes the epitomes and the like); Jane D. Chaplin edited the Oxford World's Classics Livy of Books 41-45 and the so-called *Periochae* or summaries (*Livy: Rome's Mediterranean Empire*, Oxford, 2007).

6 *Epistulae* 114.17-19.

7 Strabo 11.523.

8 *Suasoriae* 1.7.

9 The appellation is credited to Marcus Valerius Messalla Corvinus.

10 *Antony* 59.6-8.

11 Cf. *Vita Bruti* 40.11; Appian also attests to his command.

12 The honourable detail is preserved by Velleius (2.86.3).

13 Tacitus, *Annales* 4.34.1; cf. Suetonius, *Tiberius* 61.3.

14 *Claudius* 41.1-3.

15 42.2. On Claudius' literary and historical works, see especially Donna Hurley's Cambridge edition of *Suetonius: Divus Claudius* (2001). Claudius was the scholarly one of the Julio-Claudian *principes*; unfortunately we have next to no sense of the style and manner he would have displayed in his historical writings.

16 *Naturalis Historia, Praef.* 20.

17 *Suasoriae* 6.18, 23.

Chapter 8: Octavian Himself

1 85.1.

2 *Antony* 68.1-2.

3 There is a convenient edition by P.A. Brunt and J. M. Moore (*Res Gestae Divi Augusti: The Achievements of the Divine Augustus*, Oxford, 1967) with Latin text, translation and notes; note also Alison Cooley's text, translation, and commentary for Cambridge (2009). The standard scholarly edition now is likely John Scheid's 2007 Budé edition (with extensive French commentary). The Loeb edition conjoins the *Res Gestae* with the histories of Velleius Paterculus.

4 3.4; half from Sextus Pompey, and half at Actium. Plutarch cites Augustus' autobiography for his mention of this figure.

5 Smith and Powell have produced an edited volume (see the bibliography) that provides the best available guide to the likely antecedents of the work (cf. the memoirs of Sulla), and the purpose of the work in the context of the transition to the principate. With Smith and Powell cf. John Henderson's characteristically lively review at *Bryn Mawr Classical Review* 2010.05.23.

6 There is a revised Loeb edition in two volumes, and both Penguin Classics and Oxford World's Classics translations. The *Augustus* has been served with a major commentary by David Wardle (Cambridge, 2014), with extensive notes with a particular focus on matters historical; Michael Adams' 1939 'Macmillan Red' edition of the life offers valuable commentary as well. There is also a lengthy French commentary in the *Collection Latomus* series (*Commentaire historique et traduction du Divus Augustus de Suétone*, Bruxelles, 2010) by Nathalie Louis, on which the Bryn Mawr review of David Wardle (2011.11.12) is essential supplement.

7 17.2.

8 Suetonius also notes the establishment of the quinquennial memorial games at Nicopolis (18.2) and the story of the man with the ass before the battle (96.2).

9 *Epode* 9.35-36.

Chapter 9: Florus' and Eutropius' Detached Accounts

1 The Loeb edition of 1929 was published with the work of Cornelius Nepos; it was released separately in 1984.

2 ... *captus amore Cleopatrae quasi bene gestis in regio se sinu reficiebat*, where *rebus gestis* certainly recalls the opening words of Augustus' *Res Gestae*.

3 The apparent limit in size for the warships in question would have been three banks of oars; the differences in size were accounted for by the number of men who were stationed at each oar. Of course the more rowers the ship had, the greater the size of the vessel would have needed to be to accommodate the larger crew. There is no way to know for certain how the men were arranged, or what configurations may have been established for the different sizes.

4 The purple for the sails is also mentioned by Pliny, *Historia Naturalis* 19.22.1, when he notes the origin of the custom of tinting sails purple from the time of Alexander's navigation of the Indus; Pliny observes that Cleopatra arrived at Actium in purple, and fled with the same colour. The colour was inextricably associated with high office; in the case of the flight of the queen, part of the point was to appear to her subjects as if she were returning in victory to the harbour of Alexandria; there would have been an eager watch for what had happened in the wake of the grand campaign, and the omnipresent threat of rebellion and mutiny.

5 Cf. Plutarch, *Antony* 89.

6 The best available edition is probably the Budé by Joseph Hellegouarc'h, with generous notes and introduction in addition to the text and a French translation (Les Belles Lettres, 1999); there is an English version by H.W. Bird (Liverpool, 1993), with introduction and commentary.

7 Cornelius Gallus is a mysterious figure in the history of the early years of Octavian's power. We are not sure of his birth year; it may have been around 70 or 69 B.C.E. – he was thus a bit older than Octavian. He was clearly a key player in the settlement of Egypt after Actium; he served as its first *praefectus* or 'prefect' – obviously a position

of great trust and power. He suffered a fall from power that led to his suicide in around 27 or 26 B.C.E.; the circumstances of his disgrace are not entirely well known. He is of great significance to students of Augustan poetry, given that he was an elegist and the composer of some four books of *Amores* (at least we think this might have been the title). Gallus' work – or, more accurately, what pitifully remains of it – can be accessed in Adrian Hollis' *Fragments of Roman Poetry, c. 60 B.C.-A.D. 20*, Oxford, 2007, 219-252). Ovid states (*Tristia* 2.445-446) that the criticism against Gallus was not that he loved Lycoris (who had been a mistress of Antony), but that he could not keep his mouth shut after too much wine. Tourists to Saint Peter's Square in the Vatican might care to know that the obelisk in front of the basilica originally carried an inscription of Gallus that commemorated his foundation of an Alexandrian forum. Most all we know of the poet's actual writing comes from nine mutilated verses that were discovered in 1978 on an Egyptian papyrus; they speak of both the poet's *amour* Lycoris and the question of praise of Augustus and the offerings of spoils from his achievements that will decorate the temples of gods. If the account in Book 53 of Dio can be believed, Gallus was a rather foolish man, given to self-praise and extravagant works of self-aggrandizement and promotion – and a man who could not be trusted to refrain from frank criticism of the *princeps*. Suetonius (*Vita Augusti* 66.1-2) argues that Gallus was one of those figures who was raised from quite humble beginnings to the heights of power – and that Egypt's first prefect was decidedly ungrateful for the favours Augustus had shown him. Hollis' edition provides extensive commentary on the surviving *testimonia* and verses, with consideration of the minority view that the 1978 papyrus should not be credited to Gallus (and the more extreme view that it is a forgery). Absent new evidence it is impossible to do much more than speculate on Gallus; clearly he was a trusted member of Octavian's inner circle at the time of Cleopatra's final defeat.

Chapter 10: The evidence of Orosius

1 The Budé edition in three volumes by Marie-Pierre Arnaud-Lindet offers the most convenient text, with French translation and brief notes; there is no Loeb or Penguin version.

2 Cf. the Oxford monograph of Peter Van Nuffelen, *Orosius and the Rhetoric of History* (2012), which offers an engaging study of the today relatively unknown work.

3 6.19.6.

4 Again, just possibly with a pun on the title of Augustus' celebrated monument, though the Latin ablative absolute is conventional enough.

5 Improbably high casualty figures.

6 *Prior* of Cleopatra refers, nonetheless, to Cleopatra relative to Antony – she did, after all, flee before her husband – but should not be pressed too far with reference to the actual progress of the campaign.

7 That is, founded in something other than a mere desire to have an ostentatious fleet.

8 Admittedly, a casualty of the rise of naval air power – but the vivid ancient narratives of Octavian's rapid strikes on Antony's fleet carry something of the spirit of the air attacks on huge and vulnerable naval targets of a later age.

9 For those who would doubt the ability of a fish to halt a ship, we may note the remarks of E.W. Gudger: 'On this matter one of the most experienced fisherman at Key West, Florida, once gave an interesting story to me. We were trying to catch an *Echeneis naucrates*...and I spoke of this matter of retardation of the shark or a boat's speed by an attached sucking-fish and said that it seemed hardly possible. Then this man earnestly said: They sure will hold a boat. I have seen ten or twelve under a boat at one time...All Key West fishermen know that suckers will sure hold a boat.' ('Some Old Time Figures of the Shipholder, Echeneis or Remora,' in *Isis* 13.2 (1930), 340-352). We have no way verifying the likelihood of Pliny's account, but it adds an interesting detail that may explain something of Antony's actions.

Chapter 11: The Shield of Aeneas

1 Cf., e.g., S. Schiff in her *Cleopatra: A Life* (New York-Boston-London: Little, Brown and Company, 2010): 'The years after Actium were a time of extravagant praise and lavish mythmaking. Her career also coincided with the birth of Latin literature; it was Cleopatra's curse to inspire its great poets, happy to expound on her shame, in a language inhospitable to her and all she represented. Horace wrote exuberantly of Actium. The first to celebrate Octavian's splendid victory, he did so while Cleopatra was still frantically fortifying Alexandria. He celebrates her defeat before it has occurred.' Jack Lindsay comments memorably on Virgil: 'The poets give us some idea of the bogey that had been summoned up of Cleopatra the whore-witch with her eastern hordes' (*Cleopatra*, London, Constable & Company Ltd., 1970, 405).

2 *Hist.* 2.31-33; cf. the fragments of Book 40 of Diodorus' universal history that are collected in Volume 12 of the Loeb Diodorus.

3 Frederick Ahl has a translation in the Oxford World's Classics series; there is also a revised Loeb edition by George Goold (with excellent introductory notes and bibliographical guides). The prose Penguin version by David West is reliable. There are numerous commentaries on the poem either in whole or in part, as well as an extensive bibliography that reflects the epic's status as the most popular of the works of Latin literature.

4 The whole sequence is in imitation of the Homeric description of the forging of arms for Achilles by Hephaestus at the behest of his mother Thetis in *Iliad* 18, and become something of a *topos* for epic verse. The greatest of heroes need divine arms; the weaponry is a sign of the favour of the immortals on the accomplishment and fulfillment of the destiny of the hero.

5 1.124 ff. Neptune is compared to a man in a crowd who restores order amid chaos and dispute; the reference of this first simile of Virgil's poem may well be to Octavian/

Augustus. The god of the sea has a vested interest in the maintenance of order in his own realm.

6   The exact order of the images on the shield is more impressionistic than schematic; 'in the middle' refers naturally both to the prominent midpoint of the entire work of art, but also to the midst of the sea.

7   Virgil thus conflates the material of the shield with the imagined majesty of the vessels – again, the description is impressionistic more than not. The shield is cinematic; it tells a virtually living story that comes alive before the viewer – or the implied foe of the hero who wields it. It mesmerizes and dazzles; it brings to life telling scenes and episodes of a history that remains unknown and mysterious to its new, mortal owner.

8   He was also most certainly *not* Augustus on the day of Actium; the scene looks back rather proleptically, not to say anachronistically.

9   8.685 *hinc ope barbarica variisque Antonius armis.*

10 Mayer's commentary *ad loc.* notes that the reference could be taken to refer to a pre-battle burning of the ships, though it seems likelier that the harrowing description is of the flight from battle; Mayer also observes that the exaggeration was noted already by the Horatian scholiast Porphyrio.

11 8.688.

12 Strictly speaking this is not true; certainly Agrippa may have refined what was by the time of Actium an established practice.

13 Oxford, 1930.

14 Cambridge, 1976.

15 Virgil's depiction is especially striking in his having Italy on the one side, in opposition to the combined forces of the East (including its most distant preserves). References in Virgil to the Arabians are particularly interesting in light of how the Arabs were said to have burned Cleopatra's ships after her return to Alexandria.

16 8.696.

17 We might note, too, that Mars is the father of Penthesilea, the Amazon who is reborn, as it were, in the depiction of Camilla in *Aeneid* 11; Camilla is herself an allegorized Cleopatra at Alexandria, and so fittingly Mars and Cleopatra both are in the midst of the battle on the shield, just as Camilla will be said to exult in the midst of war. The Amazons, too, we might note were traditionally localized in Thrace, in the wild northeast of Greece into Macedonia; they had come to the aid of Troy, and just conceivably they could be imagined poetically as coming to aid of those warring in northwestern Greece.

18 On the actual declaration, with particular attention to the potential problem of how to make a civil war into a foreign one, see M. Reinhold, 'The Declaration of War Against Cleopatra,' in *The Classical Journal* 77.2 (1981-1982), 97-103.

19 Note, too, that Neptune is prominent on the so-called Actium Vase (from Capua?) that may date from 30 B.C.E.-25 C.E.; see further Walker and Higgs, *op.cit.*, 266-268. 'The vase was probably used as a cinerary urn and, in spite of its rather clumsy manufacture, it was probably a high-status piece.'

20 In all considerations of the depiction of Actium in Latin poetry, we do well to speculate on what would have happened in the case of an Antonian victory. J.M. Carter (*op. cit.*, 244-245) offers the conclusion that 'The problems that faced Octavian of settling the soldiers and restoring some sort of constitutional government would have been more difficult for Antony, associated as he was with Cleopatra and the east, and lacking the fabulous wealth of a captured treasury. But assuming that he could have overcome these difficulties, it is hard to see how he could have arrived at a permanent solution very different from that of Augustus. Antony might, of course, have abandoned Rome and the west; but the strength of Italy and the history of Rome's relations with the east were such that he can hardly have expected ambitious Romans to acquiesce for long in such an arrangement. If he tried to set himself up as a Hellenistic monarch in Alexandria, he would soon be challenged again.' This is a lucid and reasonable assessment of affairs – though I would argue that it is less than certain that Antony and his lover would have settled for anything similar to what Augustus achieved. There would have been little place for Cleopatra in such a system, and Antony would have had to have decided between Rome and the East as the seat of his power – and whichever realm did not receive the benefit of his direct presence, that sphere would need to have been surrendered to others (whether Cleopatra in Alexandria, or the senate and others in Italy). Carter notes that 'it was simply that the west refused and the east demanded the trappings of kingship in its rulers', and that may well be the best summary of the essential difference between Octavian and Antony once the problem of Cleopatra was inserted into the equation – a problem that Julius Caesar was ultimately unable to solve.

21 Books 3 and 5 of Virgil's epic have strong affinities; the briefly mentioned games of 3 are but prelude to the major ludic sequence in 5.

Chapter 12: Horace's Epodes –The Earliest Evidence?

1 Niall Rudd has a revised Loeb edition of Horace's odes and epodes; David West has a useful Oxford World's Classics edition, with annotations.

2 The translation is that of Lindsay Watson in his Oxford edition of the *Epodes* (2003), which offers a dense and comprehensive commentary on the poems.

3 Cf. Vegetius' testimony: *Sed Augusto dimicante Actiaco proelio, cum Liburnorum auxiliis praecipue victus fuisset Antonius, experiment tanti certaminis patuit Liburnorum naves ceteris aptiores. Ergo similitudine et nomine usurpato ad earundem instar classem Romani principes textuerunt. Liburnia namque Dalmatiae pars est Diadertinae subiacens civitati, cuius exemplo nunc naves bellicae fabricantur et appellantur liburnae ... Quod ad magnitudinem pertinet, minimae liburnae remorum habent singulos ordines, paulo maiores binos, idoneae mensurae ternos vel quaternos, interdum quinos, sortiuntur remigium gradus. Nec hoc cuiquam enorme videatur, cum in Actiaco proelio longe maiora referantur concurisse navigia, ut senorum etiam vel ultra ordinum fuerint* (*Epitoma Rei Miliaris* 4.33; 4.37). Vegetius' work was completed sometime between the close of

the fourth century and the approach of the middle of the fifth; there is an Oxford Classical Text edited by M.D. Reeve (2004).

4 *Op. cit.*, 224.

5 Cf. Pelling's note on Plutarch, *Vita Caesaris* 48.5 (Oxford, 2011): ' … Roman ears, receptive as they would have been to tales of decadent and arrogant eunuchs' (in the context of the machinations of Pothinus at the court of Ptolemy in the wake of Pharsalus).

6 See further here Watson's note *ad* 9.16. There may be a hint in the mention of the sun of the god Apollo.

7 Watson observes *ad loc.* that ' … for Horace the fact that non-Romans decide for the better side is a sour comment on the misplaced allegiance of the Roman soldiery of lines 11-16.'

8 See here the commentary of David Mankin (Cambridge, 1995) in the 'green and yellow series'.

9 See here Watson *ad loc.*, with bibliographical references.

10 *Horace: Epodes and Odes, A New Annotated Latin Edition*, Norman: The University of Oklahoma Press, 1991. Garrison provides a student edition of Horace's works with brief commentary and supplementary aids.

11 See further Mankin's commentary here *ad loc.* We have no idea if Antony had any military forces in Crete at this time, an island that was his as part of the settlement of the Peace of Brundisium; the reference to the Syrtes would be to Antony's known military units in the general area. Horace notes the traditional 'hundred cities' of Crete, a description that here evokes the idea of a grand, potentially dangerous foe – but also of the collapse of the ancient glories of Crete, of the splendour of a fading realm. Crete would have been a most significant place in the economic supply routes between Greece and Egypt; one has the sense that the speed of Antony and Cleopatra's own advance into Egypt meant that the defence and armament of strategic islands was rather neglected – thus allowing Agrippa to launch such successful strikes across a wide expanse of sea.

12 Watson *ad loc.* considers other views here, including the idea that the nausea was metaphorical. Some have seen argued that Octavian himself passed the battle in a state of seasickness, but there is no sound evidence for this position (cf. J. Fletcher, *Cleopatra: The Woman Behind the Legend*, New York: HarperCollins Publishers, 2011, 290). Mankiewicz's film depicts him as asleep, barely responsive to Agrippa who comes below decks to alert him to the victory. Fletcher is correct in emphasizing, however, that in the period after Actium it was Cleopatra who took on a more important role than her lover: 'Having survived previous situations when her very life had hung in the balance, New Isis came increasingly to the fore in the face of her husband's increasing inertia' (295).

Chapter 13: Horace's Cleopatra Ode

1   The Oxford commentary of Nisbet and Hubbard (1970) offers essential exegesis of the ode; David West has an Oxford edition (1995) with translation and good literary analysis, while Roland Mayer's 2012 Cambridge 'green and yellow' offers a reappraisal of the poem with fine commentary.

2   Antony was notoriously bibulous; there may be some degree of sarcastic humour.

3   Horace's ode was inspired on the literary level by the Greek lyric poet Alcaeus' account of a symposium in celebration of the death of the tyrant Myrsilus.

4   The dove and hawk imagery will prove to be a prominent part of the Virgilian allegory of Actium in *Aeneid* 11, where the heroine Camilla will be compared to an accipiter as she slays the Ligurian Aunides; the picture is ultimately Homeric.

5   As Karl Galinsky observes, 'Actium was not the beginning of the end – it was the end. The next few months were but a sequel' (*Augustus: Introduction to the Life of an Emperor*, Cambridge, 2012, 55). In this regard Mankiewicz's film does an admirable job of balancing the idea of finality and inevitability with the possibility for further resistance (even if some of the sequences are near laughably implausible).

6   We shall return to the notion of the 'savage' ships soon enough.

7   Mayer comments *ad loc.* that *ferocior* was a quality of a 'Roman noble,' an admirable trait, to be sure, almost as if Cleopatra became rather Roman at last in the manner of her death (in which she far surpasses the failure Antony). 'Cleopatra ruled an ancient kingdom. She was unscrupulously adroit, wealthy, and powerful. As a national enemy, she arguably posed the greatest threat to Rome since Hannibal (so Pelling in *CAH* x 63). Her death, strange yet glamorous, marked the end of nearly two decades of civil and foreign wars. It also added virtually the last independent territory on the Mediterranean coast to the Roman Empire. All in all, the battle of Actium and the subsequent conquest of Egypt decided the future of the Mediterranean world for centuries, and so Cleopatra's story would always figure largely in Roman, that is to say, world history' (Mayer, 224). Mayer further does well to note that 'It needs to be borne in mind as well that the poet's distance from Cleopatra relieves him of the frequently made claim that he is the voice or echo of Augustan propaganda... Such a claim assumes that H. knew as much about contemporary events in remote places like Actium and Egypt as modern historians believe they do. It might be said however that H. only knew what the agents chose to tell. There were conflicting stories at the time, and he might more fairly be seen as the victim rather than the echo of propaganda.' Of the three great Augustan poets, Horace may well have been the only one who was actually at Actium; as Mayer concludes, there is also always the possibility that Horace (I would add Virgil and Propertius) truly believed that Rome was in a better position with a victorious Octavian. For a somewhat different view, compare the comments of David West in his edition of *Odes* 1; there are sensible and sober introductory remarks by Nisbet and Hubbard (who side more with Kromayer than Tarn in the debate over Actium).

8   And one in which the queen might be all too willing to acquiesce, were she aware of the logic.

Chapter 14: The Evidence of Elegy: Propertius

1   The Oxford World's Classics edition of Guy Lee is perhaps the best place to start; George Goold's revised Loeb offers a good survey of the major controversies. The Oxford text of Stephen Heyworth should be used in conjunction with his *Cynthia* volume of textual commentary (Oxford, 2007).

2   *Fremitu* is difficult to render precisely; Goold offers 'alarms.'

3   And Phoebus Apollo is noted as the god of the promontory.

4   Note that Propertius' *amour* Cynthia, like the Delia of Tibullus, evokes the image of Apollo's sister Diana. This is especially interesting in an elegiac context, given that Diana was a virgin goddess of the hunt and thus offers an image of unattainability and eternal longing for that which one cannot have – but there is also a connection to Apollo through his sister. Cf. the close association of the Virgilian Camilla with Diana; the role of Apollo in her death constitutes something of an episode of civil war, indeed familial strife – a hallmark of Roman history, and perhaps (at least in a dark analysis) an indelible part of the Roman identity.

5   The 2011 Oxford edition of Heyworth and Morwood provides a thorough commentary on the problems of this elegy.

6   As Goold notes *ad loc.*, Propertius never mentions Antony by name; the Augustan poets in general avoid Cleopatra's. Her name in Greek evokes the idea of the glory of one's ancestors; it is a noble and revered name that might well be better not to speak – not to mention the sympathetic magic of the practice of not uttering certain damnable names/the Roman practice of obliteration of names and at least certain elements of memory.

7   *Cleopatra: Last Queen of Egypt*, New York: Basic Books, 2008, 170.

8   Where she had a palace.

9   3.11.55 *non hoc, Roma, fui tanto tibi cive verenda* (which is likely not to be taken sarcastically).

10 The sentiment in '*toto Ionio*' at the close of the poem is that Octavian achieved victories across the Ionian; cf. Agrippa's preliminary campaigns. Whoever crossed the sea first would have whatever advantages accrue to the offensive side; for the sake of the depiction of the struggle as a foreign and not a civil war, the opportunity to invade the East (as opposed to having to land in Italy) was a golden one.

11 The Cambridge 'green and yellow' edition of Gregory Hutchinson (2006) offers detailed annotation; there is also an older Cambridge edition by Camps. Note also the provocative analysis of Micaela Janan in her *The Politics of Desire: Propertius IV* (Berkeley-Los Angeles-London: The University of California Press, 2001, especially 100 ff.), which considers (*inter alia*) the placement of the Actian elegy before the appearance of Cynthia's ghost in c. 4.7 ('Poem 4.7 not only returns to erotic

elegiac themes, but renders Cynthia as mythologically commanding a presence as Apollo's...').

12 4.6.21 *altera classis erat Teucro damnata Quirino*; the translation is Goold's.

13 10.195-197.

14 We might note here that in Virgil's description of the ship race in Sicily during the memorial funeral games for Aeneas' father Anchises, one Sergestus commands the *Centaurus* (5.114 ff.). This vessel ends up ruined when it crashes on the rocky outcropping that serves as the turning post in the race; the boat is steered too close to the rock. A baleful outcome for the Centaur Virgil's boat race, then (the closest he comes to any sort of naval enterprise in the epic), *and* the *Sergestus* is captained by a man whose name recalls that of Sergius Catiline, the celebrated alleged enemy of the Republic in the days of Cicero's consulship (63 B.C.E.). *Aeneid* 5 has many parallels to *Aeneid* 11 (each book stands as the penultimate one of its respective half of the epic); if the latter book were meant to have an allegory of Actium in the matter of the cavalry battle, it is possible that Virgil wanted deliberately to balance the boat race of 5 and the equestrian war in 11 to highlight the connection. Also, note that in Book 5 of the *Aeneid* there is a display of the mock battle that is known as the *lusus Troiae* or game of Troy (the occasion serving as an opportunity for the introduction of Ascanius/Iulus as something more than a mere child); the elaborate equestrian manoeuvres of this contest are compared to the swimming of dolphins – a deliberate evocation of the world of marine life in the description of the horse event. We move then, from the boat race with the Centaur to the equestrian show that is compared to the action of dolphins as they play in the sea to the scene of an equestrian battle that is itself compared to the movement of the waves on the water – a brilliant progression of images and allegory.

15 There is a surviving fragment of a lamp's handle decoration that depicts a vessel with a Centaur warhead that was crafted in Egypt and dated to c. 10 B.C.E.-50 C.E.; the work is illustrated in the Walker and Higgs *op. cit.*, 266.

16 The sentiment would have special importance in Augustan propaganda; the *princeps* Augustus needed to be absolutely devoid of monarchical aspirations and the appearance of kingship. Cleopatra – and for that matter Antony – made this rather easy for Octavian/Augustus.

17 Julius Caesar posed a particular problem for the Augustan regime; he had been assassinated, after all, by a senatorial conspiracy that was clearly concerned with the possibility of the dictator's monarchical aspirations. And, of course, he had carried on an affair with the very queen who was now sharing Antony's bed and dreaming of shared glory and power. Caesar was also the adoptive father of Octavian and the granter of the possibility of entry into the Julian *gens* and the lineage of Caesar, Iulus, Aeneas and Venus. We might say that the best thing both Caesar and Cleopatra bestowed on Octavian was the gift of their respective deaths; the one made him Caesar, the other, ultimately, Augustus.

18 We might note here the account in Dio Cassius (51.16.3 ff.) where Octavian makes his visit to the Alexandrians and speaks to them in Greek after the death of Cleopatra.

He promises merciful treatment to them, and invokes not only the pretext of the god Serapis, but also Alexander the Great – whose tomb he soon visits. The scene is anything but reverential and awe-inspiring. He touched the body (a violation, to be sure, of what we would consider museum etiquette and protocol), and actually breaks a piece of the nose. But he refused the invitation to see the Ptolemies, claiming that he wanted to view a king and not corpses. He then refuses to enter the sacred precinct of the god Apis, noting that he worshipped gods and not cattle. The whole episode is a calculated commentary on what Octavian saw as the proper relationship between Romans and Egyptians; Alexander was to be respected and honoured (at least to a certain degree), but the rest of the history of Egypt in the Hellenistic Age was decidedly insignificant in comparison. As for Egyptian religion, that might prove useful for pacifying the Alexandrians with rhetoric about Serapis – but the Egyptians worshipped animals, and Octavian was not impressed.

19 We might underscore here that there is no emphasis in Propertius' Actium elegy on the idea that Cleopatra fled away in shame more than in simple defeat. For this we must look to c. 2.16; for savage indictment of Cleopatra, c. 3.11. In both cases, as we have seen, the context drives the content.

20 The great Numidian enemy of the Republic. The passage presents some difficulties in light of the mention by Horace at *Epodes* 9.23-24 that Octavian was greater than Marius, given that here Propertius seems to be implying that Cleopatra was not so impressive a foe. One could argue that the point is that we find here a reference to the 'real story' of how Octavian actually wanted the queen to kill herself so as to make her look all the more formidable an enemy for having escaped her conqueror by a voluntary death. Jugurtha is mentioned in both Horace and Propertius; again, the point is to underscore the African enemies of Rome, and Egypt can be associated with other realms in Africa even if geographically and culturally there were obvious differences.

21 We might note that the elegy goes on (4.6.75 ff.) to mention the question of Augustus' recovery of the standards that had been lost by Crassus to the Parthians (a major problem in Augustan propaganda); Antony had been seriously defeated in Parthia, and Julius Caesar had been killed before he could set off for his own engagement in the East. Augustus would thus finish what two powerful Roman military men had failed to do – not to mention the veritable erasure of the dark memory of Crassus and his defeat in the days of an earlier triumvirate.

22 See further here the notes *ad loc.* of R. Maltby, *Tibullus: Elegies, Text, Introduction, and Commentary*, Leeds: Francis Cairns Ltd., 2002.

23 The Neronian poet Lucan, the author of the *Bellum Civile* or *Pharsalia*, touches on the war in Alexandria and the dealings of Cleopatra with Caesar in his tenth and last book. Antony is described at 5.478-479 as already conceiving of civil war in the waters off Leucas (*doctor erat cunctis audax Antonius armis / iam tum civili meditatus Leucada bello*) – in poetry the topography of the battle and exact location can be breezily expressed in general geographical description (though Leucas played an important part in the contest, both in its capture and in the need to round its shores

to escape in the direction of Egypt). Lucan's Caesar makes an apostrophe to Antony in which he refers to him as the cause of great labour and toil for the world (5.497 *o mundo tantarum causa laborum*), a sentiment that has meaning only with a proleptic look to Actium. Lucan, in any case, is most noteworthy in Cleopatra studies for his richly textured account of the amorous escapades of Caesar and the queen; in the young Neronian poet, the queen becomes a veritable agent of madness and fury, a crazed source of decadence and potential downfall for Caesar.

Chapter 15: An Allegorized Actium?

1 Cf. L. Fratantuono, *A Commentary on Virgil, Aeneid XI*, Bruxelles: Editions Latomus, 2009, 52-53.

2 7.803-817.

3 In some sense there are three main contingents in Virgil's cavalry battle: the Trojans, the Etruscans, and the Italians; of course among the last group we can discern the separate units of the Latins, the Volscians, etc. Actium was similarly tripartite in general outline (Egyptians, Octavian, Antony); in both Virgil and history, there was division – in the former, the split allegiances of the Etruscans, and in the latter, the divided Romans. As for the behaviour of different contingents at Actium, we may note the citation in Plutarch's life of Brutus (53) that Strato – a Greek friend of Brutus from his days as a student of rhetoric in Athens – was warmly welcomed and received by Octavian, who found him a brave man at Actium (*inter alia*). That same passage includes the aforementioned memorable comment of Brutus' friend Messala Corvinus; he had fought for Brutus at Philippi and for Octavian at Actium, and when Octavian noted with admiration how he had done well for his former foe, he received the response that he was always a partisan of the better and more righteous cause.

4 The connection between a cavalry battle and a sea engagement may also owe something to the association of the marine god Neptune with the creation of the horse, an element of Neptunian lore that is prominently featured in the opening verses of Virgil's *Georgics* (which may have appeared in 29 B.C.E.): ... *tuque o, cui prima frementem / fudit equum magno tellus percussa tridenti* (1.12-13).

5 Especially Tarpeia, a notorious figure of treachery and greed from the early lore of Rome.

6 The story of Penthesilea is most extensively related in Quintus of Smyrna's epic *Posthomerica*, where Book 1 is devoted to the battle between Penthesilea's Amazons and the Greeks before the walls of Troy.

7 11.678.

8 A subtle note to his position in Octavian's battle array?

9 See here Fratantuono's commentary *ad* 11.579.

10 One wonders what happened during the actual Battle of Actium in terms of damage inflicted by accident from allied ships in the midst of a confused fray.

11 The Trojans are thus associated more closely with the trickery and deceit of the manoeuvre.

12 One is tempted to recall here the memorable words of Shakespeare's Enobarbus: 'Well I could reply, / If we should serve with horse and mares together, / The horse were merely lost: / the mares would bear / A soldier and his horse.' (*Antony and Cleopatra*, Act III, Scene VII).

13 3.3-4.

Chapter 16: The Lost Carmen de Bello Aegyptiaco/Actiaco

1 The most convenient edition is probably in Edward Courtney's Oxford 1993 volume, *The Fragmentary Latin Poets* (paperback edition 2003, with addenda).

2 Varius is cited by Horace (c. 1.6.1) as the poet who will write of Agrippa's triumphs in war. The Horatian ode speaks of the victories of the admiral/general both on sea and in cavalry battles (interestingly enough); the poet's point is to compose a *recusatio* or polite verse refusal to compose on an epic theme, and nothing can be gleaned from it about the Actian campaign – save the important fact that in a prominently placed early ode of the collection, the triumphs of Agrippa were a major theme for Augustan poetic celebration. We might note that among the early odes, we find Maecenas, Augustus, Virgil, and Agrippa as the topics of what we might call Horatian verse *hommage*.

3 A far less risky conflict, one might think, than the Alexandrian War of Octavian's adoptive father Caesar, the subject of the dramatic and abrupt close of Lucan's epic – a military adventure in which Caesar was more than once in serious discomfiture.

4 For how the two conflicts could shade into one, see especially Lange's monograph *Res Publica Constituta: Actium, Apollo, and the Accomplishments of the Triumviral Assignment*, Leiden: Brill, 2009, 90 ff. Lange considers (and ably critiques) the thesis of Robert Gurval in his *Actium and Augustus: The Politics and Emotions of Civil War* (Ann Arbor: The University of Michigan Press, 1995), where the point is developed that Actium was not, in the end, so important after all until Virgil. Certainly Actium is celebrated as an achievement of the greatest significance in Virgil's conception of Augustan epic – but it was not Virgil who made Actium important or influential in the development of the Augustan *mythos*. As Lange does well to note, 'The civil war changed Rome forever and Actium was the turning point in that war...But Augustus realised that victory was not enough, peace was what people wanted. He also realised early on that whatever he did, it needed to be justified, one way or the other...Peace just sounds so much better than victory after civil war.' (11).

5 See here the important article of E. Kraggerud, 'Some Notes on the So-Called *Carmen de Bello Actiaco* (Pap. Herc. 817),' in *Symbolae Osloenses* 65.1 (1990), 79-92.

Chapter 17: So What Really Happened?

1   *Op. cit.*, 612.

2   One does wonder about the decision of Antony to take treasure on board the ships; this course of action may raise more suspicion than the bringing of sails. Perhaps the answer is to be found simply in the matter of what the two leaders planned in the event of defeat. Any naval battle could go badly or unexpectedly, and unless one intended a fight to the death, money and treasure would be necessary. Retreat back into the Ambracian Gulf – in other words, exactly what so many Antonian ships did after their commander's flight – might have seemed impossibly unattractive as an option. The likely intention was victory at sea; if victory proved elusive, then flight back into the harbour might have been considered intolerably unpalatable. Again, modern historians can note that flight spelled the end of the cause in any case; Antony and Cleopatra may well have known this (or at least feared the possibility) – but in the weighing of bad options, Alexandria seemed more pleasant a destination than Ambracia. Different commanders will make different decisions, not least in straitened circumstances and under duress.

3   *Op. cit.*, 611.

4   Not to mention Alexandria, as Lange notes.

5   Mankiewicz's film version of *Cleopatra* takes an independent course from the ancient evidence; Richard Burton's Mark Antony notes that he faces an enemy with 'fewer ships'. The cinematic Antony, of course, carries a cup of wine into battle – a characterization that one cannot entirely discount as improbable.

6   Cf. Virgil's cavalry allegory for a naval battle.

7   In Volume X of *The Cambridge Ancient History* (*The Augustan Empire, 43 B.C.-A.D. 69*), 58. Pelling follows more or less the 'orthodox' view that a breakout was always planned; the nuance in some accounts of this argument comes in the acknowledgment that breakout and an attempt at victory are not mutually exclusive propositions.

8   We have no clear sense of how orders were conveyed in Cleopatra's fleet, i.e., if she were in direct control of her ships or had a naval intermediary.

9   *Antony and Cleopatra*, New Haven, Connecticut: Yale University Press, 2010. Goldsworthy's book is the most reliable of the vast bibliography on Egypt's queen. As with Alexander the Great, so with Cleopatra it seems that scarcely a year goes by without some new treatment of Egypt's queen; one study has even devoted itself to a 'forensic' examination of the case for Cleopatra having been murdered in Alexandria by Octavian's order (Pat Brown, *The Murder of Cleopatra: History's Greatest Cold Case*, Amherst, New York: Prometheus Books, 2013). Note also Duane Roller's 2010 Oxford volume, *Cleopatra: A Biography*, a book which seeks to offer as complete a portrait of the queen as possible through an example of evidence both literary archaeological. Roller concludes that for Actium, 'the outcome was hardly ever in doubt' (139).

10   Admittedly, several of which he spent away from her, sometimes in the company of Octavian's sister Octavia, with whom he had two children.

11 Of course in either case his situation would have been gravely compromised; his honour, however, and the possible effect on the morale of his men, might have persuaded him to rejoin Canidius.

12 Goldsworthy notes (369): 'At Actium, Antony failed to display the courage and military skill – the *virtus* – expected of a Roman senator. With the utter assurance of an aristocrat, Antony had never felt any particular need to obey conventions. He was an Antonius, and nothing would change or mean that it was not his right to be one of the great leaders of the Republic. In the past he often displayed courage, even if he was far less experienced and capable as a commander than his own myth-making suggested and posterity has believed. At Actium he abandoned fleet and army to escape. This alone would have been enough to doom him, discrediting him forever in the eyes of his peers. It seemed to confirm all that Octavian's propaganda had been saying about him, a man so enslaved that he was an emasculated in spirit as Cleopatra's eunuchs were physically. Antony's cause was broken, with no reason left beyond personal obligation for any Roman to rally to his cause. In practical terms he had lost the great army and fleet he had assembled and had no realistic chance of replacing them. The war was over and Antony had lost. It was only a question of time before the end came.'

13 Tarn's view is perhaps most easily accessed in the Tarn and Charlesworth *Octavian, Antony, and Cleopatra* (Cambridge, 1965).

14 Pat Southern sums up the situation well: 'The surviving record is very brief, much too obscure to retrieve the details of a campaign that occupied several months, but ultimately it is certain that all the odds were stacked against Antonius when he failed to achieve anything very rapidly against Octavian. It was all or nothing, instantaneously, and Antonius lost by his delay' (*Augustus*, New York-London: Routledge, 1998, 97).

15 Was there a successful performance of the Egyptian fleet that was considered surprising by the Romans on both sides?

16 We may mention here the situation of the intervention of night in Agrippa's engagement with the Pompeians at Mylae. Appian notes in his *Civil Wars* (5.108) that Agrippa was ready to fight a night battle after his victory by day, but that his associates urged him to be wary of both sea conditions *and* the exhaustion of his men after a most strenuous day – also that earlier, Agrippa was prevented from running his large vessels aground in shallows. That passage offers another good instance of the cooperative nature of Agrippa's and Octavian's navy.

Chapter 18: The Birth of a Romantic Legend

1 It is possible that the elegist Propertius was the first to write of the infatuated Antony – but less likely that he simply invented his facts out of whole cloth, under the instruction and advice of propagandists or not.

2   The matter is explored in full in Fratantuono's commentary on *Aeneid* 11, with consideration of the speculative argument that Camilla may be lycanthropic.

3   We may recall, too, Dio's description of the portent of the killing of a wolf in the temple of Fortune.

4   Propertius is the only poet who makes any reference to the names of any of Antony or Cleopatra's ships; not surprisingly, none of the Augustan poets note that the queen's flagship was named after her Roman lover. The *Centaur* as the name of a ship (with a mythological emblem on prominent display) might well have given rise to the comparison of the battle at sea to an equestrian conflict; the equine monsters would have fit well with Egyptian mythological depictions of animalistic deities, and any lore about lupine creatures would have completed the richly complex picture.

5   One wonders, too, if there was any deliberate play between Virgil's emphasis on lupine imagery and the *praenomen* 'Lucius,' which recalls the Greek word for wolf (*lykos*). Virgil's Arruns is a wolf hunter and wolf slayer; he 'becomes' a wolf himself in Virgil's brilliant simile that evokes the folklore of the wolf-priests of the Sabines – but the wolf slayer is himself slain by the god who was also a wolf slayer (in addition to the Servian evidence, cf. Plutarch's *Vita Pyrrhi* 32; the *schol. ad* Apollonius Rhodius, *Argonautica* 2.124; also Pausanias 2.19.3; Sophocles, *Electra* 7; Pausanias 2.9.7 – the last two passages where the god is explicitly called *lukoktonos*).

6   In the film, Antony has deep reservations about moving military forces into Greece; he predicts that it will mean attack on the very spot where Cleopatra and he land. This is, of course, convenient oversimplification for an audience that was perhaps considered incapable of appreciating the more nuanced reality, or was exhausted from a film that had already lasted several hours.

7   The idea of Antony sailing into some sort of trap is also used in the 1999 cable television production of *Cleopatra*, which in general depicts a computer generated Actium that succeeds (at least in this reviewer's estimation) only in making the Mankiewicz version appear all the greater in comparison. The story of the flight is essentially suppressed.

8   c. 1.37.12–13.

9   c. 3.11.29 ff.

10 See further here J. Tracy, *Lucan's Egyptian Civil War*, Cambridge, 2014.

11 3.11.51 *fugisti tamen*.

12 4.6.22.

13 There is a convenient edition by Virginia Brown in the Harvard *I Tatti Renaissance Library*, with Latin text, translation, and annotations (2001).

Chapter 19: 'Death Comes as the End'

1   With apologies to Dame Agatha Christie.

2   Grant (212) argues that the Antonian ground forces betrayed Canidius, as it were, and were allowed to 'save their faces' as part of Octavian's propaganda – the story

was spread, in other words, that Canidius had abandoned his men. For Grant, there were three key elements of the Augustan myth: first that Cleopatra had planned to flee, second that Antony had followed her sick with love, and third that Actium was a great naval battle. The truth may well have been that she did flee, and Antony did follow her – but only after a difficult struggle in what was after all an impressive naval battle. Such a story would be more than sufficient for any desire to glorify Augustus; not all propaganda, after all, is undeserved.

3 Pelling speculates that the reason for the landing at Paraetonium may have been to lessen the perils of the hazardous crossing, and also that Antony was eager to reach his troops given the fear of treachery and desertion.

4 69.2-3.

5 It is also the source of the scene in Mankiewicz's *Cleopatra* where Octavian is prompted by the discovery of the dead body of Cleopatra's trusted aide to have the poison that killed him tested on the badly wounded; in the film the scene makes Octavian look as bad as he is made to seem elsewhere in the script, while in reality it was Cleopatra (if anyone) who was executing prisoners with novel uses of poison.

6 Pelling observes here that 'The stories build on a notorious Egyptian tradition of medical experimentation on condemned prisoners, but they are not credible.' I would suggest that there is no reason to disbelieve Plutarch here. Pelling also cites the interesting detail in Galen that Cleopatra tested the snakes on Iras and Charmion, a version he terms 'tasteless.' The Antony and Cleopatra of Mankiewicz are decidedly reasonable in their cruelty; Cleopatra kills a faithless maid by making her simply drink the cup of poison that she had been sent to bring to the queen – confession calmly followed by the instruction to commit suicide.

7 Pelusium was where Pompey had put in to shore before his assassination in Egypt; it was also where the army of Cleopatra's brother Ptolemy had waited for the invasion of his sister.

8 One thinks here of the last days of the Third Reich, and the final decoration of youth defenders of Berlin by Hitler.

9 88.3.

10 Cf. the Plutarchan report at 86.4 that Antony's slave at his attempted suicide was none other than Eros.

11 82.2. Plutarch notes that Olympus testified to all this in a history of the events that he eventually published.

12 Plutarch takes care to record that Caesarion was killed *after* the death of Cleopatra (82.1); in Mankiewicz's film, the queen is made to realize that her son has been murdered after she sees his ring on Octavian's finger, thus realizing that the Roman is a liar when he claims to be willing to consider having Caesarion rule in Egypt.

13 83.5.

14 Pelling notes in his commentary on Plutarch's Caesar (51.3): '... tribune in 47 ... and Caesar's son-in-law: 'ambitious beyond character or capacity, Dolabella may be described as pseudo-dynamic' (Syme ... , speculating rather extravagantly that he may been C.'s own biological son).'

15 The film also displays a brief conflict between the two servant girls before the suicide ritual, as they jockey for the favoured place of attendance before the death – and there is an expression of hope that they might not be abandoned by their mistress without provision for their own ends.

16 In Mankiewicz, Agrippa points out the slithering culprit to Octavian.

17 9.11 ad 61. Aelian lived from around 170 to after 230 C.E.; he was a Roman from Praeneste. His fascinating treasure trove of information on animals (in seventeen books) is available in the Loeb library, as well as his so-called *Varia Historia* or 'Historical Miscellany.'

18 86.4.

19 We may compare the story told by Plutarch at the end of his comparison of the lives of Dion and Brutus. Octavian was in Cisalpine Gaul, in Mediolanum – and he saw a bronze statue of Brutus. He summoned the leading men of the city and made the accusation that they were harbouring an enemy of his in their power. They expressed shock and surprise – genuinely unaware of what he was saying. Finally he pointed to the statue, and asked if this were not an image of an enemy. At that he then smiled and noted that the Gauls were to be lauded, because they stood loyal to a friend even in time of crisis – and he insisted that the statue remain exactly where it was. Among many other aspects of consideration, the story serves to point to the fact that Brutus' action in killing Caesar was actually of great help to Octavian, in the final analysis at least.

20 51.3.4.

21 Lange's Actium article considers the sometimes debated question of how many men Antony had in Syria, at least before Actium; he comes to the conclusion that most of Antony's Syrian garrison must have ended up at Actium; the gladiators may well have taken advantage of a situation where the legionaries were not keeping order, and where the only 'Antonian defence' might well have come from such a low class source (*op. cit.*, 610, with reference to P.A. Brunt's *Italian Manpower 225 B.C.-A.D. 14*, Oxford, 1971, 504-505). Lange sums up the situation *after* the battle: 'Even if more of his Actian army had escaped with him, the outcome could have been no different. It was virtually inevitable that, once their leader had abandoned them, the land army would go over to Octavian. The same was true of the eastern provinces, and of Pinarius Scarpus' army in Cyrenaica. In following Cleopatra, Antonius was abandoning the empire to Octavian and taking refuge in his mistress' realm. Their destruction was the inevitable consequence.'

22 Mankiewicz's Cleopatra notes to Octavian that he flatters himself if he thinks that she would ever have any affection for him; the true story may have been somewhat different.

23 51.10.4-5.

24 51.11.3.

25 51.12.5.

26 51.14.3 ff.

27 51.17.4.
28 51.17.6.
29 Antyllus was also executed – he was a more dangerous figure than Caesarion in some ways, and had the misfortune of being old enough to be a legitimate target for a purge.
30 For the argument that Caesarion's death may be evoked in 'Dido's lament for *parvulus Aeneas* (*Aen.* 4.328-9),' in J. Eidinow, 'Dido, Aeneas, and Iulus: Heirship and Obligation in *Aeneid* 4,' in *The Classical Quarterly*, N.S. 53.1 (2003), 260-267.
31 *Iliad* 22.139-142.
32 2.87.1.
33 The death of Turullius is also noted by Valerius Maximus (1.1.19), who is interested in the detail that he was killed in a grove sacred to Aesculapius, whence he had taken timber for the manufacture of Antonian ships for the Actium campaign – a thus fitting end for the violator of the sanctity of the god's preserve.
34 6.19.13.
35 6.19.16.
36 On the problem of the exact dates of events in the late summer of 30 B.C.E., see especially T. Skeat, 'The Last Days of Cleopatra: A Chronological Problem,' in *The Journal of Roman Studies* 43 (1953), 98-100. Skeat considers both the question of different calendars, as well as the evidence of Clement of Alexandria that Cleopatra's death was followed by a seemingly strange eighteen-day reign by her children. Skeat concludes that Alexandria fell on 3 August, and that Antony died either the next day or on the fifth. Cleopatra's suicide is dated to 12 August, and then there was an 'interregnum' until the start of Octavian's reign in Egypt on 31 August – a period in which scholars concerned about the gap days assigned the period to children who never actually ruled anything.
37 One wonders if the Virgilian allegory of Actium was meant to highlight both Actium (primarily) and also the final settlement of the war in Alexandria, where arguably the most dramatic episode might well have been the final charge of Antony's horse (or, conceivably, an equestrian clash on land before the climactic Actian engagement).
38 It is not without reason that one of the main crises of the Augustan regime was the problem of the succession, a strain and stress that is reflected in the pages of both Horace and Virgil. The fear would prove well founded indeed.

Afterword: Actium and Roman Naval Practice

1 *Op. cit.*, 538.
2 Rodgers: 'After many centuries of naval warfare, the battle of Actium established the economic unity of the Mediterranean basin and thereafter, for over three centuries, the peace of Rome prevailed over those waters, during which period the Roman navy shrank to a mere coast guard for the protection of the public against pirates. One thinks of the 'mothball fleet' in the waters off San Diego, California in the aftermath of the Second World War.'

3 The American Secretary of the Navy wrote in 1894, 'It is astonishing how slowly, until of recent years, the art of shipbuilding has advanced: how much the barge in which Cleopatra sailed down the Cydnus to welcome Antony was like a modern yacht, and how similar the lines of the vessels with which the Greeks fought the Persians at Salamis, the Christians fought the Turks at Lepanto, and the English fought the French and Spanish at Trafalgar were to the lines of the warships of to-day. The changes the centuries have wrought in ships have not been essentially in shape, but in size, in motive power, in armament, and lastly in material.' (Hilary A. Herbert, 'The Fight off the Yalu River,' in *The North American Review* 159.456 (1894), 513-528, 516).

4 Cf. 'The *trieres* [the Greek for 'trireme'] was the first type of oared warship to be pulled by oars at three levels. No representation of an oared warship exists showing oars at more than three levels. It seems likely, then, that the types of denomination five to eight were pulled at three levels employing more than one man to an oar, in a five at two levels and in the others at all three levels.' (J. Morrison, J. Coates, and R. Rankov, *The Athenian Trireme: The History and Reconstruction of an Ancient Greek Warship*, Cambridge, 2000, 11). A simple and inescapable economy then: the largest vessels required the most men at the oars, and the maintenance of both the land and sea forces at Actium must have been a significant strain for both sides. 'All that is certain is that a quinquereme was a larger vessel than a trireme, probably in its dimensions, and certainly in the number of its crew' (J. Lazenby, *The First Punic War: A Military History*, Stanford, 1996, 28).

5 Michael Pitassi provides a useful overview of the available information on Roman (and other) ancient warships in his Boydell Press volume *Roman Warships* (2011), 26 ff., with discussion of the differences between what for convenience sake he terms 'monoremes,' as well as biremes and triremes, and the different possibilities of arrangements of rowers and oars.

6 5.106.

7 Indeed, if there was any revenge for the death of Pompey in Egypt, it was the fact that the experience Agrippa and Octavian had against his son Sextus Pompey was critical to the eventual defeat of Antony and Cleopatra of Egypt.

8 For a good overview of naval practice in the period, see further John Grainger's *Hellenistic & Roman Naval Warfare, 336 BC-31 BC*, South Yorkshire: Pen & Sword Maritime, 2011. D'Amato's *Imperial Roman Naval Forces* (for Osprey) notes that there were some 800 vessels in the service of the Roman fleet after Actium, with three praetorian bases initially maintained at Forum Iulii (present day Fréjus in the south of France), Misenum and Ravenna; the first was where most of the captured Antonian vessels were initially sent, though the base was soon enough disbanded – there was simply no need for so massive a naval presence, and the maintenance of fleets of the size that existed after Actium was financially prohibitive.

Bibliography and Further Reading

Allston, R. *Death of the Republic & Birth of the Empire*. Oxford, 2015.

Bowman, A., Champlin, E., and Lintott, A., eds. *The Cambridge Ancient History, Volume X: The Augustan Empire, 43 B.C.-A.D. 69* (Second Edition). Cambridge, 1996.

Brown, P. *The Murder of Cleopatra: History's Oldest Cold Case*. Amherst, New York: Prometheus Books, 2013.

Burstein, S. *The Reign of Cleopatra*. Norman: The University of Oklahoma Press, 2004.

Camps, W. *Propertius: Elegies Book IV*. Cambridge, 1965.

Carter, J. *The Battle of Actium: The Rise and Triumph of Augustus Caesar*. 1970.

Cary, E., tr. *Dio's Roman History V: Books XLVI-L*. Cambridge, Massachusetts: Harvard University Press, 1917.

Cary, E., tr. *Dio Cassius: Roman History, Books 51-55*. Cambridge, Massachusetts: Harvard University Press, 1917.

Cooley, A., ed. *Res Gestae Divi Augusti: Text, Translation, and Commentary*. Cambridge, 2009.

Cornell, T., ed. *The Fragments of the Roman Historians* (3 vols.). Oxford, 2013.

Courtney, E., ed. *The Fragmentary Latin Poets*. Oxford, 1993 (paperback reprint with addenda and corrections, 2003).

D'Amato, R. *Imperial Roman Naval Forces, 31 B.C.-A.D. 500*. Oxford: Osprey Publishing Ltd., 2009.

de Souza, P. *Piracy in the Graeco-Roman World*. Cambridge, 1999.

Ferrabino, A. 'La Battaglia d'Azio,' in *Rivista Filologia* 52 (1924), 433-472.

Fields, N. *The Roman Army: The Civil Wars, 88-31 B.C.*. Oxford: Osprey Publishing Ltd., 2008.

Fletcher, J. *Cleopatra the Great: The Woman Behind the Legend*. New York: HarperCollins, 2011.

Fratantuono, L., ed. *A Commentary on Virgil, Aeneid XI*. Bruxelles: Editions Latomus, 2009.

Fratantuono, L. *Madness Triumphant: A Reading of Lucan's Pharsalia*. Lanham, Maryland: Lexington Books, 2012.

Galinsky, K. *Augustan Culture: An Interpretive Introduction*. Princeton, 1996.

Galinsky, K. *The Cambridge Companion to the Age of Augustus*. Cambridge, 2005.

Galinsky, K. *Augustus: Introduction to the Life of an Emperor*. Cambridge, 2012.

Garrison, D., ed. *Horace: Epodes and Odes, A New Annotated Latin Edition*. Norman: The University of Oklahoma Press, 1991.

Goldsworthy, A. *Caesar*. New Haven, Connecticut: Yale University Press, 2006.

Goldsworthy, A. *Roman Warfare*. London: Weidenfeld & Nicolson, 2000.

Goldsworthy, A. *Antony and Cleopatra*. New Haven, Connecticut: Yale University Press, 2010.

Goldsworthy, A. *Augustus*. New Haven, Connecticut: Yale University Press, 2014.

Goold, G., tr. *Virgil* (2 vols.). Cambridge, Massachusetts: Harvard University Press, 1999-2000.

Grainger, J. *Roman Conquests: Egypt and Judæa*. South Yorkshire: Pen and Sword, 2013.

Grant, M. *Cleopatra: A Biography*. New York: Simon and Schuster, 1972.

Green, P. *Alexander to Actium: The Historical Evolution of the Hellenistic Age*. Berkeley-Los Angeles: The University of California Press, 1990.

Gurval, R. *Actium and Augustus: The Politics and Emotions of Civil War*. Ann Arbor: The University of Michigan Press, 1995.

Heyworth, S., and Morwood, J., eds. *A Commentary on Propertius, Books 3*. Oxford, 2011.

Hutchinson, G., ed. *Propertius: Elegies Book IV*, Cambridge, 2006.

Huzar, E. *Mark Antony*. London: Croom Helm, 1986 (originally published Minnesota, 1978).

Janan, M. *The Politics of Desire: Propertius IV*. Berkeley-Los Angeles-London: The University of California Press, 2001.

Johnson, W. 'A Queen, A Great Queen? Cleopatra and the Politics of Misrepresentation,' in *Arion* 6 (1967), 387-402.

Jones, P. *Cleopatra: A Sourcebook*. Norman: The University of Oklahoma Press, 2006.

Kromayer, J. 'Kleine Forschungen zur Geschichte des zweiten Triumvirats, VII: Der Feldzug von Actium und der sogennante Verrath der Cleopatra,' in *Hermes* 34 (1899), 1-54.

Kromayer, J. 'Actium: ein Epilog,' in *Hermes* 68 (1933), 361-383.

Lange, C. *Res Publica Constituta: Actium, Apollo, and the Accomplishment of the Triumviral Assignment.* Leiden: Brill, 2009.

Leroux, J. 'Les Problèmes stratégiques de la Bataille d'Actium,' in *Recherches de Philologie et de Linguistique* 2 (1968), 29-37, 55.

Lindsay, J. *Cleopatra.* London: Constable & Company Ltd., 1971.

Mankin, D., ed. *Horace: Epodes.* Cambridge, 1995.

Martin, T. *Ancient Rome: From Romulus to Justinian.* New Haven, Connecticut: Yale University Press, 2013.

Mayer, R., ed. *Horace: Odes Book I.* Cambridge, 2012.

Miller, J. *Apollo, Augustus, and the Poets.* Cambridge, 2009.

Murray, W., and Petsas, P. *Octavian's Campsite: Memorial for the Actian War.* Independence Square, Philadelphia: The American Philosophical Society, 1989.

Neill, M., ed. *The Oxford Shakespeare: Antony and Cleopatra.* Oxford, 1994.

Nisbet, R., and Hubbard, M., ed. *A Commentary on Horace, Odes I.* Oxford, 1970.

Pagán, V. 'Actium and Teutoburg: Augustan Victory and Defeat in Vergil and Tacitus,' in Levene, D., and Nelis, D., eds., *Clio and the Poets: Augustan Poetry and the Traditions of Ancient Historiography.* Leiden: Brill, 2002, 45-60.

Pelling, C., ed. *Plutarch: Life of Antony.* Cambridge, 1988.

Pelling, C., ed. *Plutarch: Caesar. Translated with Introduction and Commentary.* Oxford, 2011.

Perrin, B., tr. *Plutarch, Lives: Demetrius and Antony, Pyrrhus and Gaius Marius.* Cambridge, Massachusetts: Harvard University Press, 1920.

Pitassi, M. *Roman Warships.* Rochester, New York: Boydell Press, 2011.

Powell, *Marcus Agrippa: Right-Hand Man of Caesar Augustus.* London: Pen and Sword, 2015.

Preston, D. *Cleopatra & Antony: Power, Love, and Politics in the Ancient World.* New York: Walker & Company, 2009.

Roberts, A. *Mark Antony: His Life and Times.* Upton-upon-Severn: Malvern Publishing, 1988.

Rodgers, W. *Greek and Roman Naval Warfare: A Study of Strategy, Tactics, and Ship Design from Salamis (480 B.C.) to Actium (31 B.C.).* Annapolis, Maryland: The United States Naval Institute, 1937, 1964.

Roller, D. *Cleopatra: A Biography.* Oxford, 2010.

Sheppard, S. *Actium 31 B.C.: Downfall of Antony and Cleopatra.* Oxford: Osprey Publishing Ltd., 2009.

Shipley, F., tr. *Velleius Paterculus/Res Gestae Divi Augusti.* Cambridge, Massachusetts: Harvard University Press, 1924.

Smith, C., and Powell, A., eds. *The Lost Memoirs of Augustus and the Development of Roman Autobiography.* Swansea: The Classical Press of Wales, 2010.

Solomon, J. *The Ancient World in the Cinema.* New Haven: Yale University Press, 2001 (second edition of the 1978 original).

Southern, P. *Mark Antony: A Life.* Gloucestershire: Amberley Publishing, 2012.

Southern, P. *Augustus.* London-New York: Routledge, 1998. Syme, R. *The Roman Revolution.* Oxford, 1939.

Tarn, W. 'The Battle of Actium,' in *The Journal of Roman Studies* 21 (1931), 387-402. Tyldesley, J. *Cleopatra: Last Queen of Egypt.* New York: Basic Books, 2008.

Volkmann, H. *Kleopatra: Politik und Propaganda*, München: R. Oldenbourg, 1953 (translated as *Cleopatra: A Study in Politics and Propaganda*, London: Elek, 1958).

Walker, S., and Higgs, P., eds. *Cleopatra of Egypt: From History to Myth.* Princeton, 2001.

Wardle, D. *Suetonius: Life of Augustus.* Oxford, 2014.

Watson, L., ed. *A Commentary on Horace's Epodes.* Oxford, 2003. West, D. *Horace Odes I: Carpe Diem.* Oxford, 1995.

White, H., tr. *Appian's Roman History* (4 vols.). Cambridge, Massachusetts: Harvard University Press, 1912-1913.

Woodman, A., ed. *Velleius Paterculus: The Tiberian Narrative (2.94-131).* Cambridge, 1977.

Woodman, A., ed. *Velleius Paterculus: The Caesarian and Augustan Narrative (2.41-93).* Cambridge, 1983.

Zanker, P. *The Power of Images in the Age of Augustus.* Ann Arbor: The University of Michigan Press, 1988.

Index